Street Lit

Teaching and Reading Fiction in Urban Schools

Andrew Ratner

City College of New York

ISBN: 978-0-07-337843-5
MHID: 0-07-337843-7

Editor in Chief: *Michael Ryan*
Editorial Director: *Beth Mejia*
Publisher: *David Patterson*
Sponsoring Editor: *Allison McNamara*
Editorial Coordinator: *Sarah Kiefer*
Developmental Editor: *Jill Eccher*
Marketing Manager: *James Headley* and *Yasuko Okada*
Project Manager: *Rachel J. Castillo*
Cover Designer: *Mary-Presley Adams*
Design Manager: *Margarite Reynolds*
Senior Production Supervisor: *Louis Swaim*
Composition: *Laserwords Private Limited*
Printing: *45# New Era Matte Plus, R.R. Donnelley & Sons*

Library of Congress Cataloging-in-Publication Data

Ratner, Andrew.
    Street lit : teaching and reading fiction in urban schools / Andrew Ratner—1st ed.
      p. cm.
    Includes bibliographical references and index.
    ISBN-13: 978-0-07-337843-5 (alk. paper)
    ISBN-10: 0-07-337843-7 (alk. paper)
    1. Young adult fiction, American—Study and teaching (Secondary) 2. High school students—Books and reading—United States. 3. Middle school students—Books and reading—United States. 4. Urban youth—Books and reading—United States. I. Title.
    PS42.R37 2010
    813.009'92830712—dc22

                                                                                    2009033826

About *The Practical Guide Series*

New teachers face a seemingly endless set of challenges—classroom management, assessment, motivation, content knowledge, cultural responsiveness, inclusion, technology—just to name a few. Preparing for the profession can at times seem overwhelming. Teacher candidates may begin to see solutions to some of the anticipated challenges as they progress through a program of study but know that there are many that await them in their first classroom. Support by mentors and colleagues is crucial for beginning teachers, and this series is designed to bolster that guidance. *The Practical Guide Series* provides another level of support for these new and future professionals.

The series was conceived in response to concerns about teacher retention, especially among teachers in their first to fourth years in the classroom when mentorship and guidance play a crucial role. These titles offer future and beginning teachers a collection of practical advice that they can refer to in student teaching and in the early teaching years. Instructors of pre-service teachers can use these books to reinforce concepts in their texts with additional applications, use them to foster discussion, and help guide pre-service students in their practice teaching.

Besides addressing issues of basic concern to new teachers, we anticipate generating a level of excitement—one that a traditional textbook is hard-pressed to engender—that will further motivate entrants into this most essential profession with a contagious enthusiasm. A positive start to a teaching career is the best path to becoming a master teacher!

Alfred S. Posamentier
Series Editor
Dean, The School of Education,
The City College of New York

To Yoon, Ethan, and Sasha: my reward after long days of teaching and writing.

Contents

Preface: Beyond the House on Mango Street

—My kids can't relate to the literature we read in class; it's so foreign to them.
—They feel like it has nothing to do with their lives.
—They can't see themselves in the characters and settings of these stories.
—They speak a completely different language.
— The books can't compete with video games and music videos.

These are the voices of the in-service and pre-service teachers attending my English and English education graduate courses. They are the voices that provided the impetus for the writing of *Street Lit*. Most of the students teach, or eventually will teach, in high-need schools located in inner-city neighborhoods like the Tremont section of the Bronx and Bedford-Stuyvesant in Brooklyn—schools with students who share much in common with those I taught in Harlem, Newark, and New Orleans. Despite the literary merit and universally powerful themes of classics like *Catcher in the Rye* (Salinger 1951), *To Kill a Mockingbird* (Lee 1960), *Lord of the Flies* (Golding 1954) and other mainstays of the high school English canon, the teens they encounter in their classes struggle greatly to locate themselves in these stories. Despite their teacher's efforts to present fun and engaging lessons, too few students view middle and high school literature as accessible to them and meaningful in their lives.

In middle schools, a small but growing number of contemporary stories and novels are widely used by teachers hoping to offer their students literature that presents characters and settings more representative of the cultures and experiences of children living in America's urban centers. While my teachers appreciate books like Walter Dean Myer's *Monster* (1999) and Sandra Cisneros's *The House on Mango Street* (1991), they lament the limited number of selections within this emerging genre. They roll their eyes when supervisors and professional developers suggest they teach books, novels, plays, and poems that their students have already read two or three times in earlier grades.

With a mixture of bewilderment and alarm, my teachers also report finding increasing numbers of students in hallways, cafeterias, and classrooms independently reading fiction titles like Nikki Turner's *Forever a Hustler's Wife* (2007) and Wahida Clark's *Every Thug Needs a Lady* (2003). The burgeoning genre of "hip-hop" fiction, replete with gratuitous sex and violence and lacking serious literary merit, has captured the imagination of city students where the traditional canon has failed to do so.

In recent semesters, I invited in-service teachers to try their hand at writing original short fiction and poetry that aspired to fill the gap between lowbrow hip-hop fiction and the conventional high school English offerings that students so quickly dismiss. The best of the stories I received were accomplished pieces of writing that clearly grew out of the daily contact these authors had with the high school students upon which they based their characters. They read not as distant writers' *ideas* about the lives of children and families in the inner city, but rather as sensitive and intimate portrayals of the students and communities that touch them on a daily basis. As presented in this book, they are a collection of stories written *by* teachers *for* teachers and the students they encounter every day in the hallways and classrooms of city schools.

The topics and issues contained in these stories—teenage pregnancy, body image, race relations, illiteracy, and the vitality, beauty, and ugliness of life in the inner city—matter to high school students; the settings and voices of the characters are familiar and accessible to them. At the same time, if you consider incorporating these stories into your high school curriculum, you will confront a number of difficult instructional decisions. The foremost of these decisions will be, "Can I use these stories in my English classroom at all? Are they appropriate and educationally beneficial for 15-, 16-, and 17-year-old students?" Ultimately, you will reach your own conclusion based on the particulars of your school setting, pedagogy, personal beliefs, and values. Two elements of the text will help you in making these decisions. The stories are presented in reproducible form so that you can pick and choose which ones are appropriate for your instructional purposes and present them to students. Secondly, each story is followed by a "focus group discussion" in which middle and high school English teachers examine the very issues and concerns surrounding the teaching of alternative literature in the urban school setting. These concerns range from "How do I ensure that students respect each other's opinions and feel safe participating in literature discussions that touch on risky topics?" to "What can I do so that families and administrators support me in teaching nontraditional stories that I feel would benefit my students?" In other words, you will receive guidance from those who are in the best position to help you navigate the more sensitive aspects of literature instruction in urban settings—your peers in the field.

Finally, each chapter will conclude with detailed lesson plans containing clear and practical reading, writing, discussion, and extension activities for integrating *Street Lit* stories and others like them in the high school classroom. The lessons, like the stories themselves, are informed by the day-to-day experiences of teachers who understand the challenges and opportunities of educating students in city schools.

✴ How to Use This Book

Organization of the Text

Each chapter that follows is divided into three sections: a Reproducible Literature Selection, a Teacher Focus Group Discussion, and Classroom Activities. Ideally, the three sections should be read in the order given, as each section makes reference to content in the previous one.

Reproducible Literature Selection

The authors of the original stories in this section are teaching or have recently taught in or attended urban middle and high schools in various locations around the country, including New York City, Newark, New Orleans, and Los Angeles. While only two of the selections ("Permanent Record" and "Snitch") are set in schools, all of them are inspired by the students, families, and communities that the teachers/authors have come to know through their work in city middle schools and high schools.

The genesis of the book began with a challenge to the authors: write something different from what is currently offered in the body of contemporary literature targeting urban young adults. This is exactly what they did. Topics such as teen pregnancy, violence, illiteracy, race relations, and suicide appear routinely in contemporary young adult literature used in schools; however, the manner in which the selections in this book address these sensitive issues, and even more so, the language of the narration and dialogue in the stories, test the boundaries of appropriate reading content in the secondary classroom. For this reason, we encourage current and future teachers to consider each story on a case-by-case basis when deciding whether or not to include it in their English curriculum.

Why offer stories that teachers, administrators, or parents may not view as suitable for high school students?

I believe that the selections in this book have literary merit and that there are compelling reasons to share them with your students. The writing is refined, the characters are memorable, and the underlying themes and questions raised by the stories are vital, particularly for the current generation of teenagers living and attending school in the inner city. From my own teaching experience and my work with city teachers, however, I also recognize that diversity is the hallmark of today's urban schools—both diversity within and across schools. You may, for instance, currently teach ninth-grade English in a small, recently established alternative high school in Washington Heights, New York City, with a student population that is predominately first- and second-generation Dominican-Americans from tight-knit, devoutly Christian families; the school is run by a young, "progressive" principal who encourages his teachers to experiment. Or you might teach in a comprehensive high school in central Brooklyn with a population of 5,000 students split evenly between African American students and first- and second-generation Haitian, Mandarin Chinese, Bangladeshi, Russian, and Ukrainian Americans with a sprinkling of recently emigrated students from West Africa; the assistant principal of English who supervises you has 18 years of experience, eschews experimentation, and champions the "classics." The highly unique composition of individual schools—indeed, classes—suggests that an unconventional literature selection may be completely right for one English teacher to offer students but completely wrong for another teacher. For this reason, we have designed this book so that city teachers can pick and choose which stories to use in their classrooms. Even if you decide that a particular selection does not make sense given your instructional context and your teaching objectives, the very process of making this decision will contribute to your growth as an educator; you will find yourself addressing and gaining insights into some of the fundamental questions confronting teachers of English in city schools: What function should literature serve in the academic development of students? What function should it serve in the identity development and personal growth of students? How has the role of literature instruction changed in recent decades? What motivates students to read literature? What discourages them from reading literature? And to what degree should we take into account the cultures, language varieties, and life experiences of students and their home communities when choosing literature for our curricula?

To assist in teaching those stories that you choose to share with your students, each reproducible literature selection includes the following features:

- About the Story—A brief overview presenting the story topic.
- Words to Consider—A helpful wordlist that introduces students to unfamiliar vocabulary and idioms in the section.
- Discussion Questions—A series of questions designed to engage students in responding to literature at three levels: reading "in the lines" (surface-level decoding and recall), "between the lines" (interpretation), and "beyond the lines" (evaluation and application).

Teacher Focus Group Discussion

In both content and style, each story in *Street Lit* presents future and current teachers with pedagogical, moral, and ethical questions related to the teaching of literature in urban high schools. The section begins with the author posing "talking points" pertinent to these issues, followed by a "discussion" in response to the talking points. The focus groups were conducted during sections of a graduate English education course I taught on the teaching and reading of literature in secondary schools.

This section of the book is not intended as a reporting of formal research; in light of the small sample size (13) and absence of a formal procedure for selecting participants, readers should not view the focus group as representative of all English teachers in urban schools, or teachers in general. To help you contextualize the discussions, however, and draw your own conclusions regarding the applicability of the group's perspectives to your own teaching circumstances, I provide the following description of the participants: three of the individuals had yet to enter the classroom at the time of the focus group discussions; the remaining 10 participants were all full-time English teachers in New York City working in high-need public high schools in the Bronx, Brooklyn, or Washington Heights sections of upper Manhattan. The mean teaching experience of the group, including the three pre-service teachers, was 2.6 years.

Of the 13 individuals who participated in one or more of the discussions, 5 were black (2 African American, 2 West Indian, 1 African), 2 were non-black Hispanic, 5 were white, and 1 was Asian. Nine were women and 4 were men. The ages of participants ranged from 22 to 58.

The dialogue reproduced in the Teacher Focus Group segments is drawn from transcripts of audiotapes of the focus group discussions. Real-time spoken discussions are not orderly affairs, and verbatim transcriptions are insufficient for capturing the paralinguistic features of spoken discourse (facial expressions, intonation, and so on) that aid in making meaning of the discussion. To increase the readability of the reproduced discussions, I revised segments of dialogue that I thought would be particularly distracting or confusing to readers. With the exception of my own name, pseudonyms are used to identify participants in the discussions. I have also used pseudonyms to identify schools that were mentioned on occasion.

You will notice that the discussions do not focus exclusively on the chapter's literature selection but rather that the stories serve as points of departure for teachers to trade ideas and experiences on matters of general concern to city teachers. The title of the discussion in Chapter 2, "Street Lit: Too Much, Too Often, Too Early for City Kids?" refers to a recent article in the *American Educator* critical of what its author views as adolescents' overexposure in schools to "problem novels" (Feinberg 2004); in response to the *American Educator* article and the *Street Lit* stories, the discussants address the question of whether or not urban school teachers should have particular concerns about their students reading stories that include harsh depictions of life in the inner city. The Chapter 3 discussion, "Keeping It Real: Authenticity and Responsible Representation in Urban Fiction," grapples with the tensions between authorial freedom and social responsibility in depicting cultural groups, particularly those with which your students identify. Chapter 4, "The N-Word," presents teachers' views on the increasingly common use of the epithet "nigger" in the everyday discourse of city students, and how this development shapes students' and teachers' response to its appearance in contemporary literature. The Chapter 5 discussion, "Girlz in the Hood: Gender Representation in Urban Literature," focuses on the potential for literature to reify or reshape a teenage girl's concept of gender. Chapter 6 asks you, the reader, and your classmates in English to comparatively assess the literary, instructional, and ethical value of three versions of *Snitch*, the final story in this volume.

Whether the school settings and students described in the Focus Groups have much or little in common with your own teaching context, I am confident that the questions addressed in the discussions and the perspectives of the teachers will interest anyone who teaches literature to adolescents and teens. As you read through the discussion, insert yourself as a participant, taking sides on points that matter to you most. My hope is that you will continue the conversations begun in the pages of Focus Group sections with colleagues and other educators you encounter in faculty lunchrooms, university courses, and other venues for professional collaboration.

Classroom Activities

The instructional lessons, routines, and projects described in the Classroom Activities section were chosen to support the chapter's short literature selection but are versatile enough to be used in conjunction with teaching any literature title and genre. Each Classroom Activities section contains the following subsections:

- *Introductory Activity*—"Do Now's," mini-lessons, journal prompts, prereading exercises, and other activities that introduce the topic of the story and motivate students to read it.

- *Writing Project*—Exercises and long-term projects that emphasize writing as a vehicle for analytic and personal responses to literature.
- *Community of Readers Extension Activity*—Drama exercises, literature circles, team research, and other group projects that instill appreciation for the reading of literature as a social activity and promote literary analysis from diverse points of view.
- *Language in Context Study*—Brief excerpts from the story selection that illuminate instructional topics in English grammar and usage. Particular attention is given to dialogue in the stories that illustrates language patterns and conventions associated with regional and ethnic dialects of English. The lessons and activities presented in the section aim to highlight for urban students the legitimacy and richness of the language variations they bring to school as well as aid them in the acquisition and mastery of the language patterns and conventions privileged in academic settings.
- *Text Connections*—Each chapter ends with short descriptions of literature and academic texts referenced in *Street Lit,* as well as other reading resources that will support teaching of the stories and lessons contained in each chapter. The *For Students* subsection contains resources that will supplement students' reading of the chapter's short fiction selection. The *For Teachers* subsection contains resources for middle school and high school educators who seek to further explore the focus group topics and instructional activities offered in the chapter.

⚔ Windows and Mirrors: Students Seeing Themselves, Seeing "Others" in Urban Literature

We pass the word around; we ponder how the case is put by different people, we read the poetry; we meditate over the literature; we play the music; we change our minds; we reach an understanding. Society evolves this way, not by shouting each other down, but by the unique capacity of unique, individual human beings to comprehend each other.

Lewis Thomas, *The Medusa and the Snail* (1979)

As you read through the Classroom Activities sections, you will notice the absence of a single instructional philosophy or theoretical framework shaping the instructional practices described in them. If anything, the theory informing the selection of activities, lessons, and routines is that teachers are best served when exposed to a wide variety of instructional approaches and principles from which they can make informed decisions about what to teach and how to teach it.

By contrast, a consistent instructional objective runs through each of the lessons: to develop in students an approach to reading literature that fosters empathy. If empathy is a uniquely human capacity, I believe that creative literature is uniquely positioned to nurture this capacity. Why? Because fiction, poetry, and drama allow "unique, individual human beings" to not only "comprehend each other" but also to *know* each other; that is, to know each other as we know danger, hunger, and joy—in the gut. Isaac Bashevis Singer, fiction writer and Nobel Prize winner, observed: "The very essence of literature is the war between emotion and intellect, between life and death. When literature becomes too intellectual—when it begins to ignore the passions, the emotions—it becomes sterile, silly, and actually without substance" (in Burgin 1978, p. 39). The same holds true for the teaching of literature; when we limit our instruction to developing students' skills and knowledge for understanding (intellectually) stories, poems, and plays, we have ignored what Rosenblatt first described as an "aesthetic" response to literature—one where "the reader's attention is centered directly on what he is living through during his relationship with that particular text" (Rosenblatt 1994, p. 25).

At the very moment I reveal that the lessons introduced in this book aim to develop students' capacity for empathy, I remind myself that today's inner-city students—the reading audience targeted by the authors of the stories in this text—are often misrepresented, underrepresented, or not represented at all in literature typically offered in the high school classroom. Yes, the novels, stories, plays, and poems we read serve as windows for gazing upon and gaining appreciation for people, places, and experiences that are foreign to us. However, they should also serve as mirrors for looking inward and for grasping what it means to be "me" in relation to others. I am afraid that the literature currently used in inner-city classrooms seldom serves as a mirror for students, and when it attempts to do so, the mirror represents a distorted, barely recognizable reflection of city youth. And while experiencing literature containing familiar people, places, and circumstances does not guarantee self-understanding, the absence of such reading experiences will turn many young readers away from literature as a source for both self-understanding *and* understanding of unfamiliar people and experiences. As a single package, then, the stories, teacher discussions, and lessons contained in *Street Lit* are intended to prepare city teachers to help their students approach literature for dual purposes: as a mirror for exploring their own experience and that of their families and communities, and as a window to "envisage possibilities of acting and feeling that transcend their past and present experience" (Wells 1997).

Acknowledgments

Street Lit: Teaching and Reading Fiction in Urban Schools honors the power of collaboration. It emerged from a belief that secondary school teachers and university-based educators can—and should—work together not only to design curriculum and develop methods of instruction, but also to compose the literature read by students in English classrooms. While the contributions of the *Street Lit* authors—Amy Alvarez, Amberdawn Collier, Terrence Hughes, and Grace Park—will be obvious to those who read this book, there are many others who made this project possible and to whom I am most grateful.

Annette Santiago and Ilana Garon's written and spoken feedback were instrumental in revising my manuscript. They are proof that students are often our best teachers. Thanks also to my colleagues Beverly Falk, Sondra Perl, and Betsy Rorschach. Their wisdom and guidance were invaluable at key junctures in this project. A heartfelt shout-out to Elroy "Big Shot" Gay, who collaborated with me on one of the *Street Lit* stories and whose spirit runs through the entire book. My graduate education and English classes at The City College of New York were the Petri dishes that cultivated many of the ideas contained in this book. Space prohibits me from individually acknowledging the hundreds of students who attended these classes. They should know that the enthusiasm and insight they brought to events documented in this book were a constant source of encouragement.

Above all, I would like to thank my first—and best—teachers, Ruth and Richard Ratner.

Andrew Ratner
City College of New York

Creating a Need to Read in the City Classroom

Now that I am teaching at a university rather than a middle or high school, most of my contact with teenagers occurs on the New York City subway. Not much seems to have changed in the past few years. Before, it was the Discman; now it's the MP3 player. Regardless of the technology, it is still pretty hard to find kids between the age of 13 and 18 without some kind of electronic device in their palms and plugs in their ears. They're still obsessed with popular music, still stuffing their faces with bar-b-cue flavored potato chips and guzzling obscenely colored juice drinks—even at 8:30 in the morning. Apparently, they still consider mercilessly ridiculing each other as a form of entertainment. I miss them, really I do.

My time on the subway had also led me to believe that students still rarely read—books, newspapers, or anything else in print—outside of school. And then about a year ago, I was riding the #2 to work and noticed a girl wearing a uniform from a New York City middle school where I had recently observed a teacher. (It is not uncommon for city public schools to require uniforms these days.) She sat across from me with her face buried in a thick paperback. One moment her eyes would expand to the size of hard-boiled eggs. Then she would break into a grin or bite her bottom lip as if concealing some guilty pleasure. For a former middle and high school English teacher, the sight of a teenager engrossed in a book on the subway induces the kind of warm, fuzzy feeling that I suppose a priest feels when he notices a long-absent congregant in the pews. Of course I had to know the title of this book she found so gripping, and I waited anxiously for her to expose the cover before either she or I exited the subway. When she finally tilted the book at a sufficient angle, I glimpsed the words, "Bitch Reloaded" and "by Deja King." In the foreground of the cover illustration, a woman in stilettos had her skirt hiked up to reveal a sheathed knife held in place by a black lace garter. A powder-blue sports convertible waited for her in the background.

In the months that followed, this scene repeated itself to the point where on nearly every subway ride to work I would see school-aged kids—usually, but not exclusively, girls—reading paperbacks with titles like *Whore* (Lynch 2006), *Forever a Hustler's Wife* (Turner 2007), and *Thug Matrimony* (Clark 2007). Each novel I came across in the genre that has come to be known as "street lit" (or alternatively, "hip-hop lit" and "ghetto fiction") had a cover that dripped with sex and fast living.

During this same period of time, in-service and pre-service teachers attending my graduate education classes reported observing the same phenomenon in schools: kids who *never* read were walking obliviously down hallways, eyes cast downward on paperbacks like *Hold U Down* (Ervin 2006). Instead of following along in textbooks during math and English class, students were using them as fronts to obscure the teacher's view as they turned the pages of *Payback Is a Mutha* (Clark 2006). The teachers in my courses expressed curiosity about their students' newfound interest in literature but also concern; some who had read or skimmed through selections of street lit quickly dismissed them as print versions of the rap music and videos that glorified violence, materialism, homophobia and the objectification of women. The music, television, and film industries already pandered enough to gun play, drugs, money lust, and idealized portrayals of "pimps" and "'ho's" to urban teens. Was literature to be yet another vehicle for cynically marketing nihilistic lifestyles to kids in the inner cities?

Teachers also reported that the novels were replete with mechanical errors—not deliberate deviations from standard English, but rather unintended mistakes and typos. Later, as I began to investigate street lit, I learned that the spelling mistakes, grammatical errors, and improper word usages were as much a product of the genre's production quality as the authors' grasp of standard English conventions. Many of the authors had self-published their books and did not have access to editors. Others were contract writers for small, independent houses like Triple Crown Press that lacked the resources of more established publishers. The English teachers I encountered, however, cared little about why street lit novels lacked polish. Regardless of the reason, it troubled them to see teens reading published books containing the very mistakes that teachers struggled mightily to correct in their students' writing.

It was predictable that mainstream publishers and booksellers would eventually recognize the earning potential of hip-hop fiction. An article in the February 2006 *New York Times* book section recounts the story of Dewitt Gilmore (a.k.a. Relentless Aaron), who began writing street fiction while serving time in New Jersey federal prison. After his release in 2003, Gilmore printed 12 of his 30 completed manuscripts through a small company in New Jersey. He then built a literary reputation by hawking his books at correctional facilities and on city sidewalks. After three years of going it on his own, Gilmore created enough buzz in the literary world through sales of *Platinum Dolls* (2004) to land a six-figure publishing contract with St. Martin's Press.

Today, Gilmore's first novel with St. Martin's, *Extra Marital Affairs* (2006), sits on the shelves of chain bookstores like Borders Books and Barnes and Noble. You can find it and many other street lit titles in the African American literature section alongside novels by celebrated authors like Toni Morrison, Terry McMillan, and Zora Neale Hurston. In a 2006 *New York Times* op-ed, magazine editor, novelist, and award-winning journalist Nick Chiles lamented how his books and those of other mainstream African American authors had been "surrounded and swallowed whole" by a body of literature that he described as "almost exclusively pornography for black women":

> As I stood there in Borders, I had two sensations: I was ashamed and mortified to see my books sitting on the same shelves as these titles; and secondly, as someone who makes a living as a writer I felt I had no way to compete with these purveyors of crassness.

> That leaves me wondering where we—writers, publishers, readers, the black community—go from here. Is street fiction some passing fad, or does it represent our future? It's depressing that this noble profession, one that I aspired to as a child from the moment I first cracked open James Baldwin and Gabriel García Márquez about 30 years ago, has been reduced by the greed of the publishing industry and the ways of the American marketplace to a tasteless collection of pornography (Chiles 2006).

The English teachers in my courses are also left wondering "where to go from here." They understand that writing in all literary genres ranges from regrettable to pedestrian with a sprinkling of masterpieces. Should they then turn their attention to identifying the masterpieces of street lit and getting them in the hands of their students? They also recognize that like selections of street lit, there are many examples of stories, novels, and poems in the Western literary tradition that marginalize and foster negative stereotypes of people based on race, ethnicity, class, and sexual orientation. Do we ignore the entire body of Elizabethan literature because it contains instances of prejudice against Jews and blacks?

And yet, teachers cannot help but share Chiles's reservations about street lit. Particularly because the majority of their students are African American and Latin American, my English teachers fear their students will associate literature written by and for people of their own heritages with *Homo Thug* (Kahari 2004) rather than masterpieces like Ralph Ellison's *Invisible Man* (1953), Ernest Gaines's *A Lesson Before Dying* (1993), or even highly regarded contemporary work like Junot Diaz's *The Brief Wondrous Life of Oscar Wao* (2007).

Regardless of how English teachers or others feel about the literary or instructional value of books like *Bitch Reloaded,* one cannot discount the reach of street lit in urban communities. In one of the few scholarly articles in education written on street lit, Hill, Perez, and Irby (2008) explain why the genre cannot and should not be ignored by educators: "[Street lit] has not only become a familiar feature of bookstores, sidewalk bookstands, and public libraries but also a growing part of African-American popular culture . . . the growing importance of street fiction in the lives of students demands that we take notice of this phenomenon" (p. 76).

To understand the significance of urban teens' enthusiasm for street lit, one must consider it within the context of the overall teenage population's declining interest in reading in recent decades. *To Read or Not to Read,* a 2007 National Endowment for the Arts comprehensive analysis of reading patterns in the United States, reports that "less than one-third of 13-year-olds are daily readers" and that "the percentage of 17-year-olds who read nothing at all for pleasure has doubled over a 20-year period" while "the amount they read for school or homework (15 or fewer pages daily for 62% of students) has stayed the same." (U.S. National Endowment for the Arts 2007, p. 7).

In light of these statistics, some might take the position that any reading done by teenagers outside of school is a good thing. This is a weak argument, akin to saying that *Entertainment Tonight* viewers are at least keeping up on current events. Furthermore, we can hardly assume that those 15 pages (or fewer) read daily in school or for homework are drawn from quality literature. In the pages that follow you will hear from English teachers working in urban public schools who tell a different story. Responding to the federal No Child Left Behind legislation's emphasis on "accountability," school leaders are under extraordinary pressure to increase standardized test scores, especially in reading and mathematics. In *Many Children Left Behind* Ted Sizer explains that NCLB purports to address the educational needs of disadvantaged children, but "the educational need is defined as a narrowing of the (test score) gap between rich and poor" (Meier & Wood 2004, p. xxi). Such a narrow vision of "need" results in a narrowing of the focus of schooling to preparation for standardized tests. Teachers spend inordinate amounts of time conducting "test prep," which often entails the use of test practice materials prepared by companies like Stanley Kaplan and Princeton Review. At a time when literacy scholars are calling for early exposure to a breadth of topical and cultural knowledge as a means of improving academic performance (Hirsch 2003), test preparation deprives students of a crucial access point to culturally significant people, places, events, and artifacts—authentic literature from a diversity of sources and genres.

Many of the city teachers I encounter are steering away from literature that they once considered indispensable in an English curriculum. Harper Lee's *To Kill a Mockingbird* (1960) is a book that many remember fondly from high school and consider highly accessible to teens. And yet they avoid teaching it to their own students, not because they believe it has lost its relevance, literary value, or instructional consequence, but because they view students as either unwilling to read it or incapable of doing so. In place of "essentials" like *Great Expectations* (Dickens 1861), secondary English teachers find themselves choosing literature (or having literature chosen for them) not on the merits of the writing, but simply because the print is large and there are a limited number of big words and unfamiliar references. I remember my astonishment when I heard from a group of New York City English teachers that *Slakes Limbo* (Holman 1974) had become a common item on ninth-grade English curricula in their schools. *Slakes Limbo* is a 126-page, large-print children's novel about a boy who is chased by bullies into the NYC subway and undergoes a life change as he survives in the tunnels for four months. I'm familiar with the book because I taught it to fifth graders at a public school in Harlem in 1994.

I do not want to overstate the case. There are plenty of schools in New York City and other urban centers where teachers assign, and students read, the likes of Walt Whitman, Shakespeare, Homer, Charles Dickens, Ralph Ellison, Arthur Miller, and Toni Morrison. My point is that in addition to not reading outside the classroom, there are far too many students, particularly in poor, urban neighborhoods, whose 15 or fewer pages of reading a day are largely pages drawn from test preparation guides, uninspiring textbooks, and second-rate literature. It is hard to imagine how such a recipe helps "prepare students to be life-long readers" or ensures that "all students . . . have the opportunities and resources to develop the language skills they need to pursue life's goals and to participate fully as informed, productive members of society" (National Council of Teachers of English 2006). If educational leaders and teachers are serious about meeting the lofty goals we state in our English language arts standards and guidelines, we need to find a way to instill in young urban students a "need to read" literature that will prepare them to thrive in the world as it is and to change the world to make it become what it could be.

Some urban English teachers see positive signs in the publication and increasing appearance in city schools over the last two decades of a small but growing body of young adult novels that, like "ghetto fiction," are written by authors of color and focus on contemporary urban life. While novels like Walter Dean Myers's *Monster* (1999), Sandra Cisneros's *The House on Mango Street* (1991), Angela Johnson's *The First Part Last* (2003), and Gary Soto's *Taking Sides* (1991) broach many of the same topics as street lit—crime, premarital sex, single parenting, poverty—they explore them seriously and without appealing to the baser impulses of readers. As in street lit, the characters in many of the novels speak in dialects approximating those used on the streets of places like Harlem and the barrios of Chicago, but they rarely use the coarse language that litters books like *Thug Matrimony*. Excerpts from the books commonly appear in Language Arts and English textbooks published by established houses like Pearson/Prentice Hall and McDougal Littell.

Relative to street lit, then, the body of contemporary young adult fiction used widely in urban schools is published more professionally, is more wholesome, and apparently focuses more on conveying life-affirming messages to city kids than cheap thrills. But what about the writing quality and literary value of the multicultural young adult literature that has made inroads into urban middle and high school English classrooms? How do these literary works compare to other novels and stories from the larger body of young adult literature taught in schools? When is it advisable to use this literature alongside or in place of the classics? These are all debatable questions that need to be argued on a book-by-book basis. Based solely on my subway observations and my own experiences as an English teacher at the middle school and high school levels, I will draw one blanket conclusion: contemporary young adult multicultural literature has not captured the interest and imagination of teen readers to nearly the degree that hip-hop lit has done in recent years. Perhaps I will feel differently when I see teens reading a Walter Dean Myers book on their own time, or witness a pair of high school girls simultaneously drawing their breaths in exhilaration as they huddle over *The House on Mango Street* (Cisneros 1991). Until then I will conclude that street lit is winning the competition for the hearts and minds of urban youth.

The six original stories that form the nucleus of *Street Lit* were not written by professional writers. They were written by current and former English teachers employed in high-need public secondary schools in urban centers around the United States. (One of the stories was collaboratively written by me and a former student of New York City public schools.) The authors regard their efforts as a response to the challenge that street lit/hip-hop fiction presents to English teachers working in these settings; it is the challenge of presenting students with literature that will engage them as fully as the girl I observed reading *Bitch Reloaded* (King 2007) on the #2 subway, while also enriching their minds and spirits as literature did for so many of us when we were young. Ultimately, you will draw your own conclusions about the value of these stories and decide if you will share them with your current or future students.

Whether or not you view these particular selections favorably, I hope that you find inspiration in the very fact that they were written by members of your current or future profession. I see in their efforts an important message for English teachers: we can (literally) compose our own teaching lives. Teachers too often see themselves as powerless to change the conditions that influence their everyday work in the classroom. The list of factors that teachers view as acting upon them and limiting their choices as professionals is long: overcrowded classrooms, under-prepared students, mandated curricula, No Child Left Behind, and so on. A common complaint of English teachers is how hard they have to struggle to locate quality literature that actually motivates their students to read. But rather than waiting for a "can't miss" novel to magically appear in your school bookroom, or for a school administrator, state curriculum, or university professor to decide for you what literature "works" for city kids, I hope that *Street Lit* motivates you to at least entertain an alternative response to this problem, one that seems in line with the qualifications and interests of English teachers: write your own classroom literature.

Feed the Block
by Terrence Hughes

❖ **About the Story**

*Every city block seems to have at least one "old-timer" who has seen it all and done it all. The **resident sage** who narrates the following story voices his frustration with the lack of progress he has seen over the years in this unnamed apartment building. Nevertheless, he has stuck around since 1895, and when a desperate teenager has nowhere else to turn, the narrator provides a mysterious way out of the boy's troubled home life.*

Been on this block since 1895. Seen 'em come and go. You know what? In all that time, ain't nothing changed. What I mean is, the people change but they don't improve. Act like trash, think like trash, do like trash. It's trash and garbage all over, on the floor, in the hallways, in their hearts. And it hurts me. Personally. All a' these stupid girls chasing styles so boys can knock 'em up before they quit growing. And forget the boys. Dumber than the girls, ready to fight and kill over imaginary insults and fake problems. No use telling them what they real problems are. No, man, they don't want to listen. They afraid to understand what the real deal is, because they'd fall into despair, which is what a little reality will do to you if you're an ignorant dickhead. Rather go to Rikers than school. Rather do time than make a nice living. Rather stay on this block than go out and find the world. Rather be somebody on the block than a nobody living in a decent house on Long Island. Yeah, that's real smart. Like I said, they come and go but they don't improve.

WORDS TO CONSIDER

resident: A person who lives in a particular location. Example: Before she moved to New York City, Juanita was a resident of San Juan, Puerto Rico.

sage: A person with a reputation for good judgment and wisdom. Example: For the wisdom of his decisions as a U.S. Attorney and Supreme Court Justice, Thurgood Marshall was considered by many to be a sage in the justice system.

stagger: (1) To move unsteadily. Example: The referee stopped the fight when he saw the boxer staggering on his feet. (2) To overwhelm with severe shock, pain, defeat, or misfortune. Example: The champion staggered the contender with a quick right to the ribs.

I'm holding this block together. That's why I put up with it. If I don't, what will happen to the good ones? Like right now. Look there. On the landing outside 3C. See that kid, about 12, 13? His old man's no good. Druggie. Beats him up all the time. He's a good kid—nice boy who does his schoolwork and helps his mama out with the chores and the little brothers, cause she's the one who works in that family. A lonely boy, all them heavy responsibilities. And all that fear. Look at him now—**stagger**ing around, face all swole' up and bruised. See him leaning up against the wall?

"I can't go back inside," the boy mutters. "I can't take this no more. Go jump off the roof. Better than this shit life."

I hear him. How many times have I seen this, heard it. And maybe he's right. No way out.

And maybe not. I know a way. It ain't so bad. And he'd be with others just like him. Not lonely no more. Whaddaya say? Shall we invite him in? It's 4 AM. Silence. No TV, no cursing, no sex noise. Sssh. The best time for this. The quietest, deadest hour of night. Yeah, it's time. Time to feed the block.

See. Now the boy's putting his swole-up cheek against the cool wall. He moves his whole body close, places his ear exactly so's he can hear. He don't breathe. *Feel* him listening.

"I hear you," the boy whispers. "Your heart's beatin'." He steps back, looks hard at my wall. "You're alive." He places both his palms against me. His hands sink into the soft, warm surface. The boy's red eyes and mouth open wide.

Come on in, son. Keep me company.

Discussion Questions

In the Lines

1. What do we know about the narrator of "Feed the Block"? What don't we know? What do we know about the boy from 3C? What don't we know?

2. What are some of the problems that the narrator sees in his neighborhood?

Between the Lines

3. What does the narrator mean when he says, "People change but they don't improve"? In what ways might people have changed on his block over the years?

4. The narrator tells us he has "Been on this block since 1895." How likely is it that he is still alive at the time he is telling the story?

5. The narrator describes the boy from 3C as "lonely." What might be the source of his loneliness?

6. It is impossible to walk through walls. This suggests that the "way out" is not literally through the apartment wall, but rather that the narrator's invitation for the boy to join him on the other side of the wall has symbolic meaning. What does the story suggest is the "way out" for children who are overwhelmed by the conditions in their home life or neighborhood?

Beyond the Text

7. For ages, scientists, historians, philosophers, and creative artists have debated the relative importance of an individual's innate qualities versus personal experiences in determining differences in human behavior. This is sometimes referred to as the nature versus nurture debate. The boy from 3C has decided that there is no escape from the life he is living. From your own observations, how much control does a young person have over his or her path in life? How much is determined by external influences such as one's family and neighborhood?

✗ Teacher Focus Group Discussion: Street Lit: Too Much, Too Often, Too Early for City Kids?

Participants were asked to read the following introduction prior to the focus group discussion.

Barbara Feinberg's feature article in *American Educator* (2004–2005), "Reflections on the Problem Novel: Do These Calamity-Filled Books Serve Up Too Much, Too Often, Too Early?"—raises questions that are pertinent to our discussion of teaching and reading of stories presented in this book. After observing her 12-year-old son's growing unease with the "dark" novels assigned to him at school, many of them recipients of the highest awards in children and young adult literature, Feinberg conducts her own review of "problem novels":

> While making my way through them, I have encountered: kids whose parents are drunk and cruelly neglectful (*The Pigman*), a child's uncle so demented by grief that he hallucinates his dead wife throughout the whole book (*Chasing Redbird*), atrocities of foster care and abandonment by one's mother (*They Cage the Animals at Night; Monkey Island*), more abandonment (*Dicey's Song; Belle Prater' Boy*), alcoholism (*The Late, Great Me*), kidnapping (*Ransom; The Face on the Milk Carton*), child abuse (*Bruises; Don't Hurt Laurie*), family violence (*Breathing Lessons*), sexual abuse (*Speak*), incest (*Abby, My Love*), teen suicide (*Tunnel Vision*), death of a friend (*Bridge to Terabithia*), running away and child prostitution (*A House for Jonnie O.*), and self-mutilation (*Cut; Crosses*)—to name but a very few. (Feinberg 2004–2005, p. 14)

Dark, depressing, weighty—how aptly do these terms apply to "Feed the Block" and other stories presented in this collection? What impact will they have on middle and high school students—the intended audience for this collection—versus students of similar age to Feinberg's son?

Beyond her concern with the troubling themes and events that serve as centerpieces in this genre, Feinberg compares contemporary young adult (YA) titles unfavorably to older adolescent classics such as *Huckleberry Finn* (Twain 1885), *A Tree Grows in Brooklyn* (Smith 1943), and *The Watsons Go to Birmingham—1963* (Curtis 1995), which also take on weighty events and themes such as racism, broken families, and alcoholism but do not, according to Feinberg, lose the "authentic" voice and perspective of children. Despite the troubles in their lives, the children and adolescents in these novels are unselfconsciously drawn to "play." Unlike their contemporary counterparts, whom Feinberg describes as "knowing too much," they can be blissfully and genuinely naïve; the darker elements of these stories are buffeted by a grace and levity born from the youthful character's embrace of the "animate" world:

> And it is precisely this dimension to childhood experience that is absent from many realistic novels and virtually all problem novels. No magic, manifest or latent, vibrates within them. Instead, in all of these self-proclaimed realistic stories, "reality" is understood as the opposite of imagination and fantasy, as if childhood were a dream from which children must be awakened—when, in fact, reality is not divisible from imagining, for children. But in these books children's imagination is regarded as something that must be tamed, monitored, barred. The child protagonist, while presented with the darkest and most upsetting situations imaginable, is denied what in real childhood would exist in abundance: recourse to fantasy. (Feinberg 2004–2005, p. 15)

In this reader's view, "Feed the Block" avoids a number of the pitfalls Feinberg identifies in the contemporary "problem novel." From the little we see of him, the boy from 3C does not "know too much." What he does know is that he "can't take no more" and that jumping off a roof is better than his "shit life" as the punching bag of an abusive father. His salvation is not the result of soul-searching reflection, nor does it come in the form of a benevolent adult outside the troubled family—at least not one from the material world. His communion with the "man" on the other side of the wall can be interpreted as a disturbing portent of the boy's retreat into a fantasy world. Or, the reader can view it as a resilient child's survival response to circumstances that leave him with no other recourse than finding solace in an imaginary, parallel universe. What is important, Feinberg tells us, is that "the author doesn't shout out 'the problem' and/or 'the meaning' but leaves room for the reader to connect with the story—the beautifully told story—on the level that is meaningful to him." (Feinberg 2004–2005, p. 15)

Beyond the literary merit of the story, however, the question remains: does a story like "Feed the Block" "serve up too much, too soon, too often" to an audience of urban high school students? In this same article, Feinberg relates a conversation she had with a psychiatrist working in a "city" clinic who has an abused 12-year-old patient living in foster care. According to the psychiatrist, the child "can't get enough" of books like *They Cage the Animals at Night* (Burch 1985)—a story about a child whose mother drops him off one day at an orphanage with no explanation. "This makes sense to me," Feinberg writes. "I can imagine how reading about others in trouble could feel like a lifeline. . . . But how do the books hit a 12-year-old or 10-year-old who still has a mother, whose life has all its parts more or less functioning, but who is just beginning the process of becoming more independent?" Behind Feinberg's concern for the child "whose life has all its parts more or less functioning," one senses a tacit assumption that "problem" literature offers more (and is potentially less damaging) to "city" kids whose lives have more in common with the characters inhabiting stories like *They Cage Animals at Night* and "Feed the Block."

I wonder, however, if teachers who work closely with inner-city youth agree that stories like "Feed the Block" and Feinberg's "problem novels" affect these students differently from those in more affluent, "sheltered" districts. Here are two more talking points to consider for our discussion:

- Some argue that inner-city students are already overly exposed to the violence and harsh living conditions portrayed in "Feed the Block." Do you feel that "Feed the Block" is particularly appropriate (or inappropriate) for students from poor, inner-city communities? What aspects of the story concern you? What aspects of the story do you find appealing as teachers of urban students?
- Beyond the bleak tone and violent elements of "Feed the Block," the story is notable for its absence of a simple, unambiguous resolution to the serious problems it presents. As adult readers, you may find the ending engaging and thought-provoking. How do you anticipate your students will respond to the ending, and how would you prepare for their response?

Discussion

Ed: I don't have any problem with the ambiguity. I found the ending completely satisfying. It left me with a question that continues to resonate with me: how do "we"—the narrator, the boy, school teachers, responsible parents, caring citizens, anyone who hopes for positive change, etc.—respond to circumstances that are unlivable yet seemingly impossible to alter? What do we do? Should we simply "press on" and endure in the face of such misery?

Angela: I think the ending does give an answer, kind of. I see it as saying to seek wisdom and comfort from people who have kept their dignity and humanity despite the harsh conditions.

Holly: Yeah, but what about the fact that the person the kid gets help from is not real? I see the narrator just as a figment of his imagination. So then what is the message here? Escape to a fantasy world of imaginary guardians and talking walls?

Colleen: For me, the ending suggests any or all of those possibilities. We all know what it's like to work in schools where sometimes it feels like students, teachers, administrations, curriculums, policies, etc. "change but they don't improve." Maybe the very point or effect of the story is to show just how consuming it is to observe human misery, and to seek answers without becoming cynical or completely detached from reality.

Christina: Honestly, I think it may make some kids feel a little angry. If they're going through a similar situation it may make them feel a little angrier—like there's no way out. And, if they're reading stories where children are living better lives than they are living, maybe it might open up doors for them and show them a different life. Like, "There is something different from this."

Ginette: I also thought that they might have an angry reaction. I think what I notice about many of my students is that they don't see the bigger picture in things. One of the things they might do is jump on the line about "the dumb girl and the dumb boys" and take it, maybe, a little personally. I've seen them do it before. You make a comment and then they take it like, "Oh, well, why are you saying that about me?" And I'm like, I'm not! It's just in the story. Particularly students who are poor readers or who have not read a lot of literature have trouble differentiating between a fictional narrator and the author. They see them as one and the same. And I'm wondering if they might become guarded suddenly because they perceive that someone is making a judgment about them.

Holly: I'm actually more worried that rather than being angry, some of my students will get into the violence and deviant behavior. Their journals are full of entries about relatives and friends in jail, or "juvies." When they write about these things or we discuss *Shawshank Redemption* (King 1982) or *Monster* (Myers 1999), some of my students get really freaked out about jail. It's just a snapshot, but it freaks them out. Others, though, appear more excited than scared. Being in a gang for some of them appears to be cool, and so is it that their cousin went to jail. It isn't scary to them, and they *should* be scared, in my opinion.

I think that there are some subjects which are too much; I wouldn't want to touch incest with any group of high school students. But I'm not saying that we should avoid literature that contains violence or "adult" topics altogether. If these are common aspects of their lives, then we have to help them work through these issues in a thoughtful, constructive manner. I think it is good to give them a short story once in a while and say, "Okay, well, what do you think of that, now? A guy just got raped in jail. What do you think of that?"—and have them talk about it.

Ed: I don't know. What's the alternative? All the topics Barbara Feinberg lists as "too much, too soon" are the very topics that I read about in high school—alcoholism, cruelly neglectful parents, crazy uncles, etc. You can find all of these things in classics like Mrs. Dalloway, anything written by James Joyce, Faulkner, Richard Wright.

The bigger issue in my mind is that a lot of the contemporary young adult literature being used in schools is just poorly written. Like Feinberg says, they read like "guilty soap operas." That I agree with, but it's not the dark and depressing content that's "too much," it's the quality and variety of writing style that's lacking. Reading *Monster* and other Walter Dean Myers novels is not bad in itself; it can be really helpful if you're using them to get somewhere else, to get them into reading. But relying on these books grade after grade, even in high school, which I see as a trend in education, *is* problematic.

Colleen: It's interesting that we should bring up *Monster* because I'm reading it right now with my freshman classes. It's written half as a journal, and half like a screenplay that the narrator is writing about his trial for murder. And he calls it *Monster* because in the opening arguments, the prosecuting attorney says, "There are monsters in our community preying on the peace loving people." She means him, and he takes it very personally, saying things like, 'I can't believe I'm in jail, I'm a good kid,' and you find out he goes to Stuyvesant[1] and all this stuff.

    The problem is that it's really not well written, in my personal opinion. The characters are very stereotypical, particularly all of the lawyers and judges. I noticed that they are not even two-dimensional, they're one-dimensional. As far into it as I am, I haven't noticed that much development in terms of the main character. All we get is this sense of injustice, and I mean, that's fine, but you need to develop that. And I compare that to a book like *The Shawshank Redemption* (King 1982) which I've read with students as well as shown the movie, and it's more masterfully done. I noticed that when I read *The Shawshank Redemption* with a class, they really got into it, whereas when we started *Monster,* half of my class was like, "Oh my God, Miss, do we really have to open that book again?" And I feel like, in a sense, they know they're being pandered to. It's as if they're being told, oh you'll like this because you've walked down 145th Street and maybe you know someone who's in jail. Is that really the reason we should be reading the book? Maybe, as Ed said, we should be looking to expose our kids to something bigger. You can get to themes that touch them while still maintaining a high standard in terms of the quality of literature.

Glen: I find *Monster* pretty deplorable, actually. I like some of the Walter Dean Myers stuff, especially some of his short stories. There's a lot of humanity in them, but the novels are not structured very well. And I think he's much better with the short form, personally. That aside, in *Monster,* the screenplay format allows for less description, and that's why my kids like it—which always makes me cringe. I spend half my time saying, "Write more descriptively. Don't just make a blanket statement," and here they are gravitating to a book that's written in sound bites. And also, they like the fact that it reminds them of a procedural TV show. They love that. They make that connection.

Holly: Yeah, they're very familiar with that formula.

Glen: Yeah, they're very familiar with it, and my kids like what they feel comfortable with. And of course when the books contain stereotypical characters they get right into them. "Feed the Block" is not the same old, same old, which is exactly why I used it in my English classes. Yes, it's set in the inner city, and the language and predicaments of the character are familiar to them. What's different is the perspective that the characters have on the

---

[1] A selective public high school in New York City.

problems they face, and how they resolve them. It's not a so-called "gritty" television drama where grittiness is an end in itself.

Here's the interesting part: I used it in my English class and the first batch of kids I gave it to "got" the magical part of it and everything. It wasn't an issue for them because I prefaced it by saying, "Who is the narrator? Characterize this. Is this narrator a person or something else?" And they got into it, they loved it, they really did. They understood it and they weren't shocked by it or depressed by it, and they didn't feel condescended to. Mission accomplished. Then, recently, I tried this with my kids on Roosevelt Island, which everyone thinks is a middle-class enclave and it's not, but it's certainly not the South Bronx. And the kids—this was my honors class, by the way—they just went "Oh, well, what's this? Is he being molested?" And they were all being very silly and immature about it, so I just said, "Okay, class is over, we'll just move on to something else." In the meantime, the kids in the South Bronx, I'm happy to report, got it and seized upon the story as a basis for meaningful discussion. Maybe the point is that it's just a little too particular for some audiences. Not quite a broad-based appeal.

Holly: Did the students from the South Bronx respond with anger at all?

Glen: Oh, hell, they're always in a rage about something. What teenagers aren't? But no, they weren't particularly angered by this. Actually, the more concerning response was that they accepted it as very normal. "Well, this is what I have in my house, this is me." Actually, some of them seemed to view it more as documentary than fiction, which was really frightening. But the reaction was great.

Angela: I was surprised that someone said that the possible student response would be anger, because my impression is that parts of the story are so reflective of what these kids are going through that if there should be anger, it should be at the situation, not the author or teacher. When someone mentioned anger, I was like "Huh?" I'm not a teacher yet, but in my own personal experience, growing up in these neighborhoods and with these kids, it's a fact of life. You know, you talk about your friend who's pregnant, or whoever's getting beat up at home, and you're not getting angry or taking it personally. When I read this, I wasn't taking it personally. It's the way it is.

Ginette: It's a fact of life.

Ratner: Let me bring this conversation back to one of the first concerns voiced in the discussion: the possibility that kids will just find this depressing. Think about how some of the authors you have characterized as "pandering" would have written "Feed the Block." One could easily imagine the insertion of some benign sort of fatherly figure who would tell the boy that life is a struggle, and then point to the "way out," whether it be by finding a goal in life, studying hard, hanging out with the right people, or fighting oppression. Furthermore, the message or moral would somehow be made transparent in the narrative. It's not nearly as clear-cut with "Feed the Block." It seems to me that a reader could draw the perfectly reasonable conclusion that the story underscores the thin line separating hope from fantasy; it's the uncertainty at the end of the story that makes it, in my view, very, very interesting. But how about kids who don't get it, or do get it but say, "Well that's fine, but where does it leave me?" Is there a danger in introducing a story that some will interpret as suggesting that fantasy is a viable—perhaps the only—response to confronting destructive conditions beyond one's control? That's sort of depressing, don't you think? It's a hard notion to stomach for a teenager, much less an adult. How do you respond to that potential danger, if you want to call it that?

Colleen: Well, to a large degree that's what you want. I don't want the kids to "get it," necessarily. I teach high school English, so I expect them to dig deeper into literature and penetrate the more elusive elements of stories. How else will they be ready to read Shakespeare or Faulkner? I don't want them to get it. If they got it, I wouldn't be there. I would much prefer to be in a situation where we could write about it, discuss it, and together get a hold on what's going on in the story.

In terms of "getting it," to me the central issue is not the transparency of the themes or stylistic sophistication; it's more about prior knowledge of the book or story's cultural context. Is it better to give students literature about people and places that they are familiar with, or not? I don't think it's a yes or no question.

Glen: I'll tell you, there was another specific reason I used this in my class. When you have a classroom of low to average reluctant readers in seventh or eighth grade, and it's hard to engage them in a novel, even one like *Monster,* it helps to give them a sense of accomplishment, of having read something in its entirety, something that's whole. Short as it may be, it's not an excerpt or a chapter of something that they haven't the stamina to read yet. Early in the year I think something short, a page or two, is good to get them back into the idea of reading again. And something with a context and topic that's directly meaningful to their lives. That's what I'm aiming for.

Ed: I think both of you have it right. You're entering into two battles. You're entering the context battle: I have to create a context somehow for the kids to approach a story that involves cultural references of which they may be completely unaware. I have kids who live in the Bronx and have never seen or even heard of the United Nations, who couldn't recognize the Brooklyn Bridge or know that it's New Jersey on the other side when you look across the Hudson River. So you have a lot of filling in to do when you read a book like, say, *Nectar in a Sieve* (Markandaya 2002), which is set in rural India during British rule.

And then at the same time you have to contend with the reading battle, which is what Glen was describing. Many of the students I've been working with still struggle at the basic reading level. They get intimidated simply by the sight of multisyllable words and will just shut down.

I had a weird experience last year with this issue. First semester we read something called *I, Juan de Pareja*. Not a good experience. In terms of the prose, it's definitely written for students but in terms of context, it's not as accessible as "Feed the Block." And then we read things that were more accessible, like *Animal Farm* (Orwell 1946), which to me is very easy prose, and at least on the literal level, pretty straightforward in terms of context. But they hated that also. They hated everything we read that semester until we got to *Lord of the Flies* (Golding 1954). What was surprising to me was that *Lord of the Flies* was easily the most dense prose that we'd read. It's also full of cultural references and descriptions of a physical world that is completely foreign to my students. But for some reason they really loved it. I guess it reached them thematically, and they were getting a feeling of accomplishment. They were breaking it down, looking at how characterization develops theme. When I read *Lord of the Flies* in high school I was like, "Oh man, what's this guy talking about?" and here were my struggling readers, with their supposedly limited knowledge of the world, really getting into it. You never know.

Colleen: Well, it's interesting because if you look at it thematically, *Animal Farm* has an esoteric, satirical quality that we might appreciate, but *communism* is almost a meaningless word to my students. They don't get it; they don't know about it, with the exception of a few kids. But if you talk survival of the fittest, Darwinism, they *know* Darwinism. Even if they can't label it as Darwinism, they know what it means. When I taught *Lord of the Flies*, I decided that's when we were going to delve into symbolism (the conch and the glasses), and they were able to break it down and were really good with it, largely because these were symbols that actually corresponded with something in their lives.

Ed: So what does that say? *Lord of the Flies* was written in dense prose decades ago by some guy in England who hated kids and wanted to show that kids were horrible creatures. It's set on an island, for Christ's sake, which couldn't be further from my students' everyday surroundings, yet my students were able to get into it. To me it comes down to how much the themes resonate with the students. That, and if it's really well written, the students will work through the challenging language and open their minds to unfamiliar settings.

Angela: Oh wait! Maybe there was a pop culture reference connection that helped them make sense of the book.

Ed:	You mean *Survivor*?[2] Yeah, that's true. Oh, absolutely. We talked about *Survivor* a lot, and that became part of it. But, the point was that they were reading a really difficult text.
Ratner:	They were willing to struggle with the reading.
Colleen:	And I had the same experience with *Les Misérables* (Hugo 1862), a 1400-page brick of a book, so I think we have to be really careful when we say our students can't get through a book because it's too long or the language and settings are too foreign for them. They got through it and had a good grasp on its themes. And I think this is because it speaks to things that they can understand. It speaks to things that I can understand, and I haven't lived that life. And I think instead of giving them literature that on the surface has parallels with their lives, a teacher should challenge them to challenge themselves to dig a little deeper and stay with material that might intimidate them at first. That's when you're really gonna see them connecting with literature. Yes, you have to do a good job selling a story, but still there's something about really well-written stuff that will eventually resonate in a way that's . . . that's not easily forgettable, that makes it difficult for students to dismiss the book outright.
Ratner:	We have to wrap up soon. Let's see if we can put some closure on this discussion. So? "Feed the Block"? Is it "too much, too soon"?
Kevin:	I have some thoughts on that. Saying that it's "too much, too soon" is kind of pulling the wool over our eyes. Not just my students, but all kids these days are getting exposed to it anyway. If it's not in their daily lives, it's on TV, it's in the media, and to say we just need to give them "nicer" books, that's just condescending. You can't shelter them. Can you give them a nicer book? What are you gonna give them? *Harry Potter*?[3] That has torture, evil, an orphan, death of dear friends, death of a mentor.
Ratner:	But earlier Ginette spoke about how her students could read a story like "Feed the Block" and say, "Hey, they're talking about me." Does a book like Harry Potter carry that same risk?
Kevin:	I think so. He's an archetypal character. Romeo? I have nothing in common with Romeo on the surface. I don't know what it's like to be a prince. But that doesn't mean I haven't experienced what he's experienced at a deeper level.
Cyril:	Well, I just want to say that violence is around us. I don't think that a story like "Feed the Block" is too much . . . I don't think giving them a book with violence in it is exposing them, because they're already exposed. For a child in the South Bronx, if violence isn't in the home, it's right down the hall or out on the street. Therefore,

---

[2] A popular reality television game show where contestants are isolated in a remote location and compete for cash and other prizes.

[3] The titular character of seven best-selling novels by U.K. author J.K. Rowling. The books focus on Harry's fight against an evil, murderous wizard who killed Harry's parents—and will later go onto to kill many others in Harry's circle—in his quest to take over the Wizarding world.

I think it's probably better to have them think about it in a way that they probably don't think about it every day. How do we avoid that violence? How do we live with violence if it's unavoidable? Those are healthy discussions to have with students, and if a story prompts students to engage in them, then it should be read.

Holly: I think you bring up a very good point. We have to help them to see that what they see in the world, and often accept as normal for a kid their age, is actually not the way it has to be. And I think to have another value put on the experience of violence—violence in the street, violence in the home—is really a good thing. And if that means exposing them to books or stories that hold a mirror to their lives, that have some violence or some cruelty in them, but provide a context for taking a thoughtful and critical look at what's around them, that's a good thing.

Angela: I agree, but I have to point out that it's not only in the city that bad stuff happens. There are plenty of children getting abused in the suburbs. There's plenty of people who "act like trash, think like trash" in Westchester and Long Island.

Glen: Yeah, right. Not to mention all the corporate crime and perversity behind those picket fences!

Angela: So, I think it would be wrong to flood students with stories that depict blight and violence just because they're black and brown and live in poor neighborhoods. And another thing: students need to know the historical context that made the inner city what it is today. It's not like people showed up in the Bronx one day and decided to not have jobs or education and start shooting at each other. It's not like people chose to be poor and discriminated against.

Colleen: Yeah, that's a really good point. Actually, I don't think the issue is the book's subject, though. All of the topics that concerned Feinberg in the article, I read about in high school. I read *The Bell Jar* (Plath 1963), for example, which discusses suicide. So I don't think it's the subject that distinguishes what kids are reading today from earlier generations. I think it has more to do with the highly visceral quality of the writing in books like *Push* (Sapphire 1996) and alternative press books like *Homo Thug* (Kahari 2004). It's really a question of language more than subject. If you're reading Shakespeare, you're reading about murder and slaughter. You're reading about people being raped and you're reading euphemisms for sex in every other line. So, I think it's more about the quality of language being more immediate and raw. It kind of hits you in a different way. "I can't believe they're reading this!" Well, that's what I read about, too.

Ed: It reminds me of the whole PMRC thing.[4] You have Tipper Gore saying that it's not okay for Prince to talk about having sex in

---

[4] Formed in 1985 by four mothers (Tipper Gore, wife of Senator and later Vice President Al Gore; Susan Baker, wife of Treasury Secretary James Baker; Pam Howar, wife of Washington realtor Raymond Howar; and Sally Nevius, wife of Washington City Council Chairman John Nevius), the mission of the Parents Music Resource

a song, but really it's the same thing The Crystals[5] were talking about in "Da Doo Ron Ron" in the 60s. The difference is Prince is *saying* it explicitly. That's where the problem lies. As an educator should I be concerned when language is more immediate and visceral? If they're reading a lot of this stuff, is it affecting students' ability to get through literature containing language that has little in common with what they hear and use on the street?

I think it's important to separate language and content when looking at this question of "too much too soon." The language in "Feed the Block" is raw, but the ideas behind the words are very sophisticated and challenging . . . It requires active reading.

Ratner: This is a good place to finish up. I'm glad that the issue of language came up at the end because that's exactly what we'll be focusing on for our next discussion.

Helena: Can I make one more comment? I think the one issue that hasn't been mentioned is this: Books by Triple Crown Press and Zane[6] lead kids to expect that within the first five pages of every book they read there will be graphic sex and/or violence. It really diminishes their patience with any books that don't immediately contain these elements—it creates a literary culture of immediate gratification, where they won't be interested in anything that doesn't shock them right off the bat and keep doing so throughout.

Colleen: Yes! I completely agree. Television and video games are bad enough. I would hope that my students look at literature as an alternative to all the cheap thrills out there. But I don't see much appreciation in these books for subtlety or plot development.

⚔ Classroom Activities: Feed the Block

Introductory Activity: Journal Freewrite

"The most effective way I know to improve your writing is to do freewriting exercises regularly." This is Peter Elbow's opening line to his seminal *Writing Without Teachers* (1973). Given the remarkable spread and routine use of freewriting in English classrooms today (as well as in other content area classrooms), it appears that he is not the only writing teacher who feels this way. As Elbow explained, and many other writers and teachers of writing have discovered, the benefit of freewriting is that it "undoes the ingrained habit of editing at the same time you are trying to produce. It will make writing less blocked because words will come more easily" (Elbow 1973, p. 6).

Center (PMRC) was "to educate and inform parents" about "the growing trend in music towards lyrics that are sexually explicit, excessively violent, or glorify the use of drugs and alcohol." Gore spearheaded the group after listening along with her daughter Karenna to the Prince song "Darling Nikki" which contains graphic references to sex and masturbation. The group sought to censor and rate popular music that they deemed harmful to children and teens.

[5] Written by Jeff Barry, Ellie Greenwich, and Phil Spector, *Da Doo Ron Ron* was recorded by rhythm-and-blues girl group The Crystals in 1963.

[6] See discussion in Chapter 1.

Most of the introductory activities outlined in this book are more directive and specific than "simply write for 10 minutes. Don't stop for anything" (Elbow 1973, p. 3). There are compelling reasons, however, for asking students to regularly freewrite in journals as a response to literature. To begin with, if we only elicit literature responses from students through directed prompts and questions, we are sending them a message that is probably not in their best interest; we are saying, in effect: "You do not have the authority, responsibility, or ability to initiate responses when you read; the only time you should think critically, make predictions, life connections, and generally engage in active reading of literature is when a teacher directs you to do so." In Sheridan Blau's words, when we knowingly or unknowingly send this message to students, we are treating them as "welfare recipients in the economy of literature interpretation" (Blau 2003, p. 31).

Secondly, if students are given the space and freedom to initiate their own immediate responses to literature, the range and variety of responses will increase dramatically. On occasions when I have permitted students to set the topical agenda, I am often surprised by the substance and pertinence of the concerns they bring to the reading of plays, novels, and poems. Many teachers, particularly new ones, fear asking high school students to assume responsibility for spontaneously generating written responses to literature without the assistance of a prompt. They envision blank stares, yawns, and anticipate the dreaded refrain, "I don't know what to do!"

As Elbow and Blau suggest, part of the problem here is a type of learned helplessness that students have developed in response to repeated teacher-initiated discussion questions, worksheets, and the ubiquitous "Do Now" (complete with bullet points directing students how, when, and what to do in response to a story or poem). In part then, the answer to this problem lies in simply sticking with freewriting long enough to unlearn the ingrained habit. As with any other activity that is not natural to us, resolve and patience go a long way toward making freewriting more natural and pleasurable. The teachers I know whose students have become comfortable and productive with freewriting are those teachers who have been patient and resilient enough to see it through. Even if it takes weeks, the sheer stubbornness of these teachers and their commitment to the philosophy behind freewriting communicates to their students that they mean business in terms of expecting them to become producers rather than consumers in the "economy" of literature analysis.

Nonetheless, the challenge of moving students from a teacher-driven approach to journal writing to a student-driven one might require some intermediary steps. One such step is a type of modified freewrite I refer to as a "Lit-Fueled Freewrite." In this case, the literature itself (even a single line or passage from a novel, short story, or play) serves as a jumping-off point for a journal freewrite. No prompts, focusing questions, ketchup, or steak sauce necessary here—just the story or poem straight up, especially when you feel confident that the excerpt or line is compelling enough itself to elicit meaningful responses. A story like "Feed the Block" is fitting for a modified freewrite because it is short enough to read in one sitting, it is highly evocative and emotionally stirring, and it has an ending that resonates beyond the final words, which provides the student writer with the necessary impetus to put pen to page.

For these reasons, you might consider introducing "Feed the Block" by simply reading the story while students listen, without even looking at their own text. Before beginning the reading, ask the students to have their journals open and ready with just a date written for the next entry. Immediately after reading the last words of the story, direct students to begin a 5- to 10-minute freewrite. As soon as the "sound" of students silently moving their pens across paper fills the room, quietly remind them of Elbow's simple advice for freewriting: "Go quickly without rushing. Never stop to look back, to cross something out, to wonder how to spell something, to wonder what word or thought to use, or to think about what you are doing." (Elbow 1973, p. 3) When the freewrite is "Lit-Fueled," you may also encourage the students to let the story (passage, line, and so on) seep into their minds and hearts and then . . . just write.

Writing Project: Neighborhood "I-Search" Paper

The narrator in "Feed the Block" has a particular perspective on his neighborhood that grows out of his personal experiences while living there. A man, woman, or child who lived down the hall from the narrator might have presented a very different picture of this same "block." Have students write an "I-search" paper (Macrorie 1988) that presents a perspective on an aspect of their neighborhood or block that interests them. An I-search paper differs from a re-search paper in that you are not only reporting information on a topic but also describing the journey you take in learning what you seek to know or understand. In other words, an I-search paper describes "what" the reader should know about a topic, while also relating interesting or relevant aspects of "how" the information was gathered and how it has changed the way the writer thinks or feels in regard to it. Although "I-searchers" conduct interviews and surveys, record field observations, and collect statistical information in the same manner as researchers, they often write their accounts in the first-person point of view ("I") rather than third-person point of view and, in general, use a more informal, story-like tone.

In my experience, the students who produce high-quality I-Search papers are the ones who pursue questions that genuinely interest them. For this reason, it is important to have students spend considerable time in their journals exploring potential topics for their paper and discovering inquiry questions pertaining to a topic that truly matters to them. Asking students to reread the earlier freewriting entries described above may point them to a general topic or question related to their neighborhood. You can also play an essential role in helping students to narrow topics and define research questions by conducting individual writing conferences with them.

Here are a few "I-search" questions that some of my students have pursued in response to this assignment:

- How are customers of different races and cultures treated in stores around my neighborhood?
- What qualities are girls in my neighborhood looking for in a future husband?

- What percentage of high school kids in my neighborhood carry weapons on them, and what are the reasons that they do so?
- How do parents and students in my neighborhood feel about making school uniforms mandatory in the local public schools?

Community of Readers Extension Activity: The One-Question Interview

The One-Question Interview (Figure 2.1) is an engaging and easy-to-implement activity for introducing your students to a research-oriented writing process and generating interest in conducting more substantial research projects such as the I-Search paper described above. Although it is more commonly employed in social studies and science classrooms (high school subjects that tradition-ally cover "research"), I have found that it lends itself nicely to establishing a community of literature readers. As students independently interview other students and gather a range of perspectives on topics and themes invoked by a story or poem, they begin to recognize the pleasures and benefits of seeking out other readers with whom they can share their literature reading experiences.

Materials: Newsprint, markers, tape, one-question interview form.

✖ Language in Context Study: The "Understood" Subject

It is likely that at some point your students have been taught that English sen-tences must contain a subject and predicate. Yet, even at the high school or college level, students routinely omit subjects from sentences or employ them incorrectly. If subject/predicate is the most basic building block of sentences, why do many students continue to struggle with this seemingly straightfor-ward grammar point? One possible answer to this question is that in both form and concept, subject/predicate usage is not as straightforward as it appears to those who have already mastered the form. To begin with, both written and spoken forms of English allow for sentence forms where the subject is *under-stood* rather than actually included in the sentence. This is often the case with the subject of a command, order, or suggestion, such as when "you"—the person being directed—is usually left out of the sentence without confusing the reader or listener.

[You] Take your shoes off before entering the house.

Before beginning the quiz, [you] read all directions at the top of the page.

As with many other types of grammar and usage errors, students' confu-sion may also arise from differences in spoken and written communication. Speakers of certain regional and cultural dialects commonly employ the under-stood subject even when the sentence type is not a command, order, or sugges-tion. The same can be found in written English forms that simulate speaking:

[I] Been on this block since 1895.
[I] Seen 'em come and go.

FIGURE 2.1

Procedures for One-Question Interview

1. Generate a list of questions related to a story, play, or poem (or an aspect of these) that you are using in class. Cut questions into slips. (You can also have students develop their own questions during journal writing.)

2. Distribute the one-question interview form (see Figure 2.2).

3. Tell the students to write their question at the top of the form before walking around the classroom asking other students the assigned or chosen question. For each student interviewed, they will need to take notes on the response to the question.

4. When everyone has completed interviewing a designated number of students, ask two students to sit down and turn over their form (see Figure 2.3).

5. On the back of the form, there is room for the students to analyze their information. They must look at how many people they interviewed and what responses they recorded. This will help them summarize their research and analyze it for patterns, inconsistencies, and so on.

6. It is helpful if you model the summarizing process for students. For example, on the board write, "I asked 15 people 'How many religions are represented in your community?' 5 people said 1, 7 people said 4, and 3 people were not sure."

7. You may have to define the terms *research, conclude,* and *observations.* Have a discussion with students about what it means to be a "researcher" and the value of interviews as a way to gather information firsthand.

8. Ask students to find a partner and share the results of their interviews. You may also ask students to share with the entire class.

Here is a sample list of interview questions to cut into strips and individually assign to students after reading "Feed the Block":

- What is one piece of advice or guidance that you would give to the boy from 3C?

- What character from literature, film, television, or your own life reminds you of the boy in 3C?

- What character from literature, film, television, or your own life reminds you of the narrator?

- Do you feel that "Feed the Block" contains a message or moral? If so, what is it?

- What is one word that you would use to describe your neighborhood?

- How do you think people from outside of your neighborhood would describe your neighborhood?

- The narrator in "Feed the Block" says that people on his block "change but they don't improve." What are some changes you have seen on your block over the years? Do you consider these changes "improvements"?

- If you could live any place in the world other than your current neighborhood, where would it be, and why would you want to live there?

- Choose one sentence or phrase in "Feed the Block." Why did you choose it?

- Would you recommend that other students your age read "Feed the Block"? Why or why not?

F I G U R E   2 . 2

One-Question Interview Form (front)

Name _____

Your Question: _____

_____

Student	Response to Your Question

Analyzing sentences like these from "Feed the Block" help students understand that beyond correctness, there are underlying reasons why we write differently from the way we speak. Equipped with fingers, hands, faces, and vocal cords, speakers can clearly indicate who or what has "Been on the block" or "Seen 'em come and go." Writers, stripped of these modes of communication, almost always have to use words: (I, You, They, The Carters have been on this block since 1895) to clearly indicate the subject.

⚔ Text Connections

For Students

De Trevino, Elizabeth Borton. *I, Juan de Pareja*. New York: Farrar, Straus and Giroux, 1965.

FIGURE 2.3

One-Question Interview Form (back)

I asked _____ people _____

_____ people said _____

_____ people said _____

_____ people said _____

_____ people said _____

_____ people said _____

I can conclude the following:

Loosely based on the relationship between famous seventeenth-century Spanish master painter Diego Velazquez and his black slave and assistant, Juan de Pareja, *I, Juan de Pareja* won the Newbery Medal in 1965 for the most distinguished contribution to children's literature. Written as an autobiography, it chronicles how de Pareja became an accomplished painter in his own right despite laws prohibiting slaves from painting.

Myers, Walter Dean. *Monster.* New York: HarperCollins Publishers, 1999, 281 pp.
While on trial as an accomplice to a murder, 16-year-old Steve Harmon records his experiences in prison and in the courtroom in the form of a film script as he tries to come to terms with the course his life has taken.

King, Stephen. "Rita Hayworth and the Shawshank Redemption," in *Different Seasons.* New York: Viking Press, 1982, 527 pp.
"Rita Hayworth and the Shawshank Redemption" is a novella by Stephen King, originally published in *Different Seasons* (1982). It was filmed as "The Shawshank Redemption" in 1994. Directed by Frank Darabont and starring Tim Robbins and Morgan Freeman, it is the story of a soft-spoken banker who is convicted of murder and serving a life sentence at a fictitious prison located in Maine.

Like "Feed the Block," the following fiction and nonfiction selections portray teenagers struggling to find the inner resources needed to overcome the challenges of growing up in the inner city.

Carroll, Jim. *The Basketball Diaries.* New York: Penguin, 1987, 224 pp.
    Between the ages of 12 and 16, Carroll kept an autobiographical account of "growing up hip" on the Lower East Side of New York City. While attending an elite private school on scholarship, Carroll endures poverty and a dysfunctional family life by turning to petty theft, hustling, and heroin while simultaneously excelling at basketball and poetry. *The Basketball Diaries* was adapted to film in 1995 with Leonardo DiCaprio as Carroll.

Suskind, Ron. *A Hope in the Unseen: An American Odyssey from the Inner City to the Ivy League.* New York: Broadway Books, 1998, 400 pp.
    A Hope in the Unseen is a full-length nonfiction narrative that tracks the life of Cedric Jennings from his days as talented black teenager struggling to succeed in one of the worst public high schools in Washington, D.C., to his sophomore year at Brown University.

For Teachers

Macrorie, Ken. *The I-Search Paper: Revised Edition of Searching Writing* Portsmouth, NH: Boynton/Cook, 1988, 376 pp.
    The "I" in Macrorie's "I-Search" paper is the student. Rather than removing all traces of author involvement as students are traditionally taught to do when writing research papers, "I-searchers" account for their own role and interest in the research process. Macrorie argues that when students are encouraged to explore the world outside the library for answers to questions that matter to them, and to write the story of their quest for knowledge and understanding, students begin to view research as something more than an academic exercise. The examples of student written I-Search papers in the book give teachers further direction and inspiration for introducing students to this fresh approach to the research paper.

Elbow, Peter. *Writing Without Teachers,* 2nd ed. New York: Oxford University Press, 1998, 240 pp.
    The term "freewriting" has become ubiquitous in English and composition classes from primary grades through college. It was coined by Elbow in *Writing Without Teachers,* and Elbow's description of this method for undoing "the habit of compulsive, premature editing" is still the best. The book also introduces Elbow's other major contribution to writing instruction, the "teacherless writing class," a method of peer feedback focused on helping the writer make his or her own informed decisions on how to revise a composition.

Where the Time Went
by Amy Alvarez

❖ **About the Story**

*Nadia, the protagonist of "Where the Time Went," faces a decision that could change the course of her life. The fact that this choice will also alter the life of another human being makes it particularly urgent. At only 16 years of age, Nadia faces a **predicament** that forces her to distinguish her own dreams, desires, and values from those of her mother.*

Nadia stared at the clock. It was 10:57 in the morning on Saturday. It had been a week since the end of her last grounding, two weeks since the end of her last fight at school and two days, seventeen hours and three—now four—minutes, since Isaiah had been arrested.

It was also two and a half months since her last period. Exactly.

Nadia lay on her bed and watched the clock until it said exactly 11:00. She had to tell her mother today. She had been throwing up every morning. At first, she tricked herself into thinking she was sick. She took flu medicine. But eventually, she had to face facts. She got one of those little sticks that you pee on. It said she was pregnant. She told Isaiah. He told her how great it was that they were going to be parents, that he still loved her, even if they weren't together anymore. Then he stopped returning her phone calls.

WORDS TO CONSIDER

predicament: An unpleasantly difficult, perplexing, or dangerous situation. Example: If we lose the directions, we're in a real predicament.

consultation: (1) A conference at which advice is given or views are exchanged. (2) A meeting between physicians to discuss the diagnosis or treatment of a case. Example: At the consultation, both doctors agreed that James should go through with the operation.

procedure: (1) A series of steps taken to accomplish a task. (2) A particular course or mode of action. Example: The procedure for obtaining a driver's license includes passing a road test.

At 11:01, Nadia rose and headed down the hall to the kitchen. She smelled bacon, coffee and burnt toast. Her mom was playing some sappy, Christian salsa. At least it wasn't those slow ass hymns.

"Morning, *mija.* Want some bacon and OJ? The toast will be coming up. Burnt the first batch. We have to have that toaster fixed."

"No thanks, Mom."

Now that she was in the kitchen, she felt nauseated again. Her mom raised an eyebrow. "*No!? You* not hungry? I don't believe it. Sit. Eat."

How was she going to begin this? "Um . . . I'm just not hungry. You know, I've been feeling kind of sick sometimes, like, in the morning." She waited. Sonya, her mother, was pulling a half loaf of raisin bread from the freezer and was banging it against the counter.

"Probably because you stay up so late. You know, you can't do that forever. It's not good."

"I know, Ma. I dunno though. I just have been puking a lot. In the morning." God, was she not getting it? What was she going to have to say?

"I don't know, Nadia. It could be anything. You could be drinking." Nadia looked up and opened her mouth to defend herself. Sonya cut her off. "Don't think that I don't know that you snuck out when you were grounded. Hanging out with that boyfriend . . . Now look where he's at. That's punishment enough for you."

Nadia stared at the ceiling. On any other day, she normally would have stormed off to her room, flinging curses at her mom, but today was different. She needed to do this. "Look, Ma. Whatever. I never snuck out when I was on punishment." Sonya shot her a look. "I just feel sick. I been feeling sick for a while. Puking and stuff."

Sonya stopped the bread bashing. "You been throwing up?"

"Yeah."

"In the mornings?"

"Mmmhmm." Sonya scratched the plastic tablecloth.

"For how long?"

"I dunno. A week. Maybe longer."

Sonya's olive cheeks turned red. Her eyes narrowed and moistened.

"I told you that good for nothing *moreno* would do this to you! Look at you! Fifteen, in eighth grade and pregnant! Ay DIOS!" Sonya began to alternately shout prayers and curses at Nadia. "Oh God . . . Why you give me this child? God, why? Didn't I try? I bring her to church. I give her a Bible. I tell her to do the right thing! Look at you! I tried so hard with you. But you . . . You get into fights at school, don't listen to nobody, date this boy behind my back. And look at him—in jail for dealing dope! Not even pot . . . God, you know I put in my time!"

"You don't have to go yelling at me! You always in my business, anyway. You care more about that stupid religion stuff than me! Isaiah was stupid, but he cared about me!"

"What did he ever do for you? Put a roof over your head? Carry you for nine months? Now you gonna have his ugly child. *Cristo Santo!*"

Nadia was in tears now, too. She didn't intend to say anything when her mother exploded. She tried to calm herself and to say what she wanted to say.

"*Mami,*" she reverted to baby language, the way she always did when she wanted to get her way, "*Mami,* I know I done some wrong things but I can put an end to it. I know you don't want me to have Isaiah's baby. I can get rid of it. You don't want me to have it. I can just get rid of it."

"Oh, no. This is God's wrath. God is faithful. You dated a drug dealer, now he's in jail and you're pregnant with his child. I can't punish you no more than that."

"But, *mami* . . ."

"Don't 'but *mami*' me. You played that out. You wanted to have your fun. Pay the consequences. If you dare try to do anything to that thing in your belly, so help me, I will send your stubborn ass into foster care."

"See if I care!" Nadia stormed back to her room. She slammed the door and looked at the clock. 11:09. Only nine minutes? That's all it took. She sat on the floor and rested her head against the bed. She had loved Isaiah but that was history. Word had been out about his arrest. It was even in the news. She had been upset. Even cried a little. She definitely did not want his baby, with him in jail. He couldn't help her now. And her mom wasn't going to.

Nadia paced her bedroom. She went to her mirror and picked at a pimple over her eyebrow. Her mother would leave for her waitress job by noon. She would sit tight until then. She painted her nails. She looked at her math homework. She tried a question and then threw the book against the wall. It was all just too hard. Too hard. She started to cry. She tried to pray. "Oh God," she started. "Oh God, Oh God, Oh God, Oh God . . ." she continued to mutter and cry until 11:41 when she heard the apartment door slam shut. She stuck her head into the hall. Her mother was gone.

She went to the living room and sat down on the plastic-covered couch. She stared at the TV screen and flipped it on. It was on QVC Home Shopping Network. Her mother's favorite. Nadia stared at the gold bracelet on the perfectly manicured pink hand. Her mother loved watching QVC. She loved it maybe even more than church. She would take out her credit card every now and again when some item was on—a peridot ring or a Water Pik—she would hold it and then yell at Nadia to get off the phone so she could call in and then sigh, put the card back and go back to watching.

Nadia knew where she kept the card. It was in Sonya's sock drawer. Nadia had pushed her mother's stockings aside many times before and thought about taking it. She never had. Nadia had been bad before—like the time she punched Gloria Mendez in the face for saying she was a ho. But she never, ever stole anything from anyone else.

She wasn't a crook.

This was different.

Nadia walked through every room of the house, just to make sure, and then went to Sonya's room. She opened the drawer. She pushed aside a few pairs of black knee highs and found it. A Visa Gold card.

She went back to the living room and pulled the phone book from under the phone. She looked under "A" for abortion and "C" for clinic. Nadia flipped through every page until she found something. "Pregnant? **Consultations** and **procedures** on premises." Procedures. She dialed.

"Hello, Planned Parenthood. How can I—I need an abortion. I mean, can I get an appointment for one? Like maybe today?" The words rushed out of Nadia's mouth.

"Okay, just hold on. You can schedule an appointment for today, but you'll have a consultation and checkup first. How old are you?"

"Eighteen. I have money and everything."

"What's your name, honey?"

"Sonya. Sonya Martinez."

"Okay, Sonya. How is 3 p.m. for you?"

"Fine."

She hung up the phone and hurriedly copied the information. The clinic was in Manhattan, about an hour and a half away from College Point. She showered and changed. She wore her nicest jeans and one of her mother's sleeveless sweater tops. Nadia slid the credit card and a ten-dollar Metro Card into her back pocket.

It was hot outside. She walked to the bus stop. There was a couple there, making out against the wall of the dollar store. They looked even younger than she. Nadia looked away and waited.

It was about a 20-minute ride to the train on the Q65 bus. Once she got on a train, it would be about 40 minutes to the city. She had no idea how long her "procedure" would take. She thought about the word. Like a pair of warm steel tongs or cold pink hands. She rested her head against the cool glass of the bus window. Her mother would hate her forever for killing a baby. That was certain.

She got off of the bus at Main Street and waited for a train. She stood on the platform and watched the tracks. There was an enormous rat plodding down the track, toward the tunnel's exit. It looked tremendously fat. Or perhaps not.

The next train was to arrive in five minutes. Nadia wondered how much the baby had grown from the morning until now. It couldn't be very big yet. She made her thumb and index finger into an "O" and looked at it. Or maybe bigger. She made a fist. No bigger than that. The rat was bigger than that.

Suddenly, Nadia could no longer see her fist, the rat, or the tracks. All of the lights had gone out. She heard some people screaming. There was a little light coming from the tunnel, but not enough to see by. Some transit workers appeared with flashlights. Nadia could feel people pushing against her, most of them shouting the names of other people. She heard children crying and mothers shushing. After waiting for maybe 10 minutes, Nadia was let out of the subway.

Outside, everyone was crazy. Cars and buses were honking. There were no traffic lights. The Chinese fish market was closing down. Men were hauling huge basins of dead fish, live eels and a basket of crabs down to a cellar. All of the cabs were full. The buses were packed and traffic was at a near standstill.

Nadia walked home. It took about an hour. She was sweating and tired when she got home but she stood in front of her building. It was brick covered in peeling white paint. Air conditioners and window fans droned. She wiped some sweat from her face with the back of her hand and walked down the block. A few blocks down, there was a small empty parking lot that formed a cul de sac. One side of it was the back wall of a building that had no windows. The other side was right on the water. From there, you could see the Manhattan skyline and LaGuardia airport. Planes were still landing and taking off. The shoreline was a jumble of weeds, rubble, and trash. Nadia walked through the weeds and sat on a chunk of concrete.

This was the place where she and Isaiah had first made love.

Isaiah had brought two big blankets—one for them to sit on and one for them to wrap around themselves. It was spring then and still chilly. He even bought her favorite meal from McDonald's—a Big Mac with fries and a diet Coke. They watched the planes across the bay and talked about where all of those people might be going.

"One day, me and you gonna fly on out on first class. Where you want to go in first class, baby?" Isaiah had asked her. Nadia thought about it.

"I saw a commercial for the Virgin Islands once. It looked nice. Maybe Puerto Rico, too. I haven't been there for a long time.

"All right, then that's where we'll go. Anywhere is fine with me—as long as my Nadia is with me. I love you, girl."

Nadia had believed this, too. That night, he told her how beautiful she was. He had been careful with her because he knew she was a virgin. His body was perfect to her. He had a small waist and the beginnings of muscle definition on his stomach. He had full lips that revealed perfectly white, slightly crooked teeth—even that imperfection was glorious that night.

Nadia lay down on the slab of concrete. Her hands slid down to her belly. She wondered if the baby had a face yet. It probably looked like a goblin or something now. Maybe later it would look like Isaiah. No, Nadia reminded herself, there wouldn't be a later.

She fell asleep and when she woke up, the sun was going down. She was hungry. She wondered if her mother was home. She had no idea what time it was and she didn't want to go home. She sat by the water.

The sun was a gold yolk on the yellowish white membrane of water. She thought about a goblin child with Isaiah's lips and teeth. She slid her hand into her pocket and touched the card. She wondered where the time went. She sat by the water until the sun went down.

✄ Teacher Focus Group Discussion: Keeping It Real: Authenticity and Responsible Representation in Urban Fiction

Participants were asked to read the following introduction prior to the focus group discussion.

A number of assertions gave rise to the writing of *Street Lit: Teaching and Reading Fiction in Urban Schools*: the current body of short fiction written for and about the experiences of urban youth lacks authenticity; city teachers/ authors are uniquely situated to make more authentic contributions to this body of work; and a collection of authentic stories targeting city kids would serve the interests of authors, teachers, students, and other concerned parties. One could

██

Discussion Questions

In the Lines

1. Describe Nadia's condition at the beginning of the story. How does she know that she is pregnant?

2. How does Sonya react when she realizes that her daughter is pregnant?

Between the Lines

3. Why does Nadia take the credit card from her mother's drawer? What does this suggest about her relationship with her mother?

4. Why does Nadia tell the Planned Parenthood consultant that she is 18?

5. Why does Nadia return home rather than going to Planned Parenthood?

6. Before returning home, Nadia sits by the waterfront and thinks about Isaiah. How would you describe her feelings toward him at that moment?

7. As the story ends, it is unclear if Nadia will abort the pregnancy. What do you think that she will do? What will become of Nadia's relationship with her mother? (Cite evidence in the story to support your predictions.)

Beyond the Text

8. In a feature article on the Planned Parenthood Web site,[1] Estelle Raboni writes: "It's important that parents—teens' first and most important sexuality educators—help teens navigate the confusing and distorting messages they receive from the media about sex and relationships, by providing messages that are realistic and healthy." Planned Parenthood offers the following "Helpful Hints for Parents" for communicating with their children about sexuality:

   - Set good examples that show kids how our lives are enriched by our values.
   - Reassure them that they're normal.
   - Build their self-esteem—give credit for talents and accomplishments, offer constructive advice, and avoid criticism and punishment.
   - Respect our kids' privacy as much as we value our own. Do not pry.
   - Use correct names for sex organs and sexual behaviors.
   - Take advantage of "teachable moments." A friend's pregnancy, neighborhood gossip, and TV shows can help start a conversation.
   - Include topics such as sexual orientation, sexual abuse, and prostitution.
   - Be clear about our values and let kids know that others may have different values about sexuality. Teach them that respect for differences is important.
   - Don't use scare tactics as a way to stop young people from having sex—it doesn't work.
   - Give accurate, honest, short, and simple answers.
   - Admit when we don't know an answer. We can help our kids find the answer in a book or other resource.
   - Accept questions at face value. For example, "How old do you have to be to have sex?" doesn't necessarily mean, "I'm thinking about having sex."
   - Let our kids know that we're available, and make it a habit to share what we think and feel.

---

[1] http://www.plannedparenthood.org/news-articles-press/politics-policy-issues/teens-sex-6709.htm

- Ask questions even if they don't—questions about what they think and what they know.
- Figure out what we want to say about our own feelings and values before we speak.
- Let our body language, facial expressions, and tone of voice support what we say with words.
- Get to know the world in which our kids live. What pressures are they feeling? What do they consider normal?

From the perspective of a teenager, how "helpful" do you find these tips? What would you change, remove, or add to this list? In general, how should decisions be made about teenage sexual activity and pregnancy, and who should be involved in making these decisions?

---

easily contest these premises, as well as the very definition of "authenticity" in fiction. During today's focus group we will discuss issues of authenticity and representation in urban fiction using "Where the Time Went" to ground the discussion. In preparation for our talk, spend a few minutes freewriting in response to the following questions.

1. Yokota (1993) proposed the following criteria for selecting culturally authentic multicultural literature:

   - Richness of cultural details
   - Authentic dialogue and relationships
   - In-depth treatment of cultural issues
   - Inclusion of members of minority groups for a purpose.

How useful or appropriate are these criteria? By these criteria, how would you assess the stories we have read so far?

2. Can outsiders write authentically about another culture? Should they even attempt to do so?
3. To what degree does the objective of "authenticity" in fictional depictions of the inner city complement the objective of social responsibility? To what degree do these objectives come into conflict?

Discussion

Ratner: I thought we could use Yokota's criteria for selecting culturally authentic multicultural literature to structure our discussion. So, let's begin with "richness of cultural details." How would you assess "Where the Time Went" according to this criterion?

Colleen: I totally want to jump on that because with this story if you take out the Spanish words, there would be no way to tell that this is a Hispanic family, and that to me, reflects its inauthentic quality. It reads like the author casually threw in Spanish to give it the veneer of Latin culture, but not much beyond that.

Ratner: So, it sounds like you are taking the author to task for falling short on Yokota's fourth criterion: "Inclusion of members of minority groups for a purpose."

Colleen: Yeah, some of the dialogue feels authentic, but as I read through the story, my reaction was, "So what?" Even if it contained culturally authentic details, I found myself wondering how these details contributed to the larger issues and events in the story. The whole pregnant-teen-in conflict-with-parent-thing is a situation we've seen over and over again. We read about it. We watch it on TV and movies. And so that situation doesn't push the boundaries. As a result, some of these details seem old and trite. As I was reading it, there are obvious things in the dialogue that denote this is a Spanish household, but to what end?

Debbie: To break it down by the criteria here, I'll say this: one of the things that the author touches on is tension between Hispanics and blacks in the urban community. The mother refers to the daughter's boyfriend as a "good for nothing Moreno." That, to me, came across as authentic and something that I don't see enough in "multicultural" literature presented to students in our schools. Urban communities are often painted as homogeneous groups and separated from another homogeneous culture called "suburbia." The country is painted as black and white—literally—when in fact, it's not.

Christina: Yes, that aspect of the story came across to me as an "in-depth treatment of a cultural issue." And yeah, it's true that the pregnant teen thing has been covered a lot, and of course, it's not like any cultural group has a monopoly on teen pregnancy. Still, I think the story touches on some facets of teen pregnancy that resonate in Latin cultures. First of all, there is the religious aspect: Dominicans and other Latin communities in the city are strongly Christian. This isn't incidental to a story about a girl who gets pregnant and happens to be *Latina.* Then there are the racial overtones that Colleen mentioned.

Glen: Yeah, I would agree with you but the key word you used was "touches upon." In my opinion, the story would have been more successful had the author delved deeper into this dynamic, or even more so, if she had delved into the relationship between the daughter and mother. By the time I got to the second page, I was hoping she was going to get into the punitive reactions of adults to children; I don't think she did, and in the end she went for the cheap shot instead of what was really interesting: the reaction of the mother as a parent of a baby who screwed up. That wasn't really explored and instead you have this kind of stereotypical, "Oh God, Oh God, Oh God." You know, "Ay Dios" and all that stuff that kind of makes it seem plastic. They should work for a relationship that is much more subtle than that, and a lot more interesting.

Angela: I would have to agree with Glen, and as a Hispanic woman, I'm kind of sensitive to this kind of thing. Why does it always have to be the daughter on a path to self-destruction and the hysterical, helpless mom wringing her hands?

Glen: And then there's the wise old grandmother who speaks like one or two words of Spanish every sentence. I feel like we've come across that caricature at least twice in literature we've read this year in my class. It's always, "*Mira* this, *Ay Dios!* that." And you go, "Oh, stop it. You're distancing her, and you're making her into a cartoon." The author might as well write "rice and beans, rice and beans" a hundred times.

And, you know, as soon as the girl says, "I'm pregnant," the mother picks it up immediately launches into, "Why? Why? I tried so hard." I was reminded of a parent-teacher conference where I had a kid who was a "once-a–weeker" who became a "once-a-monther." His mom came in for parent-teacher conferences. And I'll never forget, she played this stereotype to a T. She says, "I've tried so hard to save my kid. I try so hard. Where are you that you're not going to school? Where are you?" And he turned and looked at her and said, "Well, you know where I am. I'm on the couch next to you."

She had the waterworks going, and she was crying, and she was putting on the act and doing this whole thing. So, you know, that's interesting.

Ariella: But also keep in mind that this is a short story and you can't explore every issue in great depth in a short story. I think the story is ultimately about Nadia's decision whether or not to go through with the pregnancy and how she is ultimately alone in making that decision. I think that's what gives the story its drama and depth. Her alone*ness*—literally—from the moment she leaves the apartment.

Holly: You also have to remember that she wrote this for a teenage audience. I'm not sure teenagers would be as engaged if the story focused more on her relationship with the mother and the complexity behind the mother's response. If the story feels a bit inauthentic, maybe it has more to do with the fact that it's YA (Young Adult) literature than tokenism towards a particular culture.

Glen: Yeah, I see your point, although I don't know why, by definition, Young Adult has to feel contrived.

Holly: No, I'm not saying it *has* to be contrived. I saying it's really hard to write YA that doesn't sound contrived to the adult ear. I think, for the most part, kids and teens have a different sensibility from adult readers.

Ed: What I'm noticing as a reader is that when you read a good book you're like, "Wow, this is a good book" and it's apparent that the author has put care into every sentence. Some of the literature that I'm asked to teach doesn't seem like the same care has been put into it, and it is very hard for me to stand in front of the class and promote a book which I don't really think the author has put much thought into. I'm not an author, but when you read a book like *It Happened to Nancy* (Sparks 1994),[2] you want to roll your eyes, and when you read *Lord of the Flies* (Golding 1954), you say: "That's written very well," and then there are some books that are meant to appeal to kids but they are not written all that well.

Ratner: Do you see any connection between the care and attention to craft as it relates to authenticity? Do you see the result of that care as something more authentic?

Colleen: Yeah, for example, when I read *Like Water for Chocolate* (Esquivel 1992), I could actually hear the voice of the author speaking to me. Tita's voice comes through to the point where when I read it, I'm at peace with what she is trying to say.

Ed: Yeah. I think it is actually the quality of writing more than the subject matter that makes it authentic. I think a lot of difficulty the kids are having is that a lot of the books that get pushed toward them are all exposition. It's all there, you know? Everything is known throughout the entire book. There is none of that *Like Water for Chocolate* kind-of-experience where the reader is called on to come up with the subtext. There is plenty of stuff out there that is both well-written and meets Yokota's definition of multicultural literature, but what's getting pushed on the students are books that are long on exposition and short on much else. And, I think, what is ultimately behind this trend is the lack of faith that our kids can handle anything better.

Ratner: Let's get back to the story. How do others feel? Does "Where the Time Went" strike you as authentic?

Ariella: I was kind of waiting to hear what others had to say about the story, because I actually used it in my class recently. The first thing I want to say is that there were many moments when I saw students actively engaged and interested in the lesson. This, to me, is the clearest sign that they found something "authentic" about the story. I was worried about how they might approach the topic of teen pregnancy, being teens themselves, and then the obvious controversial decision Nadia must make. I was pleasantly surprised by how serious and mature they were throughout the reading of the story. They also had a ton to say in regard to the subject matter, teen pregnancy being an ever-present issue within their communities.

I remember after the first two paragraphs were read, one of my students whispered "O-D" or "overdose" which in their parlance is reference to the fact that Nadia's behavior had led to an extreme outcome. As our reading progressed, I heard a few other students say "Oh shit!" in response to the rising action in the plot. So, again I was pleased to hear students (even if it might be

[2] *It Happened to Nancy: By an Anonymous Teenager,* edited by Beatrice Sparks. Sparks, who also edited *Go Ask Alice* (1971), a best-selling anonymous diary of a troubled teenage girl, compiles the journals of a 14-year-old victim of date-rape who contracted AIDS and died.

a curse word) relating to the main character's situation; it showed me that they were involved in the story.

Colleen: Yeah, I see what you're saying, because it's the same thing when I'm reading fiction: I know it's a good story when I have that kind of gut-level response to an event or line or character. It hits you in the stomach and not just the head.

Christina: Yeah, but you hear kids say those same exact things when they're playing video games or talking about what they did over the weekend.

Debbie: Yes, but that's the point: this story is not *Grand Theft Auto II*,[3] or a recounting of some fight in the cafeteria. There's actually not much that happens at all in the story; I think what Ariella means is that there must be something that the students find "real" in the story for them to have such a strong reaction to it, and they might not have had the same reaction if Nadia was Nancy from Long Island or whatever.

Ariella: Yeah, and another important moment in the lesson took place right after the story concluded with Nadia waking up after falling asleep on the slab of concrete by the water. After the last line was read by me, a student looked up and asked in a kind of frantic way: "So, what happens? What does Nadia do?" I could see on their faces that many other students were perplexed by the ending; some seemed bothered by the ambiguity, but others appeared drawn to it. This showed me two things: one, that students were thoroughly engrossed in the events of the story, and two, that some of our students are spoiled with too much instant gratification, movies with obvious endings, etc. This story leaves a lot open to the imagination. We're not sure if Nadia will decide to keep the baby and thus, feels okay about having overslept and missed her appointment, or if she'll go home with the intention of heading back to Planned Parenthood the following afternoon.

Kevin: At first I thought she had had the abortion.

Ratner: It's not totally clear, is it?

Kevin: I don't know. No, it's not clear, but I thought she had the abortion because, toward the end where it says where she lay on the concrete slab, she was thinking how the baby looks like a goblin now but later the baby might look like Isaiah. And then she goes on to say, I mean, the narrator goes on to say she reminded herself there would be no later.

Ratner: Right, but we don't know for sure if she's saying that as a fact or as a wish, right?

Holly: See, that to me is what makes this story a cut above a lot of the YA literature. We won't ever know for sure what Nadia will do. There's an uncertainty to the entire situation; there's not one best

---

[3] The second installment of a popular video game franchise that sees the player taking on the role of criminal in a big city who must work his way up through the criminal underworld.

	choice to make. Any decision comes with pros and cons. That's life. And I think the author intentionally writes an ending that makes the reader think so that just like Nadia, we too are left to think about a life-changing decision.
Ratner:	Okay, let's move on to another question: Can outsiders write authentically about another culture? And let's again talk about these questions in relation to the objective of this book.
Ed:	Yes, I think it can be done. It's done all the time. Take *Memoirs of a Geisha* (Golden 1997). That was a white man writing about a culture, an era, and a sex different from his own. It's hard to argue that Faulkner couldn't write good literature about people other than white people, because he's white, you know?
Ratner:	Let me reframe the question in the scope of multicultural literature for kids in the city. It's not just a simple question of "can," but "should." Does a fiction writer have a responsibility to the people or culture he or she represents in a story or novel? How does one weigh that responsibility against artistic freedom? Does writing for authenticity ever come into conflict with social responsibility to the subjects and readers of one's work?
Glen:	Well, I think that if you're writing for a school-age audience with the intent of school districts adopting your book, you have a special burden placed on you. Let's face it: you don't have the same latitude over language and subject matter that you do if you're writing on your own. And frankly, based on my experience with the school system here, I think that stereotypes are routinely encouraged. You're in safe waters as long as the story or book you present has a noble person of a minority or an evil person from the oppressor class or something. So we have that kind of thing going on. They like that. The school wants that. The result is that we have all these boring books about historical heroes and heroines . . . Sojourner Truth, and all those people. But how about something contemporary and real? Most of it is not good. And it is very stereotyped, whether it is written by a minority or a white person. It's really not good stuff, and I think it's because they underestimate their audience.
Cyril:	I feel very strongly about that. I feel the responsibility is to tell the truth in some way. Even if it's in a story aimed at a kid who is 14 years old, or 15 years old. Telling the truth is something the kids, believe it or not, no matter how rowdy or jaded they may seem, respond to. And there's no magic formula. I mean if a situation or a narrative approach to a story strikes them as pertinent and honest, they will go for it. They'll get the implications. They'll get the moral, the message of the story very clearly. And to present them with something honest *is* socially responsible, even if what you present is ugly or uncomfortable.
Angela:	As far as authenticity and social responsibility go, to a degree, yes, the short story should convey the truth. And yes, I think

urban living has plenty of unhappy endings and so the literature has to reflect this. It is dark and it isn't always pretty. But I don't think that's all there is to urban life. There has to be a spectrum of images and ideas conveyed in this literature. We need to see all the different types of people and neighborhoods. You've got, let's say, Central American kids in Queens and West Indian kids in Brooklyn who live in these really nice suburban-like neighborhoods who attend decent schools and have hard-working, educated parents, but we don't see enough of that in literature and other media focused on the "urban" experience. There has to be some kind of balance.

Ratner: And there's the rub. Let me end with some thoughts I'm left with after this conversation, which revolve around the theme of how challenging it is to put together a book of this kind.

I certainly agree with Angela that the hallmark characteristic of the city is diversity—cultural diversity, diversity of life experiences, beliefs, values, etc. But in making a conscious effort to represent every plate on the smorgasbord of urban expression, it's easy to fall into the trap of tokenism and laundry listing. Yeah, I'd love to have 30 accomplished stories fall into my lap that cover every imaginable character type and culture that inhabit American cities, but that's not going to happen.

Putting aside the diversity issue for a moment, our conversation has reminded me just how hard it is to write a polished, compelling piece of fiction—and one that reads as authentic to a range of readers. You can do so many things well in a story but leave in one or two clichéd lines and everything unravels somehow. And I'm sure drafts by Robert Penn Warren and Toni Morrison had some clunkers in there. And keep in mind that the authors of these stories are not widely published authors. They're teachers, like you and me, who practice the craft that they instruct to school-age kids. If nothing else, we have to give them credit for taking the risk that all artists take—creating something from nothing—and striving to represent the lives of their students in a way that is more credible and thought provoking than the current fare.

✎ Classroom Activities: Where the Time Went

Introductory Activity: Bringing Something to the Party—Independent Reading for Literature Circles

Why do we read literature? As teachers, we fear that for many of our students the answer is that they simply have no choice. They are told to read *Lord of the Flies* for homework and so they do it, or at least they read the Cliffs Notes version of the book. Of course, we aim to instill in our students loftier motivations for reading: to dream, to laugh, to commiserate, to formulate perspectives on life and models for living. Here is another rationale that I found in a manual written for the Office of Correctional Education:[4] "Literature can free criminal offenders from the mind-forged manacles of their own consciousness by clarifying the experiences of their past and offering them opportunities to create a future" (Waxler, Trounstine, & McLaughlin 1997). It strikes me that offenders and nonoffenders alike are often prisoners of "the mind-forged manacles of their own consciousness" and that literature can be a healthy counterforce to this condition.

The introductory mini-lesson I describe below emerges from a rationale for reading literature that is less elaborate than these others, but no less significant: we read literature so that we can talk to others about what we have read. For example, I'm reading Gary Shteyngart's *Absurdistan* (2006), a comic novel about Misha, an American immigrant saddled with visa problems, trapped in the chaos of post-Soviet Russia and desperate to reunite with his beloved Rouena from the Bronx. I have already recommended the book to my friend Jack, a first-generation eastern European who grew up in New York City; I look forward to the day we can share a few laughs over Misha's antics.

Sheridan Blau writes: "Whenever we are witnesses to aesthetic or natural phenomena that take our breath away or that move us or touch us powerfully, we tend to want to share the experience with others, partly to confirm our own expertise, partly to relive it by recounting it and hear it recounted by others, and partly to gain the broader perspective that comes from such sharing" (Blau 2003, p. 54). Many other literacy researchers and theorists (Mayher 1989, Pradl 1996, Smith 1997, Schoenbach et al. 1999) have made the case for validating reading as a social process in schools by providing students with opportunities to engage in conversations around literature just as readers are naturally inclined to do outside of school.

It is even more pleasurable to take part in literature discussions when one *actively* engages with other readers of stories, plays, novels, and poems. This is the theme of *Bringing Something to the Party,* a mini-lesson I conduct in preparation for the "teacherless" literature circle that will be discussed later in the chapter.

I begin the mini-lesson by letting my students know that the day is special because we will make our first attempt to discuss our literature selection without me leading, or even taking part, in the discussion. "In about 20 minutes," I announce, "you will meet in groups of six to discuss 'Where the Time Went.' I *won't* be providing any worksheets, questions, or even topics for discussion. From now on, that's your job." A survey of the room reveals concern, dubiousness, and confusion on the faces of most students. A few students appear motivated by my challenge, while a few others appear overly enthusiastic; I assume that these individuals plan to use the time to talk with peers about video games, after-school plans, or to simply "chill out."

"The good news for those who have not read or finished the story for homework is that we will shortly begin 15 minutes of silent, sustained reading, and you can use this time to catch up with your classmates. The even better

---

[4] http://www.ed.gov/offices/OVAE/AdultEd/OCE/SuccessStories/Part2.html

news for those who have read the story is that you now have time to *re*read it *and* I have always noticed that it is the students that reread stories who bring the best stuff to literature circles."

An attentive student usually raises a hand at this point wanting to know what I mean by bringing the "best stuff."

"I'd like you to think of our teacherless literature circles as a house party, or a neighborhood barbecue, the kind where everyone brings a little something or other to the event. Now here's the thing," I lower my voice for dramatic effect, "You don't want to be the one who brings that bowl of tired-looking coleslaw or the boring coffee cake that sits on the table for hours untouched. Or worse yet, you don't want to be the guest who comes completely empty-handed and feels stupid walking through the door right behind others who come with tasty drinks and desserts. You want to be the one who brings that delicious salsa dip that folks are lined up to try. You want to be the one who brings those succulent sausages that are gone in 10 minutes." A few of the students still look perplexed, but most appear to be catching on. Linda's hand shoots up in the back of the classroom:

"So, basically you're saying we should have something to talk about when we get in our literature circle?"

"Not just anything. I want you to come prepared with something *really* good, something that will keep the conversation lively and interesting, something that will make others want to join in the conversation. As you're reading, keep an eye out for that dish that nobody else thought to bring to the party. Maybe it's a question about an event in the story, or an observation you've made about a character that other readers might have missed. Maybe you have an unusual idea about why the author wrote a line or used a particular word in the story. Maybe 'Where the Time Went' reminds you of another story you've read, a movie you've seen, or something that happened in your own life. This is the 'stuff' you want to bring to the party/literature circle."

As I'm giving my pre-literature circle pep talk, I begin a chart paper display of "Party Favors" and ask students to contribute other independent reader responses that they can imagine bringing to their literature circle. A useful list will have some or all of the following:

Literature Circle "Party Favors"

- Visualizations
- Predictions
- Questions/Wonderings
- Observations about Author's Style and Writing Strategies
- Personal Connections
- Intertextual Connections

Now it's time for the students to start reading. By definition, mini-lessons are short, so that the bulk of class time is left for what matters most in terms of literacy development: sustained, purposeful, and student-driven reading and writing. The last comment I make before silent, sustained reading begins is a reminder that party favors are sometimes mistakenly left back home, which defeats the purpose of all the thought and effort put into finding one. I remind students to record their independent reader responses as a dated entry in the "literature log" section of their notebooks. Some English teachers prefer that students record independent reading responses in the margins of texts, as this most closely resembles the habit of readers in the "real world." Others have students write on Post-it notes, especially when working with texts that will be used again by other students. There are two reasons I prefer bound notebooks as literature logs: (a) they are a more permanent record of reading responses over time, one that both student and teacher can review and return to for a variety of purposes; (b) it is easier to write in and refer back to them during the actual literature circle. Responses in notebooks also make it more feasible for me to duplicate exemplary responses on an overhead transparency and display to the entire class for future mini-lessons.

The Teacher's Role During Independent Reading for Literature Circles

As tempting as it might be to sit back at your desk and listen to the sweet sound of teenagers absorbed in reading literature or pens scratching responses in literature logs, your work is not finished when the class is quiet and by all appearances focused on the story at hand. I always emphasize to my in-service and pre-service teachers that their most fruitful instruction will occur while students are deeply engaged in the process of reading and writing rather than while the teacher is conducting a mini-lesson to the entire class. When students are actually reading and writing rather than *preparing* to read or write, their needs as readers and writers become evident to them. They will also become evident to you, as long as you are willing to use independent reading periods as a time to confer with students, where you investigate the challenges they are facing and offer strategies for addressing their challenges.

Based on the work of Lucy Calkins (1991) and Nancie Atwell (1998), the three-step approach described in Figure 3.1 has been invaluable to me when conducting independent reading conferences.

Independent Reading Conferences in Action

As she quietly reads "Where the Time Went" at her desk, I signal for "Anita" to meet me at a table in the corner of the classroom that I have designated for reading conferences. Calkins and Atwell encourage reading workshop teachers to conduct conferences at the desks of students, kneeling to their level, speaking in hushed tones, and then moving on to other students like a bee floating from flower to flower. Many teachers prefer this method and employ it effectively. My personal preference is a designated "conference table" in a corner of the classroom. When I'm in a library or movie, I find it terribly distracting when people carry on a conversation near me, even if it is done in whispers. The same, I imagine, holds true for some of my students trying to concentrate on their novel, play, or poem.

As with all my conferences, I begin by asking my student a broad question intended to put her at ease and invite conversation.

FIGURE 3.1

Three-Step Approach for Independent Reading Conferences

Research

Ask the student a few broad questions about how she reads, such as the following:

- What are you thinking about as you read?
- When did the reading become difficult, and what did you do at this moment?
- Tell me about something that you are reading.
- What are you looking for as you read?

These broad, open-ended questions are intended solely to give you a window into how the reader is approaching the text. Most often, and especially after asking follow-up questions, the student will directly or indirectly let you know how you can be helpful.

Theorize

At a certain point, you will make an educated guess regarding one possible reading challenge facing the student. For instance, you might surmise that the student is predicting what will occur later in the text but rarely entertains more than one possible outcome, or you might reach the conclusion that the student does not review in her mind what she has been reading in the preceding paragraphs.

Instruct

Based on your theory, offer the student one strategy that "expert readers" would use to address the specific challenge faced by the student. It is important not to teach more than one lesson at a time so as not to overwhelm the student. It is also important to focus on sharing a strategy habitually used by readers, rather than simply helping the student unlock the meaning of the particular text at hand.

"How's it going, Anita?"

"Good. I like the story so far."

"Great. I thought the class would enjoy it. What are you thinking about?"

"What do you mean?"

"Well, any thoughts in your head as you're reading?"

"Right now? No, not really."

It is possible Anita is simply confused by the whole notion of conferencing, or she is trying to anticipate what I'm "expecting" of her. It's also possible however, that she truly has no "thoughts in her head." I take Anita at her word. Based on my previous experience with her, I suspect that she moves through long expanses of text without employing any of the reader "moves" from the wide assortment of responses available to readers. In this respect, she is no different from other struggling readers I have encountered over the years who, even in high school, continue to treat reading as a relatively thought*less* activity, like eating peanuts or doodling while talking on the telephone.

"Anita," I continue, "Can you read from where you left off to the end of the next paragraph? When you're finished, see if you can tell me about any thoughts that are popping in your head. It's really important when you read to have thoughts in your head. They can be questions, ideas, an image you see clearly, predictions, and so on. You might even speak those thoughts under your breath. Remember how last week we had that lesson on 'talking back to your book'?" Anita nods and begins to read. When she's done, she turns her head to look at me:

"I think that she's gonna have the abortion."

"You think or you *know?*"

"I think."

"Good. That means you're making a prediction. Why do you predict that she will have an abortion?"

"Well, I have this cousin, and she had this boyfriend, and she was in the same exact situation."

"And so?"

"And so she had the abortion."

At this point, my research leads to a few theories about Anita as a reader. The first, already mentioned, is that she does not read actively or at least does not do so routinely. The second problem I see is that when she makes a prediction, it is based purely on personal experience; she does not consider previous events in the story, character traits, or any other aspect *within* the story world. Personal connections to characters and events can be helpful for making sense of fiction, but they can also limit understanding when the reader fails to recognize that our life experiences inform our reading of fiction but do not serve as blueprints for how to interpret a story or play.

Anita's prediction problem can also be framed a different way: she makes only one prediction rather than considering a number of possibilities for what could happen later in the narrative. Research in critical thinking tells us that good thinkers "withhold judgment and seek new evidence or points of view when existing evidence is inadequate or contentious" (Bailin et al. 1999) and think "open-mindedly within alternative systems of thought, recognizing and assessing, as need be, their assumptions, implications, and practical consequences" (Paul & Elder 2001). And like responsible jurors, good readers of literature keep open multiple avenues of interpretation and over the course of a narrative reach conclusions based on accumulating evidence. Many young readers I have encountered treat predictions as "open and shut cases," and many teachers encourage this approach by asking students to make a single prediction and then "check" the prediction as they read onward. I believe that encouraging students to make several predictions, rather than a single prediction, inculcates a more dynamic and purposeful approach to reading literature.

Now I am at the "instruct" phase of the three-step approach to conferring. Thinking through the multiple reading challenges outlined above, however, I am reminded of a valuable piece of advice Lucy Calkins imparted to me when I first attempted reading and writing conferences: guard against teaching more than one lesson at a time. Most learners, both adults and children, are equipped to learn only one lesson at a time. Through the years, often the hard way, I have found that the corollary is also true: teachers are equipped to teach only one lesson at a time. When we try to do otherwise, the result is frustration with the student we are trying to "help." We also feel like failures as teachers when in fact we have set ourselves up to fail because of unrealistic expectations. And so, I choose one point of emphasis as I begin to instruct Anita:

"Anita, can you think of anything else that might happen besides Nadia deciding to get the abortion?"

"Maybe she won't get the abortion?"

"Yes, that's a possibility. Can you think of a reason why she might not get the abortion?"

"Maybe she don't think it's right."

"Okay, that's a possibility. Any other reasons?"

"I don't know. It seems like her mother would hate her, and she don't want that."

"What makes you think that her mother would hate her if she had the abortion?" Anita turns her eyes back to the story as if searching for evidence.

"I think it said something about . . . Oh yeah, right here. Her mother says that she'll send her stubborn ass to foster care."

"It looks like you have a couple of good predictions now, Anita. We don't know which one will be correct at this point. It might even be that neither prediction pans out. Something else entirely can happen. That doesn't mean you haven't done the right thing. Good readers make a few predictions based on what happened earlier in the story—not just one, but a few. Then they just keep reading to learn more and check up on their predictions."

Once I feel relatively certain that Anita has understood my point, I leave her with a clear and assessable directive. This is essential for a number of reasons. First, it holds the student accountable for applying the targeted strategy. Second, it allows the teacher to check up on the student later to measure the degree to which she has understood and effectively employed the strategy.

"All right, Anita, I'll let you get back to the story now. But first, tell me what you're going to do as you keep reading."

"I'm gonna make more predictions."

"And what about the predictions that you already made?"

"I'm gonna see which one comes true."

"Great. When I come back in a few minutes you'll let me know what happened with your old predictions and the new ones that you have made."

Teachers who are new to facilitating independent reading periods and individualized reading conferences often express concern about "losing control" over what is happening moment to moment in the classroom. They have a point. Independent reading and conferring virtually guarantees unpredictable moments and a certain degree of disorder in the classroom. From a teaching perspective, it is certainly more efficient and tidy to have every student on the same page and following the same scope and sequence of instruction. If we believe, however, that from a learning perspective, students have varied reading challenges that are best met in the moment they face that particular reading challenge, efficiency is not a compelling enough reason to limit oneself to whole-class literature instruction. Instead, we need to develop methods *within* this individualized approach that imbue us with a greater sense of control and purpose. The three-step method I have outlined above, with time and practice, has helped me greatly in this regard.

Many teachers I encounter also express concern that conducting routine silent sustained reading during class time will prevent them from "covering" enough curriculum, or that there is simply not enough learning going on during these periods. In part, these concerns grow out of an entrenched notion that learning and instruction occur only when a teacher is standing in front of a class of students imparting information and writing on a chalkboard. Still, their apprehensions need to be taken seriously. There *are* many lessons to be taught, books to be read, tests to be taken, and standards to be met. However, the answer is not to avoid individualized instruction in the literature classroom but rather to find alternative strategies to ensure it is done well. As in many discussions of instructional methods and educational policy, it is counterproductive to frame this as an either/or proposition: whole class versus individualized instruction.

My travels around the classroom conferring with students reading "Where the Time Went" take me to Tariq. I notice he underlined the sentences, "You care more about that stupid religion stuff than me! Isaiah was stupid but he cared about me!"

"I'm wondering what made you underline those sentences, Tariq."

"I guess I just liked what she said, and how she said it."

"Yeah, it's a powerful line." We both look at it silently for a moment. "Any thoughts about what she means?"

"Yeah, it's like her mom is always trippin' on that religion stuff. She don't know what's up."

"I see your point, Tariq." Obviously, there is plenty more to say about these lines and we can continue this conversation. When I confer, however, my focus stays on the reader and not the text. I want to leave him with one morsel of advice from one reader to another and then move on to other students. If the discussion focuses solely on the text, I might help Tariq gain a better understanding or alternative perspective of this particular story, but I have not left him with a reading strategy that he can apply to any piece of literature he encounters.

"Look, Tariq," I continue, "I really like what you've done here. The good readers I know zone in on important lines or even a few words in a story. They know that authors plant their stories and essays with small bits of writing that are just loaded with importance. Readers underline them like you have, or use a highlighter. Some like to collect them in journals so that they can keep thinking and writing about the lines. Here's something that I'd like you to try: jot those lines at the top of the next entry in your Lit Log and just 'write off' of them. You remember we discussed the 'writing off' strategy? Just write everything that comes to your mind when you think about those lines, and don't stop until we're ready for Literature Circle. You should also think about bringing them up in your Lit Circle. I'll bet other students have a lot to say about them."

Before leaving Tariq, I ask him if I can share his "reader move" with the class. Even if it means interrupting silent reading for a few minutes, there are compelling reasons to seize this teachable moment. First, the genuine excitement I am feeling about Tariq's reader move will help me conduct the impromptu mini-lesson with greater passion and conviction. Second, my students are in the *process* of reading the story. Calling their attention to Tariq's reader move as they read independently, and not after the fact, communicates to students that readers do not respond to literature only during academic exercises; they do so by their own volition in order to make the experience of reading literature more meaningful and pleasurable.

The final reason I decide to interrupt silent reading is a practical one. Like my in-service teachers, I'm concerned that despite all the fruitful instruction and learning that occurs during these independent conferences, there are certain skills or content that have not been addressed through individualized instruction (or have been addressed but only with a few students). Occasionally suspending independent reading periods for brief, whole-class mini-lessons that grow out of independent reading conferences allows me to attend to a greater breadth of instructional points over the course of time.

"Listen up, everyone. I'll let you get back to the story in a moment." Some of the students appear happy to take a breather, others slightly annoyed by the interruption. "Take a look at Tariq's copy of the story. What do you notice?" As I walk between desks and tables displaying Tariq's story, Maribelle calls attention to the underlined sentences. "That's right, Maribelle," I confirm, and read the lines aloud. A few of the students giggle. To my right, Emmanuel blurts out, "That girl needs to check herself."

"What?" Briana interjects from across the room, stamping her foot for emphasis. "Her mother needs to check herself. *She* the one with the attitude." Heads begin to shake and eyes roll followed by a cacophony of teenage opinions.

"All right, all right," I bellow above the roar. "Save it for lit circles. Obviously you have strong opinions about those lines, which is exactly why I'm pointing out what Tariq did here. Remember: as you read, you're thinking about what you want to bring to your literature circle. Sometimes a line or even a few words from the story is just what's needed to get the party started. It's like the dance mix that someone brings which gets everybody off the wall. It's the piece of gossip that everyone can't stop talking about." At this point I need to check myself. Whole-class teachable moments that grow out of independent conferences should be just that—moments. "Okay, get back to your stories now. Ten more minutes of silent reading and journals. And remember: don't be the one to come to the party empty-handed!"

Ten minutes later I stop silent sustained reading and ask the students to form their literature circles. Once they are settled, I call their attention to the chart paper with our list of Literature Circle Party Favors. "I think we need to give a name to the reader move that Tariq made earlier, because it's a good one. What should we call it when you, the reader, underline or transfer to your journal that special line or phrase that makes you stop and think, or that makes you want to talk more about it with other readers?" A brief discussion produces a short list of candidates: "highlight lines," "conversation lines," and "juicy bits." When a consensus emerges, I update the Literature Circle Party Favor list of reader responses:

- Underline, write off of, and discuss "Juicy Bits"

Writing Project: Literature Op-Ed

Expository essay, persuasive essay, five-paragraph essay—these are a few of the terms English teachers and curriculum designers use interchangeably to describe a piece of writing that states a position on a topic and provides evidence to support that position. One would search long and hard, however, to find these terms used to describe writing outside of an academic setting. Instead, we have book and movie reviews, literary criticism, and editorials; we have political position papers and manifestos. These genres and subgenres may be expository in nature, persuasive in intent, and five paragraphs in length, but I have never encountered a published author who described his or her work as an expository or persuasive essay.

One could argue that this is just semantics. What difference does it make whether we describe a writing project as a persuasive essay or literary criticism? Besides the obvious difference in specificity, I believe that it *is* important for students to recognize that authors write for genuine purposes, target specific audiences, and guide their craft according to conventions of style and structure within established genres. Like the five-paragraph essay, the newspaper Op-Ed, for instance, tends to be short in length (though not necessarily five paragraphs). This brevity makes sense for a number of reasons. Newspaper writers who make weekly or even daily contributions do not have the time to research and write longer pieces. Furthermore, their writing competes for space with other types of journalism that occupy sections of a daily newspaper.

Op-Ed pieces are also written for a mass audience. Although the style and sophistication of writing may vary according to the targeted readership of the paper, Op-Ed authors, unlike those who write for scholarly or technical publications, must ensure that their language is accessible to a general population.

Finally, Op-Ed authors have to cover issues and topics that concern their readership. Whether the topic is chosen by the author or assigned by an editor, the topic has to matter enough to readers that they will take the time to read it. These stylistic and structural conventions of the Op-Ed provide the writer with a sense of purpose and organization for crafting meaningful pieces. Your students will also benefit from writing within the limited (but not limiting) guidelines of authentic persuasive genres like the Op-Ed.

If students write in authentic genres like the Op-Ed, they will also have an abundance of helpful models to consult as they craft their own pieces. When I am facilitating an Op-Ed writing workshop, *The New York Times* serves as my "textbook"; distinguished Op-Ed columnists like Thomas Friedman, Bob Herbert, and Maureen Dowd take on the role of my "teaching assistants." And my favorite *Times* sports columnist, Selena Roberts, demonstrates that writers publish powerful, beautifully crafted opinions related to topics less weighty than foreign policy and the budget deficit.

The majority of my lessons during the workshop begin with questions that get to the heart of what concerns Op-Ed writers: How can we begin our pieces so that the reader wants to continue reading? What kinds of evidence and examples should we include to convince the reader to take our position? When have I written too much or too little? What makes an Op-Ed piece memorable? Then, as a class, or during individual writing conferences, we scour the columns of Friedman, Roberts, and others in search of answers to our specific questions. Rather than providing the kind of canned answers sometimes offered by textbooks and teachers, these authors often surprise us with their writing strategies. While discussing Bob Herbert's "Blowing the Whistle on Gangsta Culture," (2005) for instance, my students notice that Op-Ed writers do not necessarily state their "thesis" in the opening paragraph as we often require of students when they write essays.

> BOSTON—Edwin "E. J." Duncan was a young man from a decent family who spent a great deal of time with his friends in an amateur recording studio his parents had set up for him in the basement of their home in the Dorchester neighborhood.
>
> It was in that studio that Duncan, along with three of his closest friends, was murdered last week, shot to death by a killer or killers who have yet to be found. Whoever carried out the executions, it seems clear enough to me that young Duncan and his friends were among the latest victims of the profoundly self-destructive cultural influences that have spread like a cancer through much of the black community and beyond.

"Talk about how Herbert begins this Op-Ed," I announce to the students after we finish reading the first four paragraphs of the column. "What do you think he's up to in the first paragraphs?"

Quincy, as is often the case, is the first to raise his hand.

"Basically he's saying that there's this kid who was recording music in his basement. Then, him and his friends were murdered and they don't know who did it."

"Okay, Quincy, that's what Herbert reports happened in Boston recently, but what I'm really asking is why do you think he began his piece this way?" Quincy's response is fairly typical when we first begin reading literature in conjunction with a writing project. If students are reading purposefully at all, they are not used to reading for the expressed purpose of gaining insights into the myriad strategies authors employ to communicate effectively. "Yesterday we spoke about reading as writers. If you want to learn how to dance, you watch the best dancers and check out what they're doing on the dance floor, right? If you want to learn how to play basketball better, who you gonna watch, Moochie Norris?"

Students turn to each other quizzically. "Who's that?" Quincy asks.

"Exactly. He's some scrub who played for the Knicks a few years back. If you want to learn how to play basketball, you watch the best. You watch Kobe. You watch Lebron, right? You ask yourself how they did that crossover dribble, or how they release their jump shot. Then you watch closely on TV and try it out for yourself. That's what we're doing here today and the next few weeks as we read these columns. So, again, who can tell me what Bob Herbert is doing here in the first paragraphs? What are the moves he's making?"

"I think he's just trying to let you know a little about this person. That's it," Danielle volunteers.

"I think he wants you to, like, feel sorry for the kid," Darius adds.

"That's interesting, Darius. What do you mean by that?" I ask.

"It's like they was just minding their own business, just doing their thing in the basement, and these gang bangers pop 'em."

"I like the way you're thinking, Darius. I've noticed that when I read about someone who has died, I feel the loss more strongly if I know something about the person. Even little things like what the person did in his free time or how he likes to dress. Maybe that's what Herbert is trying to accomplish here."

Our conversation continues this way, with the class offering various theories about the moves made by Herbert in his lead. In their own words, a few students suggest he is providing basic information that the reader will need to proceed through the column. Other students speculate that Herbert wants to build some suspense so the reader will want to find out the circumstances behind the executions. We agree that all the theories provided by the students have merit and that authors can fulfill multiple purposes in a lead. The product of our discussion is another display on chart paper.

Moves for Op-Ed Leads

- Give the reader a sense of place and essential background information.
- Hook the reader by creating suspense (don't give everything away too soon!).
- Introduce and bring to life main characters in the column.
- Set the tone (serious, light, angry, and so on).

When we reach the fourth paragraph, the class identifies Herbert's thesis: "It is time to blow the whistle on the nitwits who have so successfully promoted a values system that embraces murder, drug-dealing, gang membership, misogyny, child abandonment and a sense of self so diseased that it teaches children to view the men in their orbit as niggaz and the women as hoes." We agree that in most other Op-Ed pieces we have read, the authors clearly and succinctly state their major claim early in the column but not necessarily in the first paragraph. To our list, we add "State your thesis clearly and succinctly early in the piece (but not necessarily in the first paragraph)."

Ethos, Logos, and Pathos

The Greek philosopher Aristotle separated strategies of persuasion into three categories: ethos, logos, and pathos.

Ethos

Ethos is appeal rooted in the character and reputation of the speaker/writer. The goal in developing ethos in a persuasive argument is to gain the trust of the audience.

Example:

My Dear Fellow Clergymen:
While confined here in Birmingham city jail, I came across your recent statement calling my present activities "unwise and untimely." . . . Since I feel that you are men of genuine good will and that your criticisms are sincerely set forth, I want to try to answer your statement in what I hope will be patient and reasonable terms.

I think I should indicate why I am here in Birmingham, since you have been influenced by the view which argues against "outsiders coming in.". . . I, along with several members of my staff, am here because I was invited here. I am here because I have organizational ties here.

Martin Luther King, Jr., "Letter from Birmingham Jail" (1964)

Logos

Logos is appeal based on logic or reason. Logos-driven arguments target the intellect of the audience through logical chains of reasoning, literal and historical analogies, statistical evidence, and so on.

Example:

According to the First Law of Petropolitics, the higher the price of global crude oil, the more erosion we see in petro-ist nations in the right to free speech, a free press, free elections, freedom of assembly, government transparency, an independent judiciary and the rule of law, and in the freedom to form independent political parties and nongovernmental organizations. Such erosion does not occur in healthy democracies with oil.

Thomas L. Friedman, "As Energy Prices Rise,
It's All Downhill for Democracy,"
The New York Times, May 5, 2006

Pathos

Pathos is appeal based on emotions such as love, fear, patriotism, guilt, hate, or joy. Pathos-driven arguments use emotionally loaded language, images, and narratives. They compel people to take action rather than just understand an argument intellectually.

Example:

Granted, people like these die all the time in Africa of malaria or AIDS. And it's true that it's probably as wrenching for a parent to lose a child to malaria as to a machete. But when a government deliberately slaughters people because of their tribe or skin color, then that is a special affront to the bonds of humanity and creates a particular obligation to respond. Nothing rips more at the common fabric of humanity than genocide—and the only way to assert our own humanity is to stand up to it.

Nicholas D. Kristof, "Disposable Cameras for Disposable People,"
The New York Times, February 12, 2006

Traditionally, students first encounter these rhetorical concepts in forensics clubs or undergraduate public speaking courses, yet I have found them immensely useful for facilitating middle school and high school writing workshops focused on persuasive genre writing like the Op-Ed. Teachers who feel students need the structure provided by the five-paragraph essay format will find the guiding principles of ethos, pathos, and logos equally useful in this regard. And, unlike the arbitrary strictures of the five-paragraph essay, Aristotle's time-honored rhetorics keep the writer squarely focused on what matters most in crafting a compelling argument: appealing to the heart, mind, and gut of your audience.

Ethos, logos, and pathos steer *me* to sensible and constructive responses to typical questions that arise when I conference with young writers. For example:

How Long Should My Op-Ed Be?

Op-Eds are usually just a few hundred words. It should be as long as it takes to make an argument that hits your reader in the heart, mind, and gut—but no longer.

Does This Count As a Compelling Argument?

Read the paragraph(s) back to yourself. Does your argument make sense to you? Will it make sense to your reader? How can you revise it so that it makes more sense?

Or

Read the paragraph(s) back to yourself. Do your words move you? Will they hit your reader in the heart or funny bone? How can you revise the section so that it is more moving?

Or

Read the paragraph(s) back to yourself. If someone else wrote this, would you trust the author? Will your reader want to take your side? How can you revise the section to gain even more trust from the reader?

Is This a Good Conclusion?

I find that great Op-Ed writers often use the final paragraph or last sentences to make their final pitch to the heart of the reader. In other words, they often, but not always, end with pathos. Let me read your final paragraph back to you. After I'm finished, tell me if you yourself felt something in your gut or chest or felt compelled to take action. If you do, that's a good sign. If you don't, perhaps you might want to try some alternative endings.

Op-Eds in the Literature Classroom

Although Op-Ed writers do not regularly focus columns on specific works of literature, they do so periodically, particularly when a novel, poem, or work of nonfiction takes on the status of a cultural "happening." In recent years, opinion pieces have been written in major newspapers and magazines in response to books like the *Harry Potter* series, Dan Brown's *The Da Vinci Code* (2003), and James Frey's *A Million Little Pieces* (2003). I share these columns with my students so that they can come to know the types of concerns opinion writers voice in regard to literature, and how these writers approach—stylistically, rhetorically—discussing newsworthy books. In reviewing these columns, the students learn that an Op-Ed column focusing on a novel or nonfiction book is different from a book review; it is less concerned with the quality of the writing and literary merits in the narrow sense than with the reasons why a book has garnered attention and what the book and the buzz around it can, or should, teach us about contemporary society.

A story like "Where the Time Went" showcases a range of debatable topics and themes that students can address in the form of an Op-Ed or editorial.

Sample Assignment for Literature Op-Ed:

Write an opinion piece to the school newspaper that takes a position on one of the following questions:

- What is the appropriate age for a person to begin having sex?
- What message or lesson should pregnant teenage girls take away from Nadia's story?
- What is the best course of action for a teenager who finds out she is pregnant?
- What are the responsibilities of parents who know or suspect that their children are sexually active or pregnant?
- What are the responsibilities of teenage boys who are sexually active?
- Should teachers assign a story like "Where the Time Went" to high school students? Middle school students?

Remember that this is *not* a book review! The focus of your piece should not be the degree to which you liked or disliked the story. Instead, you need to persuade readers of the school newspaper which side to take on the questions listed above, using "Where the Time Went" and other sources (research, life experiences) to make your case. You may also choose a topic that is not listed, but please clear it with me first.

Community of Readers Extension Activity: The Teacherless Literature Circle

Earlier in this chapter I described how English teachers can frame an independent sustained reading period as an opportunity for students to prepare for literature circles later in the class. Having actively read their stories and updated journals with personal and intertextual connections, observations and questions about characters and the author's craft, predictions, "juicy bits," and other "party favors," they are ready to form circles and begin the party.

Some teachers bridle against the prospect of four or five groups of students simultaneously holding discussions on self-chosen topics. They regard literature circles as an invitation to classroom chaos and remark that their students "just aren't ready for that kind of thing." My response to this comment is always the same: "I know it doesn't come easily to students; it's precisely *because* it's hard for them and because students are seldom held accountable for initiating their own learning that we must do it." The truth is that students in many of the college and graduate classes I have taught or attended through the years could have used some guided instruction in how to participate in a group discussion. Some of the most unproductive group discussions I have attended were at faculty meetings in high schools and universities!

Directions, routines, and procedures matter in group discussions, just as they do with all instructional activities. They are even more crucial when the goal is for your students to conduct an extended group discussion with minimal intervention from the teacher. Here are recommendations for organizing literature circles to maximize productivity and reduce the anxiety of ceding control to students.

Pre-Literature Circle Preparation

Modeling

It is imperative that your students have a vision of literature circle in practice, especially if they are unfamiliar with holding discussions without a teacher in their immediate presence. I use the word "vision" to stress the importance of them *seeing* teacherless literature circles in action as opposed to simply reading about them or listening to a teacher provide directions. Doing so not only helps students develop a schema of the activity awaiting them; they are more likely to have confidence and motivation to take up the challenge of independently discussing literature if they see that others like themselves have done the same. The two best ways I know to provide students with this vision are video and fishbowls.

Video

Over the years I have videotaped both exemplary and less than exemplary teacherless literature circles from my own classrooms and those of other teachers. On the day before we are ready to begin literature circles, I show these videos to my students, pausing the recording every few minutes to solicit general observations, comments, and questions. I always begin with a tape of an exemplary group, and nearly every time I show it, students express their certainty that the students are "performing" for the camera or have been "coached" to speak with each other in such a civil, adult-like manner. (It is interesting to note that when I show the tape to in-service teachers, they have an identical reaction.) I tell the audience that they are both correct and incorrect: The students on the tape would conduct themselves in pretty much the same way if they weren't being filmed; however, this did not happen by magic. They learned to discuss literature well as a result of time, practice, hard work, and high expectations.

To illustrate my point, I show a tape of these same students early in the school year during literature circles. In this tape, my students see pretty much what one would expect to see when unpracticed discussants of literature are asked to facilitate their own "book talk": lots of idle chatter, uneven contributions from circle members, the occasional "What should we be doing now?" and individual students or couples physically separating themselves from the group. When a student makes an effort to talk about the story or play at hand, the conversation quickly peters out as the other members appear uninterested or at a loss as to how they should respond to the initial comment. "What we need to do over the next few weeks," I explain to my current students after stopping the tape, "is think carefully and look closely at what these students were doing and saying when the lit circle went well, and what they were saying and doing in the tape I just showed you." We begin this process by creating a list of lit circle member etiquette that helps and hinders discussion:

Do's	Don'ts
Form your circle quickly and start right away (time is limited!).	Don't use lit circle to catch up on personal business.
Track the speaker (let him/her know that you're listening!).	Don't avoid eye contact or speak into your journal or book.
Stay in the circle (body posture shows "active listening").	Don't slump in chair, drift from circle, sleep, or daydream.
Always bring your literature log and story/play/poem to group and USE them during the discussion—take advantage of the hard work you did during independent reading!	Don't leave your lit log and book at home, in your locker, at a friend's apartment, or anywhere else.
Involve every member of the group in the discussion.	Don't direct all your comments to one or two group members.
Take the opinions of others seriously; disagree respectfully ("I hear what you are saying, but . . .")	Don't roll your eyes, smirk, laugh at, or raise your voice in anger when responding to circle members.

Fishbowls

During the first few weeks of teacherless literature circles, we conduct a number of "fishbowls" in which one group (the fish) conducts their discussion in the presence of the remaining students, who have formed an outer circle around "the bowl." This gives us an opportunity to observe and make notes of the practices that help and hinder fruitful discussion. The general direction I give the observers (notepad and pen in hand) is, "As you watch the group, take notes about what you feel helps the discussion 'grow' and what hinders it from growing." Sometimes I will give a more specific direction: "Listen carefully to the types of questions the fish are asking each other. What types of questions help the discussion grow? What types of questions stop the discussion dead in its tracks?"

I have found that with a little direction, students are capable of identifying the very same discussion strategies and practices that education courses introduce to in-service and pre-service teachers. They recognize, for instance, that a question like, "Should Nadia get an abortion?" (yes/no questions) often short-circuit discussions, whereas open-ended questions like "Why do you think Nadia decides to get an abortion?" provide for more elaborate and diverse responses.

By the third or fourth fishbowl, students are becoming more sophisticated in their critical observations. Juan, for example, notices that discussions suffer when students ask too many questions with obvious answers: "I noticed that the group was sticking mainly to questions like, 'Why did Nadia take her mother's credit card?' and 'Why is Nadia's mom mad at her?' I'm not saying they're bad questions, but everyone knows the answer and there is not much more to say about them."

As a group we agree that alone these types of "detail" questions do not lead to rich discussion. What we need are more "big" questions, the kind that can provoke debate because the answer is not readily apparent. We identify Magda's questions—"How should Nadia decide whether or not to go through with the abortion? Should her mother be involved in her decision?"—as examples of "big" questions, and we agree that we should make an effort to prepare more of these questions during independent reading.

Group Monitoring

The guidelines provided earlier in "The Teacher's Role During Independent Reading for Literature Circles" (see p. 42) also apply to teacherless literature discussion groups. Yes, the goal is for students to independently facilitate the literature discussions, but this does not mean that teachers should use the activity as a time to relax or catch up on grading papers. As with independent reading conferences, some of your most productive instruction will occur while students are engaged in the process of discussing literature as opposed to when you are conducting mini-lessons to the entire class. When students are actually discussing literature rather than *preparing* to do it, their needs will become evident to both them and you.

With three or four groups simultaneously engaged in discussion, you become the proverbial fly on the wall buzzing from group to group. Students will look to you for clarifications on the text, or to play Solomon when group members have conflicting readings of a story. Discipline yourself to resist their entreaties. First and foremost, your role is to listen, observe, and when the moment presents itself, teach them to fish rather than giving them fish:

"Look. I'm not going to tell you whether or not Nadia went through with the abortion. It's your job to figure that out. I can tell you, however, what good readers and discussants of literature do when there is a disagreement like yours. Anyone know what I'm going to say?"

"They go to the text, right?"

"Exactly, Kieron. They look for evidence in the text. It could be in the narration, or even one line of dialogue. If I were in your group and you wanted to convince me whether or not Nadia ended the pregnancy, I would need evidence from the story. Read me a line or a passage and explain to me what it proves. And here is one other piece of advice that I haven't given before: Think about a third possibility. I have been in literature discussions where folks are arguing for a half hour over A versus B. Then suddenly someone suggests that maybe the answer is C, and that opens the bottleneck."

Conferring During Lit Circles

Kathleen Tolan, a former New York City public school teacher and current staff developer for the Columbia University Teachers College Reading and Writing Project, modeled for me how to instruct individual students during literature circles without interrupting a discussion. While buzzing around a group, quickly and unobtrusively whisper in a student's ear any number of situation-specific literature discussion moves that the student can immediately employ during the discussion. Here are a few examples:

- *Kieron, maybe you want to ask Justin what he thinks about Nadia's decision.*
- *Asia, everyone seems to be saying their own thing. See if you can respond to the next comment or question rather than just moving on.*
- *Hey, Daniel, I feel like the discussion is losing steam. Maybe you can zero in on a paragraph to read to the group followed by a short freewrite.*
- *Inez, I noticed that the discussion has been going off in a million directions. The group can really use a "Pull-It-All-Together Girl"* (see Figure 5.5 on p. 119) *to focus the conversation and get back to your big question.*

Discussion Breaks

Used judiciously and in limited number, discussion breaks serve the same purpose as breaks during independent reading: They allow the teacher to (a) highlight literature circle topics of universal concern to students and (b) attend to a greater breadth of instructional points over the course of time. When I feel the whole group can profit from something I heard or observed during one group's discussion, I simply call a "time out" and briefly share it with the class:

> I just made my third tour of all four groups and noticed that not one person has mentioned Nadia's boyfriend, Isaiah. Yes, he's a minor character in the story and only has one or two lines, I believe. But I think that you'll agree that he plays an important role in "Where the Time Went." The general point I'm making is that it's important to pay attention to minor characters. They give stories more dimensions and complexity. A few of the discussions seem to be running out of gas, and focusing on minor characters is a great way to get things going again.

That's all it takes—two, three minutes tops—and then I apologize to the class for interrupting and ask them to get back to business.

Language in Context Study: The "Be" Verb in Dialogue

A common feature of African American Vernacular English (AAVE) is the deletion of "is" and "are" (the copula "BE") in places where they would be contracted in standard English (Labov 1973, Rickford 1999).

It is important to help students recognize that AAVE and other English dialects are not deficient versions of standard American English but rather legitimate speech varieties with their own grammatical rules and pronunciation norms. In regard to the copula "BE," for example, deletion of "is" and "are" do not occur arbitrarily but within predictable sentence structures such as:

- Before adjectives and expressions of location:

AAVE: You always in my business, anyway.

Standard American Vernacular English (SAVE): You're always in my business, anyway.

- In future sentences with "gonna":

  AAVE: One day, me and you gonna fly on out on first class.
     SAVE: One day, you and I are going to fly first class.

- Before verbs with the -ing ending:

  AAVE: [He can] Even cure you of acne if you willing to pay for it.
     SAVE: He can even cure you of acne if you're willing to pay for it.

- Before nouns (or phrases with nouns):

  AAVE: How they gonna say that I got a 75 in English when I couldn't read the back of a cereal box?
     SAVE: How are they gonna say that I got a 75 in English when I couldn't read the back of a cereal box?

✝ Text Connections

For Students

The issue of teen pregnancy has received little attention in young adult literature and literature used in the secondary schools. The following list contains brief summaries of a few novels and stories that address this delicate topic. It also includes literature that explores mother-daughter relationships, another central topic of "Where the Time Went."

Johnson, Angela. *The First Part Last.* New York: Simon Pulse—Simon and Schuster, 2003, 131 pp.
    Bobby, the protagonist of this short novel, is a 16-year-old father struggling to raise infant daughter Feather on his own. The story is told in chapters that alternate between the day Bobby found out his girlfriend Nia was pregnant and his subsequent struggles as a teenage father. As the storylines converge, the reader gradually learns about the fate of Nia and how Bobby became as a single parent. The manner in which the mystery unfolds is melodramatic; it is the novel's only serious flaw. The presentation of teenage pregnancy from a father's perspective, and Johnson's tender but also sobering depiction of child rearing, make *The First Part Last* valuable reading for teens.

Williams, Lori Aurelia. *Broken China.* New York: Simon & Schuster, 2005, 272 pp.
    China Cameron "fools around" one night with her best friend and subsequently finds herself raising a daughter at the age of 14. When the child unexpectedly dies at two years of age from a respiratory infection, China copes with her grief by holding a lavish funeral. To pay the bill, China decides to leave school and work as a receptionist at a local "gentlemen's club" where she is faced with the advances of drunken clients and the manipulations of the club owner. When it becomes clear that her job responsibilities will include "dancing," China must decide between staying at the club and finding more appropriate ways to cope with her loss. The graphic

descriptions in some of the club scenes feel gratuitous, and *Broken China* is further diminished by a number of plot contrivances. The convincing voices of the characters, however, and their inspiring resilience as they face the corrosive stresses of urban poverty make the book an appealing and important book for young adults.

Williams-Garcia, Rita. "Wishing It Away." *No Easy Answers: Short Stories About Teenagers Making Tough Choices.* New York: Random House, 1997, pp. 261–268.

Within a compilation of short stories broaching issues facing teenagers in urban settings, "Wishing It Away" relates the experience of Belinda, a 14-year-old girl faced with the daunting reality of raising a child when she is still a child herself. Confused and feeling unloved by everyone around her, Belinda makes a series of controversial decisions that have the entire class talking. Although told in simple language, the story will create discussion around the important issue of teen pregnancy.

Mackler, Carolyn. *The Earth, My Butt, and Other Big Round Things.* Cambridge, MA: Candlewick Press, 2003, 256 pp.

Virginia Shreves is an overweight, underconfident 15-year-old left to navigate the perils of adolescence on her own. Her father is virtually absent, and her beautifully thin adolescent psychologist mother focuses most of her attention on Virginia's weight "problem." An idealized older brother attends Columbia University until he date-rapes a girl and returns home. The reader roots for Virginia to develop the inner fortitude that will allow her to come to terms with her body issues and cope with the turmoil in her family. The novel broaches a spectrum of social issues that concern teens and young adults. Some of the issues, such as date rape and eating disorders, are handled by Mackler with insight and sensitivity. Others, such as self-mutilation and parental pressure, are treated superficially.

Oates, Joyce Carol. *"Where Are you Going, Where Have You Been?"* Edited and with an introduction by Elaine Showalter. New Brunswick, NJ: Rutgers University Press, 1994.

Fifteen-year-old Connie spends her days hanging out at hamburger joints, flirting with boys, and bickering with her mother. While her family is away at her aunt's barbecue, two strangers pull up in front of her house in a sports car. The driver is Arnold Friend, a sweet-talking psychopath that Connie gradually recognizes is not the fun-loving 18-year-old he claims to be. As Friend becomes increasingly menacing in his attempts to lure Connie into the car, Connie is violently thrust from a teenage existence of pop-song inspired fantasies to a moment when she must make a life-altering adult decision. Oates masterfully weaves together a number of themes that will resonate with young adult readers, such as tensions between mothers and daughters, the sexual development of teenage girls, the victimization of women, the generation gap, and the transition from innocence to experience.

For Teachers

Atwell, Nancie. *In the Middle: Writing, Reading and Learning with Adolescents.* 2nd ed. Portsmouth, NH: Boynton/Cook Publishers-Heinemann, 1998.

Calkins, Lucy, with Shelley Harwayne. *Living Between the Lines.* Portsmouth, NH: Heinemann, 1991.

Of the hundreds of books indebted to the work of Peter Elbow, James Britton, Donald Murray, and other pioneers of the reading and writing workshop approaches to English and language arts instruction, Atwell's *In the Middle* and Calkin's *Living Between the Lines* remain the most inspiring and instructive. The workshop model focuses on developing students' literacy by engaging them in the authentic processes and practices used by readers and writers of authentic literature genres. The genius of Calkins and Atwell was in developing a language that spoke to a generation of teachers who recognized the limitations of skill-and-drill-based curriculums but needed an alternative vision of reading and writing instruction. The vision they put forward—students choosing their own books and writing topics; spending not a class period, but weeks brainstorming, drafting, revising, editing, and publishing a single narrative, poem, and essay; developing lifelong reading and writing strategies modeled by teachers during individual conferences at the point of need—has never been an easy one to carry out. The fact that legions of teachers across the country continue to do so, many with great success, is testament to the power of these two seminal texts.

Daniels, Harvey. *Literature Circles: Voice and Choice in Book Clubs and Reading Groups.* Portland, ME: Stenhouse Publishers, 2002, 260 pp.

This is the most comprehensive text on the subject of literature circles. The detailed strategies, structures, and tools for launching and facilitating literature circles will especially benefit teachers who are planning or just beginning to utilize literature circles in K-12 classrooms. Daniels recognizes that precisely because literature circles are meant to be student-led, teachers must establish collaborative routines and procedures that allow for such autonomy. Particularly helpful in this regard is a "typology" of common management problems teachers encounter when establishing literature circles and strategies for addressing them. For those experienced with literature circles or looking to expand their uses, Daniels provides "advanced" variations on the basic book club as well as a chapter on "nonfiction" literature circles for the content areas.

Permanent Record
by Elroy Gay, as told to Andrew Ratner

❖ **About the Story**

At the age of 32, Elroy Gay has just begun to learn how to read and write. Seeking answers to how he managed to make it through the eleventh grade without basic literacy skills, Elroy visits the last school he attended to request his academic record. What he finds in the records provides a window into his childhood.

The first thing that you gotta know about me is that I can't read a damn thing. It don't matter that I'm a 32-year-old man, or that I'm the president and founder of Sixth Boro Productions, Inc. (which, by the way, is the second thing you should know about me), or that I'm on the verge of signing big contracts with names like DreamWorks Records and PNB Clothing attached to it. It don't matter that they got my shirts and hats in storefronts in Rome and Japan, not to mention all over Houston and Delancey Streets. None of that matters, 'cause when it comes to reading, it don't matter if I'm reading a kiddie book or *The New York Times* newspaper. Both of them are just a bunch a jumbled-up letters to me.

And it don't even matter that I made it all the way up through the eleventh grade in New York City public schools, and that I was even elected for the High School of Graphic Art and Communications, one of the hardest-to-get-into high schools in the whole city system where you have to have a eighty-five average just to walk through the door. It couldn't have been because of my reading skills, 'cause I didn't have none then, and I still don't hardly got none today.

WORDS TO CONSIDER

gimmick: (1) a trick to grab attention; (2) a device or gadget. Example: The cheap toy on the bottom of cereal boxes is a gimmick used by food companies to sell their product. Example: When buying a new car, the quality of the engine is more important than gimmicks like voice-command radios.

subsidize: To support financially. Example: Avery's tuition was subsidized through university scholarships and government loans.

I'm letting you know that these are the main things to know about me because you put them all together, and you got some damn serious questions to consider. I mean, how does a nigga from the projects go all the way through eleventh grade, not learn to read a word except "and" and "but" maybe, and still come out running a major company, rubbing elbows with the likes of Cash Money Millionaires and Star at Hot 97 FM?

Let me tell you, though, this ain't only my story. It's the story of the whole Lower East Side of Manhattan, a.k.a., the Sixth Boro, which I love and which I'll always call my home. I say it's also the story of the LES because I am the LES, and the LES is me. The Lillian Wald Projects, that's me. The Baruch Projects, that's me. The Bingo Park, that's me. The Chinese take-out on Delancey's—me too. The corner at 1st and Avenue D, the hanging out corner, the score your dime bag corner, the flirt with the Puerto Rican girls and black girls—any girls that come along—corner. That's all definitely me, so step right up and read all about it.

But let me back up the truck a bit because already I haven't told you the whole truth so help me God. What I mean is, I can read now; maybe not *The New York Times,* but maybe a *Daily News* article, especially with a little help from my tutor Ellen or my biographer, Doctor L. Sometimes, though, it doesn't seem real to me that I can read now, so I still think of myself as "the guy who can't read." I mean, if you been wearing the same outfit for thirty-one years, it's not like you a completely different man just 'cause you wake up one day and change your shirt when you thirty-two. I'm still Elroy in the back of the sixth grade class at PS 63, asking to go to the bathroom whenever I know it's my turn coming up to read.

So I can read a little now. But either way, those questions still need asking. They still need explaining, which is why I decided to write down this story. It must have also been what Dr. L was thinking recently when he suggested that I try to get a hold of my old school records, which I gotta admit I wasn't so crazy about doing at first. It's not that I have bad memories of school, ain't like that at all. I loved school. That's where I made my name. Always had the flyest clothes. Always selling candy and shit like that. That's why I was so popular. That's why all the girls wanted to get with me and all the boys wanted to be me. Spending all them days in the cafeteria. Snapping on people in the back of class. Those were good days back then, even if I couldn't read. Nobody seemed to notice much anyways.

Nah, the reason I wasn't so keen on going back for my old school records is because sometimes it's just better to let things from the past stay right where they is. This seemed like one of those times. Just had a feeling that I might not like what I find over there at the old school office. But Dr. L kept mentioning it to me, so one morning I roll outta bed and head for the C train just like it's 1986 and I'm hustling to get to Graphic Arts so I don't get marked late. The subway is packed with people going to work, and kids with book bags on their way to school crowding around in little groups and talking shit already, even though it's only eight in the morning. But I manage to find a seat just like I always did, and I put my earphones on just like I always did, except this time instead of closing my eyes (like I always did), I find myself looking at all the advertisements in the panels above the windows. I musta seen them same ads a million times, the same colors, the same smiley faces, but now I'm actually reading what they say. And let me tell you something, now that I'm reading a little, I'm realizing that sometimes people write some pretty fucked-up shit. There's one with some Doctor Zitsmore, smiling his ass off and telling you he could remove any kind of wart you got on you. Even cure you of acne if you willing to pay for it. Then there's something by Microsoft with a pretty butterfly logo but instead of just one or two of them butterflies there's a whole army of them running from one end of the subway to the other with no end in sight, like when Moses punished the Pharaoh by making the sky dark with a whole big swarm of insects.

But the one that really got me was an old one that must have been from a few years before. It must have been behind some other ones that they ripped down so that they could put up newer ads. It had a picture of two cops on either side of a little old black lady with one of them old-lady hats on her head. She look like she might topple over any minute, but these two cops are holding her up by her skinny arms. In the background it's smoky, like they just pulled her from a fire or some other disaster. Then below the photograph, in big letters, it say, "Cops Care." And I'm thinking, Now what the fuck does that mean, "Cops Carry?" Yeah, they carrying that old lady, but why is someone gonna make a big poster about how cops carrying old people and shit?

But then I remember something Dr. L told me when we first started our reading lessons: sometimes when you got that "e" at the end of a word, you got to actually think of it as being connected to the letter that's two before it because that's the way it used to be way back in the times of knights and queens. So a word like "fake" used to be spelled f-a-e-k or like "bone" was b-o-e-n. Then one day the powerful priests, who were the only ones that knew how to read, start worrying that some of the common people was starting to get their reading skills too. That's when they decided to put in a little trick just to confuse all them poor niggas who just wanted to read a little. Instead of writing "lake" like they always did—l-ae-k—they would just always move that "e" sound over to the other side. The sound picture got split up but the sound would stay the same. Of course, they didn't let the common people in on their little **gimmick** 'cause then they'd also get the power and the knowledge.

So anyway, I just made a long story of telling you that the poster on the subway with the cops and the old lady didn't say "Cops Carry" but "Cops Care," which to me is still kind of fucked up. I mean, I don't need no advertisement telling me whether cops care or don't care. Some of them do and some of them don't. Some of my good friends are cops and they got me outta some bad situations. I'll never forget what they done for me. But I seen some bad ones too. You show me one black man or Puerto Rican in the LES who ain't been harassed or disrespected by a cop for no good reason. Good luck, 'cause there ain't a one of them. Either way though, I don't need no poster telling me "cops care" like it's Pepsi tasting better than Coke. C'mon now.

So while I'm so busy thinking about all that, the subway pulls up to 50th Street and Eighth Avenue, which is where the school's at. I begin walking and thinking some more. What if they ask me questions? What if they ask me to fill out one of them visitationer's forms? What trick am I gonna pull outta my sleeve for this one? I walk right past Graphic Arts and wind up instead in front of Park West High School, which is on the same block. I bust a U and head back down the block, still worried about what forms they gonna stick in my face and then, I find myself looking right through the chain link fence at the basketball courts in front of the school. That's where I used to bring my B+ game around fourth period. Of course, I'm talking about my Magic Johnson moves à la 1985. Up and down that court ninety million times, but before you know it, the damn period is over; I'd scored forty but still get marked absent from homeroom just the same. That would be bad news 'cause like the homeroom teacher Mr. McDaniel told me, "Just show up, Elroy, and you'll pass."

But here now I'm thirty-two and walking through the metal detector like I'm at Rikers Island on a visitor's pass. They didn't have one of them back in my day, but I had heard enough that I knew to leave my best friend back at the crib. Just to be sure, I check my pockets before heading through the metal detector. You could never be too safe at Graphic Arts and Communications. The lady security guard starts buggin' out when she sees my ID:

"Where you been? This says 1985!"

"I just come back for my records."

"Records? You sure they still got them so far back?"

"They better have them 'cause I sure don't, and I got some research to do!"

Still looking confused, she writes me up a pass and I take the elevator right up to the fifth floor. I want to explore but I'm nervous. Security is tight these days. Then from behind me I hear:

"Big Shot? What you doing here nigga?"

You know I can't see too good without the contacts so I'm like, "What-up nigga!" and keep heading straight to the office not even knowing who I'm talking to. Gotta keep moving. In the office, I walk up to the counter separating the students from the secretaries' desks and the principal's office. Everything looks just like I left it fifteen years ago. Piles of paper on every desk, phones are ringing off the hook, and the secretaries with that "don't bother me now" look on their faces except for the one who sees me. First she got the "not you again" look on her face but after checking me out a second time she looks more confused than anything else.

"Can I help you?" she wants to know, spying me up and down.

"Yes, please," I say to her, a little nervous now that the moment is here. "My name is Elroy Gay. I come to get my old school records."

"School records? You said Elroy Gay, right? I thought you looked familiar."

"Yes, Elroy Gay. I was here in 1984 and 1985."

"That's when you graduated?" she asks before turning to yell at a few boys who are making a racket as they waiting to see the principal

"Um, no, Ms. Lopez. I didn't graduate. I left in the middle of eleventh grade." Ms. Lopez looks surprised that I remember her name. It's just a talent I got. If I looked in someone's face enough times, chatted them up a few times, that's all it takes. Their name stays with me forever.

"Well, I'm sorry, Elroy. You'll have to go to the school that you attended after here. Your records follow you from school to school."

"I'm sorry to keep bothering you, Ms. Lopez. I know you're busy, but I didn't graduate from nowhere. This was the last school I went to."

"I see. Well, I'll try to dig them up, but it might take a few minutes." Then she asks me the question that I figured would be coming sooner or later. "Do you mind if I ask what you want them for, Elroy?" I hesitate a moment and then I'm kind of amazed how easily the words start to leave my lips. For thirty years I'm hiding my reading problem from the whole world and now I'm telling anybody who I got a reason to tell.

"It's for a book I got coming out soon. I'm writing about me going through school and never learning how to read. It's about a lot of things but that's one of them. So, I thought it might help to see what kinda grades I was getting back then." She had started to warm up to me, but now Ms. Lopez looked a little suspicious again.

"I have to tell you Elroy, I've been here over twenty years and nobody ever needed records for that reason. It's an interesting project you have, but if you ask me, I just hope that you're careful with it. People could get in trouble for that kind of thing, you know."

"Oh no!" I tell her, "I'm just gonna write the story like I see it."

"And besides," she says, looking past me at the two boys who are now taking turns punching each other in the shoulders, "You kids aren't so easy to teach, you know."

"Believe me, Ms. Lopez, I remember all that, and it's going in the book too."

While I'm waiting for Ms. Lopez to come back with my records, I hear that same voice behind me that I heard earlier in the hallway: "Yo, Shottee. What the fuck you doing here?" "Shottee" is short for Big Shot, which is how most people in the LES know me. I turn around now and it's Malik Foster, a young brother who lives right in my same building in the Lillian Wald projects.

"Malik? I didn't know that was you back in the hall. What-up nigga?"

"What the hell you doing here?" he asks again. Next thing you know I be telling him the whole story too. And you know what else? It feels good! Now that I started telling people, it's like I want to tell the whole world. Look at me! I'm Elroy, a.k.a. Big Shot, thirty-two and never learned to read shit. Shottee who lived down the hall from you and helps you take the groceries from the elevator. Shottee, president and founder of Sixth Boro Productions. Shottee, record producer of Bones, Thugs and Harmony. Shottee, creative force behind Sixth Boro Day and dozens of murals painted on school walls and storefronts all over the Lower East Side. Shottee, whose shirts and hats and scarves with his Sixth Boro logo you wearing right now. First I get a little nervous, a little hot in my collar, but once I get up the courage to make it known, people all say the same thing, including Malik:

"Yeah Shottee? That's cool. That's real cool. I never knew that about you, Elroy. I'll buy that book when it comes out. Put me on your list, man." And then, as soon as people tell me, "It's cool" and are still giving me the love the way they always gave me and I gave them right back, it's like I can finally come out of that hiding hole I been stuffed in for thirty years. I feel as free and light as a little bird.

When Ms. Lopez come back with my records in a manila envelope, I thank her with all my heart. Maybe she don't know it, but I'm thanking her not only for finding the records but just for helping me get through those years in whatever way she knew; not just her, but all those secretaries and the teachers, and the cafeteria workers and the janitors and the security guards, who were all trying to figure things out just like me. Nobody ever said it's easy starting out with a little boy and helping him become a man.

Before heading out I see that same security guard who I seen coming in. "All right, baby," she say, "You get everything you came for?"

"Yes, thank you. I got it all right. See, you never too late to get the school records."

"I guess not, baby."

Then I'm back out on the block heading to the subway. Soon as the fresh air hits me, that old feeling comes back. Fifteen years later and I still got that happy hop in my step. Nothing feels so good like leaving school after that last bell, even if I haven't been around for fifteen years.

Back on the C train, it's quiet now. I got the car almost to myself, except for a homeless man way to the other end laying across the seats with his head resting on a bundle of rags. I make sure to get as far as possible from the stink, and I sit down to open the envelope. All the papers spill out, papers and more papers. I skim through them and start trying to figure out what it all means. I hardly understood all them letters and grades when I was in high school, trying to get a sneak peek at the report card before Moms got a hold of it; even though I could read a little now, it still takes a few minutes to make sense of it all. Some of it just don't sound right, at least not like I remember it. Look at seventh grade, for example, where it say:

Term Ending 1981
English 75
Social Studies 75
Math 75
Science 75
Reading 75
Health Education 70
Hygiene 80

English 75! C'mon now. How they gonna say that I got a 75 in English when I couldn't read the back of a cereal box? And how they gonna give me that same grade in Social Studies when I couldn't even read the social studies book and none of them ditto sheets. Come to think of it, I don't even remember ever having one of them Social Studies books. The teacher always be like, "Elroy, could you please take out your Social Studies book." And I be like, "Sorry, teach, I forgot it at home this morning." Trouble is, I'd forget it at home every morning. In fact, I don't even remember ever taking one home, period. Maybe I was absent the day they giving them out.

Math 75. I remember spending a lot of them math periods in the hallway and bathroom selling Bubbalicious bubble gum, Tootsie Pops, and Kit Kats from wholesale boxes I got from my sister Lilly's store. I remember figuring out the change for all them school boys and girls buying up my candies. That's about the only Math I be doing in seventh grade. And still there's Mr. Fowler giving me a 75 for selling Snickers bars in the boys' bathroom. All right, maybe I could see getting that 80 in hygiene, 'cause I always come in looking clean and well-groomed. Mama Gay wouldn't have it no other way. Also, this was about the time when my brother Otis started teaching me to dress nice with all the money I be making from the candy. But 75 in reading? C'mon now.

It's when I work my way over to eighth, ninth, and tenth grade though, that things really start to get crazy. It's when I have to start clearing my eyes every few seconds 'cause the tears are starting to fall and I can't see the writing and all the numbers and even when I can see them, I can't believe them because somehow, for some reason, the grades keep going up and up. According to this here school record, I'm an A student! Nineties and eighties across the board. Three years in a row they giving me 90 in English. Social Studies 90, 85, 90, Math 88, 90, 90, and on and on. They grading me like I'm Albert Einstein when I been spending nearly half of every school day selling crack-cocaine in Hell's Kitchen at 50 cents a cap!

The subway keeps moving and I see my hands are shaking now because something has come over me: I'm holding a history of me right in my hands but it ain't no real history. It's a history of lies. It all hits me at once: all them years I thought I was getting over on them, it was them getting over on me. Here I am, 32 years old and I can't even get a library card 'cause I don't know how to fill out the mother-fuckin' application. Here I am 32 years old and I'm calling it progress when I can understand the sign about Dr. Zitsmore removing bunions from your feet. All at once, I remember what they was telling me like it was yesterday: "Just show up to class, Elroy, and you'll pass. Just make sure that you don't get any more absences."

There was so many of us kids failing that they didn't know what to do with us all. Everywhere you went in the LES it was like half, maybe even three quarters of us, wasn't learning shit all day. Some of them was just like me, just little kids that never learned how to read and write back in elementary school, and moved right through the years never knowing what to do about it, and still they keep moving you through with the other kids, except maybe once in fourth grade when, like me, they leave you back to see if it scares you straight. But then they put you right back on that train; the whistle blows—fifth grade, all aboard! Whistle blows—sixth grade, all aboard! Whistle blows—seventh grade, all aboard—until you just start believing that the lie is true. Maybe there ain't no problem with your reading. Maybe you really is a passing student since here you are sitting in the cafeteria eating Sloppy Joes and Tater Tots with all the other tenth graders.

And you know what else? They got my family riding on that same train with me. When you got eleven brothers and sisters there's gotta be some of them that know you have a reading problem. And some of them did know, like my brother Albert. I know he knew, because even today I can picture us fighting in the kitchen like brothers do, going back and forth, looking for each other's weak spot until Albert would say:

"Shut up. You can't even read."

"Can't read? I can, too, read, crackhead!"

"Oh, yeah. I bet you can't even spell your name."

"I can too spell my name."

"Yeah, then spell it."

"E-L-R-O-Y"

"Ah! See, I know you couldn't do it."

"Now how you gonna tell me I didn't spell it right? I know how to spell my own name, you crackhead!"

"I said, spell *it*. That's I-T. You said, E-L-R-O-Y. See, you can't read *or* spell, Elroy." So yeah, they knew about my reading problem. My Moms knew. My sister Lily knew because sometimes she read me letters I got from my friends at the Fresh-Air camp. Mostly they all knew. But they was seeing those same 85s and 90s that I was looking at right then on the subway. So what they gonna say? "I'm sorry. I think you got it all wrong, Mr. Principal. Elroy don't even read as good as our baby cousin Shakearah, and she only in the kindergarten." Hell no! They was thinking, if it ain't broke, then why should we fix it; so that's why they got on the train, too. The report card said, "Ain't Broke." So why fix it?

I'm crying like a little boy with all them thoughts rushing through my mind when the subway doors open and the cold air hit. I poke my head out and something don't look right: we at the elevated stop on Carroll Street in Brooklyn. Passed my stop at Houston Street probably ten minutes ago. When I get out to cross over to the uptown side, I gotta put my hand beneath my shirt because it feel like that homeless man in my car snuck up and kicked me in the stomach when I wasn't looking.

By the time I get back to the 'hood, though, things have settled down. Back in the crib, the room I love so much, my little paradise in the projects, I feel pretty good again. Rested. I feel like I got something accomplished. Sure, I'm holding a pile of lies, but at least I got my hands on them now. At least they're not hiding in some file cabinet where nobody can never find out what was really going down at Seward Park and Graphic Arts and JHS 22. Now, you all gonna hear about it, and not just about the school. True, I didn't have the reading skills for a long time, but I always had my ears and eyes. When you live in the projects, you hear and see everything long as you willing to look and listen. Right from my little own crib here in the Lillian Wald, seeping through these thin walls tagged by some of the greatest graffiti artists in the six boroughs, I heard it all. That's why I call my crib the "Rat Hole." To the outsider, it's just another 8-by-5 block of **subsidized** housing, but to the insider, to the rat, it's the center of the universe.

Ignore that bullhorn you hearing. We got Public School 97 right across the street. Kids in the schoolyard yelling at the top of their lungs, and that bullhorn yelling right back, "Line up! Get in line! You're late! Line up!" Don't worry. Just keep your ears and eyes open. Those crazy kids be heading back inside in less than five minutes anyway.

Then we'll get down to business.

Elroy Gay
December 2002, New York, NY

Discussion Questions

In the Lines

1. Why is Elroy heading back to his old high school?
2. What are some of the observations that Elroy makes about the advertisements on the subway?
3. Describe Elroy's grades in high school? Why is he surprised that these were his grades?

Between the Lines

4. After Ms. Lopez gives Elroy his school records, why does she say, "It's an interesting project you have, but if you ask me, I just hope that you're careful with it. People could get in trouble for that kind of thing, you know."
5. After reading his school records, Elroy says, "It all hits me at once; all them years I thought I was getting over on them, it was them getting over on me." What has led Elroy to this conclusion?
6. By the time Elroy gets back to his room, he says he feels "pretty good again" and that he "got something accomplished." Why do you think Elroy feels this way? What exactly has he accomplished?
7. "Functional" literacy has been described as the ability to read and write in order to accomplish everyday tasks, such as reading a bus schedule or filling out a job application. By contrast, "critical" literacy emphasizes reading and writing as a means of understanding the world and reshaping attitudes, values, and beliefs in order to make the world a better place. What type of literacy, or literacies, does Elroy demonstrate over the course of the story?

Beyond the Text

8. Governments, schools, and teachers, family members, friends and neighbors, neighborhood institutions like churches and community centers, and cultural media such as television and radio all have an impact on a child's education. Children's innate abilities and character will also shape their educational development. Elroy did not begin to read and write until he was in his thirties. In your opinion, who is most responsible for this? Based on your own observations and experiences, who is ultimately responsible for ensuring that a child becomes educated and literate?

❈ Teacher Focus Group Discussion: The N-Word

There is much to be gained by allowing people of all backgrounds to yank nigger away from white supremacists to subvert its ugliest denotation, and to convert the N-word from a negative into a positive appellation.

RANDALL KENNEDY, *Nigger: The Strange Career of a Troublesome Word* (2002)

It is time to blow the whistle on nitwits who have so successfully promoted a value system that embraces murder, drug dealing, gang membership, misogyny, child abandonment, and a sense of self so diseased that it teaches children to view the men in their orbit as niggers and the women as hoes.

BOB HERBERT, "Blowing the Whistle on Gangsta Culture,"

The New York Times, December 22, 2005

Discussion

Ratner: Tonight's discussion will focus on "offensive" words and offensive language in the high school classroom literature. We'll pay particular attention to the term "nigger" or "nigga," a word that is used repeatedly in "Permanent Record." Obviously the term is fraught with controversy; historically, it has been one of the most charged racial epithets in the English language. The fact that some will find it uncomfortable to talk about in this setting only serves to illustrate this point.

It's interesting to note that in the Kennedy and Herbert quotes above, we have two highly educated individuals—a Harvard Law professor and a *New York Times* columnist—who have reached polar opposite views on the same subject. Herbert is writing about "Gangsta Culture" in general, but my assumption is that he would also prefer that we "blow the whistle" on the word "nigger." And then you have a Harvard Law professor who sees something positive in contemporary uses of the "N-word" in popular culture and everyday discourse; he suggests that it signals a healthy appropriation of the term by those who have historically been on the receiving end when it is used maliciously.

Huckleberry Finn (Twain 1885) was, and remains, the most widely read novel in American schools. Since the 1950s, students, teachers, parents, civic groups, scholars, authors, and legal professionals have debated whether a story in which the word "nigger" is used hundreds of times belongs in high school English classrooms. In these three quotes, however, one can see that the tenor of the discussion surrounding the term has changed dramatically in recent years, coinciding with transformations in the word's meaning and use. It's hardly news to those of you teaching in city schools that more than a few students use the "N-word" as regularly and casually as Englishmen refer to each other as "lads." You may have also noticed that the word has become increasingly commonplace in popular music, literature, and film. These developments pose some challenging questions for English teachers. While some find Twain's use of the word "nigger" (and what critics describe as his "minstrel" portrait of Jim) egregious, others defend him by saying that he uses it ironically and that it should be viewed within what is clearly his denunciation of antebellum society and the morally bankrupt institution of slavery. No less than Ralph Ellison is reported to have agreed that those who have a problem with Huck's liberal use of the epithet are "making the same old mistake of confusing the narrator with the author" (Fishkin 1995). But how about the narrator's use of the word "nigger/nigga" in a story like "Permanent Record"? What purpose, if any, does it serve in the narrative "Permanent Record" or in other examples of contemporary literature and media where the term is used casually? Does it have a place in the English classroom? Here are some other questions to consider:

- What does the word signify to you personally and to you as a teacher or future teacher? What does it signify to your students?
- Is there an important distinction between "nigger" and "nigga"?
- Is there an important distinction to be made when blacks and non-blacks use the term?
- If you were to use "Permanent Record" in a middle or secondary school setting, how would you address the repeated use of the word "nigga" and other instances of strong language in the narrative?

Ed: It seems like I've heard this argument before in the 80s with the Silence Equals Death campaign. HIV/AIDS activists used the pink triangle as their logo, which was an appropriation of the symbol that was sewn on the shirts of homosexuals by the Nazis. Gay and lesbian groups co-opted the pink triangle to take its power away, and I think this is exactly what has happened with the word "nigger." No longer does it have a bad connotation, you know? The word has no power. I use that word.

Cyril: I wouldn't say it has no power. It depends on who is saying it and in what situation. When a rapper like Ice-T says, "Does America look like South Central to you?" he's basically saying that everything has to do with the perspective from which you're talking. It's a completely different thing for a black person living in South Central Los Angeles to use the word "nigga" or "nigger" than when a white person living in entirely different circumstances says it.

Debbie: I don't think a rapper like Ice-T is saying that we need to take the word and change its connotation. He's not saying that he is a "nigga" because he is a black person. He's saying that he's a "nigga" because of his life experiences and he's not apologizing for this. It's just what it is. The Harvard professor is obviously saying something different: that we need to take the word and change its connotation. As a black person, I never thought about it this way. If nigger means somebody who is ignorant, somebody who is uneducated, and somebody who is crude and all those things, and you are those things and you choose to call yourself "nigger," then that's your prerogative. I feel much better with that argument, as opposed to the argument that we should reinvent the word so that it becomes more acceptable.

Ariella: I think it's also important to note that these men are successful in their own right; for instance, Ice-T is making a lot of money off of marketing the image that he's struggling. The truth is that he will never have to struggle for anything. I get upset and I tell my children that if they use this word in a corporate setting, they're going to be judged by others. What if people hiring them are uncomfortable with the word or don't have ownership of the word? Many high-school-age students are ignorant about its history; they don't even know from where the word originated. If they were more aware of the negative history around it, they would choose not to use it in any form or for any purpose. I get annoyed because these rappers are removed from it. Their bank accounts are filled, they can speak any way they want, use offensive or inoffensive language, and interpret words to mean whatever they want—and they're safe. They are safe from judgment, their albums are selling, but these kids just hear that word and think, "I can speak like that and there will be no penalty." The truth is that there will be! If you look at our country, the people who are in power are people that aren't using the word. They would be offended by the word or assume that the people using the word are ignorant or have been raised in a certain environment. So it's foolish to say to our kids, "Oh yeah, you can use that word!" and not tell them, "Well, here's the history of the word you are choosing to use, here's what these people had to go through and endure to fight against that word, and it's been great that a letter has been dropped and a vowel added, but let's look at who has profited from its appropriation."

Angela: So, my first question just from reading the Kennedy quote is "What is the positive use of the word N-I-G-G-A?" I've yet to hear one, other than guys referring to friends on the street in a welcoming kind of way. I think that's as positive as it's going to get. That's just my own personal opinion.

Colleen: Well, it's interesting to talk about the positive connotations of the word "nigga" because it brings back a memory from my first year of teaching when I had a class of twelfth graders. There was this one kid, Johnny, who annoyed me every day but was also one of those kids who constantly made me laugh. I substituted for a class that Johnny attended with his friend Xavier. His friend was giving me problems, and I told him: "You just need to get up out of that chair and move right now," and he was like: "Who are you?" And Johnny says to him: "Nah, it's all right Xavier. She's my nigga." And I'm thinking, was that a compliment? I think I just got complimented. I took it to mean, "You're with me in this." It's more than just "buddy." It's something a bit tighter than that, like somehow we are going through the same experience. That's how I've seen it used.

Ratner: So, an expression of solidarity?

Colleen: Yes, solidarity. I also want to go back to what Ariella said earlier and divide the argument somewhat. She was saying that students should not use the word because they'll be judged for it. I'm not completely comfortable with that line of reasoning because there's something a bit hypocritical about white people, the very ones who invented "nigger" in the first place, telling students of color that they can or can't use a word because it's going to keep them down in society. As a white teacher, it troubles me to say that you just have to do this if you want to participate in this system. Why should we teach them to conform to the very system that oppressed people of color in the first place? It doesn't seem like a valid reason for instructing students to stop using the word, you know?

On the other hand, Adrianna makes a valid point that there is a long, awful history behind the word that our students might not recognize. I teach with an African American woman, Latisha, who grew up in the South and has had that word directed at her in a derogatory sense, and she cannot abide it. She tells her students: "Don't use it in my classroom. Don't try to mainstream it; it is never, ever, going to be cool." She even introduced her students to a slave narrative, *Our Nig* (Wilson, 1859) to force the point home about what "nigger" really means to people. As presented in the book, "nigger" is *not* about brotherly love, not an expression of solidarity. It's derogatory in the worst sense. And *yet*, a couple of the smartest kids in the class picked up on the word and now they use it like "Ahhh, my Nig." Latisha couldn't believe that after all that, they were using it as a joke. They still couldn't contextualize it.

Ratner: So, they even appropriated a variation on the word that she introduced to call attention to its historical meaning as a derogatory term?

Angela: Appropriation has been going on since the word was coined. Even slaves were calling other slaves "niggers" and it wasn't meant in neutral or positive sense. It wasn't meant like, "Hey you, pass me the salt." It was meant to belittle and subjugate. I don't think it is ever going to escape a negative connotation, no matter how many times we try to appropriate or change it.

Ratner: It might seem that way to many people, especially those of us who did not grow up in the current youth culture where the word can be tossed around so casually. It's hard to imagine that it could ever have a neutral or even positive connotation. But then again, when I walk through the hallways of this college, or go to the cafeteria for lunch, I encounter undergrads—blacks, Dominicans, Asians, even white kids—who seem completely at ease using the word. And these are kids who have supposedly "made it" and at least on paper have more formal education than your middle and high school students. Does this suggest that, even if their purpose was making money or whatever, celebrities like Ice-T and Jay-Z have, in fact, "defanged" the word?

Glen: Well, I have to tell you that in my experience, especially when I was teaching in a school in the Bronx where 80 percent of the students were Hispanic, they would use the word all the time. And I have to tell you that they never used it positively. It was always hurled at each other like daggers. Every once in a while somebody would use it affectionately, but that was one percent of the time. It was overwhelmingly negative and very hostile, and when they wanted to be nice to each other, they did not use that word. They just didn't.

Ratner: Thanks for sharing that, Glen. Let me interrupt for a second to say that it's one thing for a bunch of lawyers and academics to sit around in a courtroom and discuss whether or not you should have *Huckleberry Finn* in the curriculum, but it is teachers who have firsthand knowledge of how and why kids are processing this type of controversial language. You are coming from a different perspective; it's one person's perspective, but I think it's a very important one.

Ariella: Back to Colleen's point, I don't see it as telling students to conform. I would never do that. But I don't feel that they are given the proper tools to choose their words. Without providing them with the history of the word, I don't feel that they can make an informed decision about if, when, or how to use it. They are bombarded with it to the point where now they think the word has always been positive, and I am hypersensitive now because my students are studying the Civil War and reading *Uncle Tom's Cabin* (Stowe 1851). It's just so scary to be studying and reading about how Africans and African Americans were raped of their culture; this word was so demeaning that it's hard to imagine how it can become positive. I'm also hypersensitive because although I am white, I tell my students that I have experienced racism firsthand due to my darker skin tone. Anybody who has a remotely darker skin tone belongs to a culture that has been enslaved somewhere and at some point in history. It's just wrong to assume that they're smart and mature enough to recognize that each time they use the term, they are "choosing" to be ignorant, and "choosing" to enslave themselves in a way. We shouldn't conform simply to avoid the judgment of a racist society, because life *is* a game, with rules. They need to know that there is a risk in using that word, just like there's a risk if I always wanted to call my girlfriends "bitch" every time I went somewhere. Women have been oppressed forever so if I want to casually call my friends "bitch," as some women do, I have to be willing to accept that somewhere along the line someone will view me as trashy or ignorant. Now, if a college student comes to me and says, "I've studied the word and I'm okay with using it," that's fine. But not one child in my class has an inkling, and nor do I, what it would be like to be a slave for one day. They can't even bear writing a one-page paper, so I can't imagine if they were being beat, separated from their family, and forced to work under grueling circumstances. Then they feel completely free to blurt out the word "nigger"? This gets me really going because they haven't earned that right.

Debbie: I think we choose when to be offended. I think that's what it comes down to in the end. When my students use the word, I'm a bit uncomfortable but not offended. Now if a white person on the street was angry at me and screamed the "N-word," I would be offended. I don't know why it has to be more complicated than that. I don't see why we have to tell black people not to use it when they want to use it to communicate solidarity. I don't see why we have to take it away from them, nor do I feel that this would be akin to condoning offensive use of the word.

Glen: Can I jump in a second, please? To me, what you're saying can be applied to the controversies we have had over *Huck Finn* and the way the word is used in that book. People shouldn't try to make the past pretty and nice when it isn't that way, and they have to realize that when that word is being used, it reveals a lot about Huck.

I have these students who think it's funny to use the word "nigger," but when we read *Raisin in the Sun* (Hansberry 1959) and Walter says he's going to take the money from the White Block Association so he won't have to "live with a bunch of stinking niggers," the kids go, "Ohhhhhhhh!" That context hits home with them; they understand that in that instance the word is meant to be a knife to cut through someone. So, my point is that maybe students have more understanding of context than we think.

Ed: I'm not sure that I agree. I think that their contextualization is as simplistic as, "If a white guy says it, that's bad, and if a black guy says it, that's okay." Last year with my class, I said, "I understand that there is this new word, "nigga," and it's used as a pronoun. Then there's that other one." And they said, "Oh, that's 'Nig*ger*.'" The interesting thing is that I had the class create a concept web of other words they associate with "nigga" and what they came up with was all bad stuff. Every word or phrase had something to do with "gangsta culture," but it's essentially the same culture you saw on Wall Street in the 80s. It's all about being selfish, about getting what you want whenever you want it and doing whatever it takes to make that happen. At least to this group of kids, that's what "nigga" meant to them. Sure, there is playfulness and an element of bravado when they use the word, but what scares me is when the play-acting and posing become a prophecy, when they start to actually pursue that lifestyle.

Debbie: My student said to me a couple of years ago: "You know, Miss, I don't think there are really any bad words, I think people just choose to get mad at some words—like, take the "F-word"—what is really bad about the "F-word"? If it is sex, we can say the word *sex* and that's not bad. What's so bad about the word? Why can't we say it?" and I was thinking about it for a while and I was like, "What *is* so bad about this word?" But as a culture and a society we have decided that this word is offensive, and whenever we hear it we should be offended. Now, if I tell you that the only thing you can really say to offend me is to accuse me of having a big nose, guess what you are going to do the next time you are really mad at me and you want to offend me? You are going to point out my big nose. So, I don't understand the argument that says, "Let's not use the word at all, no one should use it at all," because as soon as people mean to offend you, they know that this is the thing that you are hypersensitive about. This is the most obvious thing to say to offend a black person; therefore, you are going to say it. You know? So when the recipient is capable of saying, "This word has these connotations, and I do not associate myself with them," it takes away the power of the word.

Angela: I agree with you, but I'm finding that maybe the context is important just because when a black person uses it with another black person, or a Hispanic person uses it with another Hispanic person, and they're all from the same neighborhood and they're all on the same level, on the same page, it's not meant to hurt. On the other hand, can broader popular culture ever use the word without signifying its hurtful or defamatory origins? So is there harm in it? I can see both sides of the issue.

Ratner: I want to bring our discussion back to the story and questions we've raised about teaching literature containing words that offend. What purpose does it serve, if any, in a narrative like "Permanent Record"?

Ariella: Well, my students would love this story. After reading the first paragraph, I thought, "I have to give this to them," just like I did with "Feed the Block." They would love it because they would view it as having "street cred."

Ratner: OK, but we all know there are things that kids like that are not good for them. I assume we are not going to make enjoyment the only criterion, although obviously that is an important one.

Ariella:	It's also a good model of a narrative. The strong language is just one small aspect of the story. I think I would approach the strong language within the larger topic of voice—how writers can use different words to convey a different emotion or sentiment. The great thing about the strong voice is that they will be drawn to it, which would then allow us to explore some of the more subtle aspects of the story. In fact, we can discuss the very same things we're talking about now. My only concern is that some of my students would see the narrator as completely reliable and take a literal message that they can get far without learning how to read.
Colleen:	I am not one for censorship at all; I hate it in any sense. I think if this is the author's voice and it's a valid voice, and the word is not simply being tossed around for shock value, there is no reason to edit this. Just like you don't edit *Catcher in the Rye* (Salinger 1951), you wouldn't edit this. I don't know if I would give this to my ninth-grade class, because they're too immature to be able to see beyond the shock value of it. Most of my twelfth graders are close to 18, though. They could handle it.
Debbie:	That's my point, too. For instance, with my sixth graders, I wouldn't be able to use *The Color Purple* (Walker 1982) because I don't think I would get past the first page. I mean, they would die laughing over the lesbian themes, and they wouldn't get the point of the story. But if there's something to be learned from a story, I don't see the harm in using something with derogatory words.
Ratner:	I am interested in Holly's perspective as someone who just started teaching this year. How do you feel about all this?
Holly:	I actually don't allow the word in my class at all, and there are serious repercussions if it is used. In terms of exposing students to literature with strong language, I find the Ice-T lyrics to be a bit "too much." I take it case by case, however. I'll use *To Kill a Mockingbird* (Lee 1960), for example, as long as students know that they can't just start throwing the "N-word" around. It's not allowed in my class at all, and students need to know that there is a difference between the "N-word" being used by an adult author with a specific historical purpose, versus their casual use of it in my presence.
Debbie:	Why have people attempted to ban *To Kill a Mockingbird?*
Ratner:	Well, like *Huck Finn,* individuals and school boards have tried to censor *To Kill a Mockingbird* because it uses the word "nigger" repeatedly.
Debbie:	I just don't understand why one would choose to get offended by a book that is bringing attention to the issue of racism. It doesn't make any sense.
Glen:	Well, I think a lot of school boards are full of people who don't know very much, and they get wind of something and act without full awareness of the situation.

Ratner: Cyril, what about you? Any thoughts about this story? Would you feel comfortable using this in your classroom?

Cyril: Quite honestly, I'm on the fence. If I did use this in a class, one objective would be to reinforce the concept of "code switching," which is something we discussed recently. For example, when Elroy [the narrator] is speaking with the school secretary, he switches into a more formal, standard English, and then when he runs into that kid from his neighborhood, he switches immediately back to African American Vernacular English. My students used to call this "street" or ghetto English, but I want them to see that it's a legitimate language—with or without curse words—and that people who do well in life know how to "change codes" according to situations. I would ask them, for example, what would have happened if Elroy spoke to the secretary exactly the same way he spoke to the kid, or vice versa.

Colleen: I actually wouldn't bring this story into my class, not because of the language but because of some of the themes. I was reading this on the C train and crying because it totally subverts everything I am trying to do in my classroom.

Ratner: How so?

Colleen: Well, I want my students to value literacy. And here you have this guy who made it all the way through eleventh grade and now runs a company without ever having learned to read or write. Even if it's just talk, and he hasn't accomplished everything he says he's accomplished, I'd be worried that my students would get the wrong message.

Holly: I agree. I often feel like my students are looking for a reason to get out of anything they don't want to do. From freshmen to seniors, I would not hand them this story because it seems like I am giving them a "get out of school free" ticket.

Ariella: If I had to pick only one text to use, would I pick this? No. But our students see examples of people who get by all the time. This is why life is not fair. I think it is wrong to lie to them and say if you work hard, you get what you deserve. We talk about it all the time, and they ask me: "Why did so-and-so get passed along to high school? He failed everything!" And I say, "You know what? That's a great question, but he will only get passed along so far." Elroy is a dreamer, and part of that innocence is to be able to dream, but there needs to be a way to balance that against the importance of education and hard work. I mean, people of all ages and races get away with stuff. They know that there's a lazy way out, and sometimes giving them a text like this puts everything on the table, lets them know that they aren't fooling you and you aren't trying to fool them either.

Glen: I would agree with that, and in fact, Elroy at one point says something like, "All those years I thought I was getting over on the teachers, when in fact they were getting over on me." Keep in mind the narrator is over thirty years old and only recently could read the back of a cereal box. There's nothing appealing about that aspect of his life. I think it will hit home to some students. To me the story is a wonderful example of how a society sets up certain rules, how the rules serve some people and not others, and how sometimes people break these rules when they see they have little alternative. It's about the responsibilities of the individual versus responsibilities of society. I think many students will get the idea that it's a story about these tensions.

✕ Classroom Activities: Permanent Record

You never really know someone until you climb into someone's skin and walk around in it.

— Atticus Finch, *To Kill a Mockingbird* (Lee 1988)

Introductory Activity: Walking Around in Someone Else's Skin

The wise council of Atticus Finch to his daughter Scout serves as the theme for the instructional activities covered in this chapter. Take a walk down the hallway of any high school and you will see that the egocentrism associated with infants remains largely intact through pubescence and the late teens. This is not to say that teenagers are inherently selfish, but simply that when they form circles in the middle of the hallway, oblivious to passing traffic, or when their close-quarters greetings and taunts leave your ears ringing, they can appear, well, rather indifferent to the needs of anyone other than themselves. To my mind, the greatest benefit that reading literature has to offer teens is this: its singular capacity for drawing us beyond our immediate experience and into the very sinews of the "other."

For over a month now, I have been reading Maurice Sendak's *Where the Wild Things Are* (Sendak 1963) to my two-and-a-half-year-old son before bedtime. No matter how many times Max first encounters the Wild Things as they "roll their terrible eyes, gnash their terrible teeth," Ethan grows visibly distressed—"No, no, no!"—and begs me to turn the page. It is quite obvious that during these moments Ethan is not simply reading about Max. He *is* Max. Jeffrey Wilhelm argues in *You Gotta Be the Book* (1996) that when an adolescent reader's response to literature lacks depth and analytic rigor, it may be because adolescents are "often asked to interpret a story by gazing and reflecting upon something that they have never experienced" (Wilhelm 1996, p. 89). And while high school readers may never lose themselves in fictional characters as fully as toddlers, I have found that the following activities help students tap into what Wilhelm describes as the "evocative dimensions"[1] of reading literature.

---

[1] Reader responses that Wilhelm groups under the "evocative dimension" include "entering the story world," "seeing the story world," and "relating to characters." (Wilhelm 1996, p. 46).

Community of Readers Extension Activity: Literature Improvisations

Heart-to-Hearts

The procedures for the literature-based improvisational activity I refer to as Heart-to-Hearts are listed in Figure 4.1. Simply ask students to assume the role of fictional characters and carry on a dialogue where they speak openly and honestly with each other concerning matters that the characters could not, or would not, address within the actual pages of the fiction.

> *Frankly Scarlett, I don't give a damn.*
> *It was the best of times, it was the worst of times.*

When we think of great literature, we think of memorable lines of dialogue and narration, lines that reverberate with wisdom, pathos, or humor. We also think of unforgettable scenes that have been seared into our visual consciousness. The mention of John Steinbeck's *Of Mice and Men* (1937), for instance, immediately conjures for me the indelible image of the hulking, simple-minded Lennie on his hands and knees with his best friend George pointing a pistol to the base of his skull.

It strikes me, however, that the spell cast over us by finely crafted literature has also to do with what is *not* said or never happens in its pages. Here, for instance, I think of Paul D. in Toni Morrison's *Beloved* (1987), the ex-slave whose shame and repressed desire to commune with Sethe is symbolized by the iron bit that he was once forced to wear at the Sweet Home. What would he, and could he, say to his lover Sethe, and to others, had he not been the victim and witness of such brutality? Like Paul D. with "that tobacco tin buried in his chest where a red heart used to be . . . its lid rusted shut" (Morrison 1987, pp. 72–73), fiction is replete with characters yearning to express themselves but

FIGURE 4.1

Directions for Heart-to-Hearts

1. Pass out slips of paper with the names of major and minor characters in a story, novel, or play.

2. Inform students that you will ask for volunteers representing two or more characters to face each other across a table and have a heart-to-heart discussion.

3. In preparation for the activity, ask students to prepare questions and comments that they wish to pose to one or more of the characters with whom they will have the heart-to-heart discussion.

4. Direct students in the audience to "listen in" to the heart-to-heart discussion and take notes regarding the plausibility of each character's responses (i.e., whether the volunteer's comments are "in character" and reasonable in light of what the reader has learned about the character in the actual story).

5. Review and assess the conversation using the original story to evaluate the degree to which each participant has remained "in character."

unable to produce the language necessary to do so. Whether due to inhibition, bad timing, or simply the immensity of an idea or sentiment ("Ah, Bartleby! Ah, Humanity!"), words often fail narrators and characters when they most need them.

While there is much to be gained from students adapting literature in the English classroom for theatrical performance complete with memorized lines, blocking, body movements, props, and costumes, I find the preceding literature-driven nonscripted drama activity particularly suitable for stretching students' capacity to empathize with literary characters. My experience has been that once we remove the demand of memorizing or reading from a script, students loosen up and actually enjoy performing in front of teachers and peers. More importantly, without their faces buried in a text or minds occupied with remembering their lines, students are more likely to gain a felt sense of the characters they dramatize.

Another important advantage of improvisation over scripted readings is that by definition, improvisation requires students to project how their fictional personas would respond to events, or to individuals who have not been depicted in the actual story, play, or poem. Doing so requires them to think beyond a character's function in the plot and focus instead on the character's inner life and core qualities in a way that requires deeper-level textual analysis.

Here is another improvisational activity that I have found particularly suitable for stretching students' capacity to understand and empathize with the characters they encounter in the high school literature classroom.

Chance Meetings

What kind of interaction would Iago and Othello have if they found themselves sitting next to each other at a Yankees game? If they ran into each other while shopping at a Circuit City, how would Elroy act towards Mr. McDaniel, the homeroom teacher who told him to "just show up"? Chance Meetings (see figure 4.2), such as the ones envisioned above, help students develop a deeper, lived-through empathy for literary characters and get a sense for what it would mean for these characters to exist in a social world. Again, for students to reap the full benefit of this activity they should maintain their roles for substantial periods of time. It is one thing to dramatize a single line or stretch of dialogue in the role of an adult illiterate or cunning villain. It is an entirely different experience to play Elroy or Iago for 15 or even 20 minutes. It is usually when students lose themselves in the role that they gain new insights into a character and respond viscerally to "walking in their skin."

A Note on Minor Characters

In "Permanent Record," Elroy tells us that a homeroom teacher once told him, "Just show up and you'll pass." This is all we know of Mr. McDaniel, and yet even he provides the reader with material for reflection and discussion. Why might an individual charged with educating youth say something so unethical and seemingly harmful to Elroy? What might be the cultural, professional, or

FIGURE 4.2

Directions for Chance Meetings

1. Provide each student with an index card (or something similar) upon which is written the name of one character from a chosen story or drama.

2. On the back of each index card, have students write two adjectives that they believe best describe their assigned character. (Next to each adjective, they should also identify a line or passage from the story that supports their choices of adjectives. This encourages accountable, text-based interpretations of characters.)

3. Students then wear their nametags with the name of the character visible to other students.

4. Provide the students with a scenario that they will then enact in the role of their assigned character. The scenario should *not* be one that occurred in the actual text. For example, you might ask students to take the role of various Romeo and Juliet characters walking through a shopping mall or political rally, or working together on completing tasks like preparing a meal or decorating a Christmas tree.

5. Ask students to walk around the room in character while engaging in short conversations that might take place in the designated scenario. After a minute or so, direct the students to move on to a conversation with a new partner.

6. Following the literature improvisation, ask students to reflect on their choices of adjectives for the characters, and to modify or add to their choices based on their experience during the improvisation.

7. In a follow-up group discussion, share individual experiences of the literature improvisation and explore how these experiences changed or reinforced students' perceptions of the various characters.

8. For a variation on Chance Meetings, prepare character nametag headbands or place adhesive tags on the backs of students so that they are not immediately aware of their assumed character.

---

personal pressures motivating him to make such a comment? Based on what we know of Elroy, what aspects of Elroy's personality might have influenced Mr. McDaniel? Figure 4.3 presents an excerpt from a Heart-to-Heart conversation between a tenth-grade student playing the role of Elroy Gay and his actual teacher playing the role of Mr. McDaniel.

Writing Project: Copy/Change

Whereas Heart-to-Hearts and Chance Meetings promote empathetic readings of fictional characters, Copy/Change invites students to climb into the skin of another writer and "walk around in it a while." Teachers choose a passage from a poem, play, or story and direct students to alter part or all of the original text. In some cases, teachers will ask students to Copy/Change a limited number of specific items that illustrate a targeted writing strategy, skill, or grammatical element. Students might be directed, for example, to Copy/Change a

F I G U R E   4 . 3

Sample Heart-to-Hearts Improvisation

Student: I just wanna know, Mr. McDaniel, why all you teachers let me pass tenth grade?

Teacher: I don't understand.

Student: I mean, you knew I couldn't read, didn't you? How can someone pass tenth grade if they can't read?

Teacher: Well, I guess I knew that you had some trouble reading, but . . .

Student: Some trouble? I couldn't read at all, Mr. McDaniel. Not even the back of a cereal box!

Teacher: Really? I didn't realize it was that bad.

Student: So why did you do it, then?

Teacher: Like I said, I don't think that anyone knew the extent of your reading problem.

Student: My English teacher must have known it. My Social Studies teacher must have known it.

Teacher: Don't be so sure, Elroy. Classes were so big back then, and when you're teaching 150 students a semester, it's hard to keep track of them all. And kids can be pretty sneaky, you know. They know how to hide things. They cheat on tests, have other students do their homework. They make all kinds of excuses. Sometimes they refuse to read or even open their book when you ask them to do it.

Student: Well, why do you think I would do all those things?

Teacher: I guess I see now, but it's not so easy to see it when you're in the middle of teaching a class with a million things going on.

Student: Still, someone should have recognized that I had a reading problem and done something about it, even if I was playing the fool back then. I'm not blaming you, Mr. McDaniel. It's just that people don't know how hard my life has been because they only see Elroy with the nice clothes and my company and the book I'm putting out soon.

Teacher: Look, Elroy. If I had to guess, this is how it happened: you were always a nice kid . . . very likeable. And it's hard failing students, especially the ones that you like. It's hard looking them in the eye and telling them that even if they made the effort, they just can't handle grade-level material. And keep in mind that teachers have their own pressures. You have principals telling you that you have to pass a certain percentage of students, even if you know certain kids shouldn't move on to the next grade. You have parents who accuse you of being unfair for failing students and who say that the problem is your teaching rather than bad parenting or the fact that a kid came to your class already three or four grade levels behind.

Student: I see your point, but it just don't seem right.

Accomplished authors bring complexity and depth to their plays and stories through their rendering of minor characters. The most fully realized of these minor characters not only illuminate facets of the major characters, they have their own histories, motivations, and life-altering dilemmas. Whether through the drama activities described in this chapter or other lessons, calling students' attention to minor characters fosters close reading of literature and increases the potential for students to have meaningful encounters with stories and dramas.

passage of Tim O'Brien's story "The Things They Carried" (1990) from its original third-person narration to a first-person point of view. The class could then discuss how such a change alters a reader's impressions of Lt. Jimmy Cross as he leads his combat platoon in Vietnam. Depending on the teacher's objectives, the changes that students will be directed to attempt may or may not alter the original meaning of the passage or author's purpose.

When working with middle and high school students, I introduce Copy/Change as an opportunity for my students to temporarily "get inside" an author's head and writing hand—that is, to "be" that author and thereby better understand the author's style and writing process. Rather than assigning a specific passage or element of a passage to Copy/Change, I invite students to write about anything—their best friend, a memory, a recent sporting event, and so on—but to do so in the voice and style of another author. Describe, for example, their walk to school in the morning in the style of Toni Morrison. Paint a picture in words of a family member, but do so in the voice of Elroy Gay in "Permanent Record."

Based on my experience with middle and high school students, I offer the following guidelines for conducting Copy/Change:

- *Guide students to study and mimic stylistic elements of targeted authors, rather than episodic elements.*
  You can anticipate that students will experience initial confusion over writing in the voice or style of another author. The very notion of style and voice may be foreign to them, as may be even the most basic concept that writers have the power and freedom to create a unique voice and style. As a result, certain students will respond to Copy/Change by simply inserting themselves or other foreign characters into a plot event described by the targeted author. In this case, it may be helpful to have the students initially write a narrative in their own voice. Afterwards, ask students to compare their writing style with a specific aspect of the author's style, such as the length and variety of sentences, choice of verbs and nouns, or characteristics of dialogue. Students can then attempt to revise their narratives by incorporating the targeted element of style.

- *Push students to write relatively lengthy Copy/Change pieces.*
  Writing teachers too often treat Copy/Change as exercise in sentence-to-sentence translation, directing the class to move from line to line of a poem stanza or scene in a play while substituting different adjectives, changing nouns to pronouns, and converting dialogue to regular text. Truly understanding and internalizing the writing strategies, challenges, and psycho-emotional state of another author requires not only climbing into the skin of that author but walking around in it "a while." For this reason, when I invite students to Copy/Change a narrative or poem in the voice of Holden Caulfield or the style of Zora Neale Hurston, I encourage them to immerse themselves in this experience by writing continuously for 20 minutes or by not putting their pens down until they have filled two pages of their journals.

- *Facilitate discussions and post-writing activities where students describe the experience of "walking in the skin" of another writer.*

  It is the process of Copy/Change and what students learn from this process about themselves and other writers that matters, not the production of a pitch-perfect imitation of the author. After a period of silent, sustained Copy/Change writing, I ask students to share what it felt like to be Gwendolyn Brooks or Ernest Hemingway. Ask students questions like these:

  - What particular aspect of the author's style surprised or challenged you?
  - What insights did you gain about why the author chose to write in his or her particular style?
  - How did writing about your subject in the voice of another author change the way you think or feel about the subject?

Invariably, these discussions not only lead to insights about the writing process of great authors but also shed light on students' own approach to writing and the writing process in general.

✂ Language in Context Study: Absence of Third-Person Singular "s"

Although the absence of third person "s" may occur in other varieties of English, it is a common feature of African American Vernacular English (AAVE). Describing the police department advertisement on the subway, Elroy says: "She look like she might topple over any minute, but those two cops are holding her up by her skinny arms."

Ask students to compare this sentence with its Standard American Vernacular English (SAVE) equivalent:

> She looks like she might topple over at any minute, but these two cops are holding her up by her skinny arms.

Rickford (1999) writes that the absence of third-person singular in AAVE also explains the AAVE use of "don't" in place of the SAVE "doesn't." Since this word has a third-person singular "s" in the SAVE affirmative version (he "does"), it is replaced by the plural equivalent in AAVE:

> AAVE: Maybe she don't know it, but I'm thanking her not only for finding the records but just for helping me get through those years in whatever way she knew how.

> SAVE: Maybe she doesn't know it, but I'm thanking her not only for finding the records but just for helping me get through those years in whatever way she knew how.

In "Permanent Record," Elroy's narrative contains sentences where the third person "s" appears as it would in SAVE, and other sentences where it is absent. It is important for students to recognize that individuals who speak AAVE do not use all the features all the time (Rickford 1999). Factors that influence the degree and variety of an individual's use of AAVE include age, social class, and gender. Using Elroy's narrative or other texts that contain AAVE, ask students to track those instances when the speaker or narrator uses language features associated with AAVE versus SAVE forms. See if they can detect any patterns as to when and how often a speaker will use features associated with one or the other vernacular.

⚔ Text Connections

For Students

Wilson, Harriet *Our Nig; or, Sketches from the Life of a Free Black.* New York: Penguin, 2004.

Written in 1859 and rediscovered in the 1980s, *Our Nig* is the first novel written by an African American woman. Frado, the subject of the narrative, is given away to servitude at the age of six. The death of her black father and abandonment by her destitute white mother leaves her an indentured servant to the Bellmont family of Singleton, New Hampshire. Frado's fortitude in the face of deprivation and isolation in an antebellum New England town is testament to the resiliency of the newly "free" African American child.

Sapphire. *Push.* New York: Knopf, 1996, 192 pp.

Impregnated by her own father and suffering repeated abuse by her mother, 16-year-old Precious Jones of Harlem is also completely illiterate. When her principal sends her to an alternative literacy program, a dedicated teacher and fellow students who have led equally harrowing lives thrust her into a journey of self-discovery and redemption through the power of words. Told in the stark, unvarnished voice of Precious, *Push* suffers from clichéd and underdeveloped storytelling. Despite these flaws, Sapphire's relentless depiction of society's indifference to the welfare of poor children leaves its mark on the reader.

Gaines, Ernest. *A Lesson Before Dying.* New York: Vintage, 1993, 272 pp.

Grant Willis, a young, university-educated black man, returns to his home in 1940s Cajun country to teach elementary school. While there, he is browbeaten by his aunt and other community members into teaching Jefferson, a black youth on death row, how to read and write, so that Jefferson can "die like a man." Though initially reluctant, Grant and Jefferson forge an intricate bond, and together come to understand the heroism of resisting.

For Teachers

Rose, Mike. *Lives on the Boundary: A Moving Account of the Struggles and Achievements of America's Educationally Underprepared.* New York: Penguin, 1990.

Before he became a professor at the UCLA Graduate School of Education and Information Studies and a nationally recognized expert on language and literacy, Mike Rose grew up as one of the educationally underprepared children that have been the focus of his scholarship and teaching. Rose poignantly recounts growing up poor in South Central Los Angeles; his placement, due to a clerical error, in classes for remedial students; and ultimately, how he overcame the stigmas and everyday impediments to learning facing those labeled as poor, illiterate, and intellectually deficient.

Wilhelm, Jeffrey. *"You Gotta Be the Book": Teaching Engaged and Reflective Reading with Adolescents.* New York: Teachers College Press, 1996, 208 pp.

Wilhelm's book begins with a few questions that keep English teachers up at night: Why do some students love reading literature while others loathe it? And what can be done for reluctant readers so that they find pleasure and meaning in this essential activity? He tackles the first of these questions through comparative case studies of engaged and reluctant teenage readers. Drawing from the case studies, intensive reflection on his own teaching practices, and relevant theory from a wide range of scholarship in literacy, Wilhelm creates a system of classifying the range of student reactions to literature along 10 "dimensions" of reader response. He then argues that struggling readers only experience a fraction of this range because their focus on the mechanical tasks like word identification and pronunciation prevent them from experiencing literature on an "evocative level" (p. 46). The second half of the book offers a number of easily applied visualization and drama strategies that help struggling readers "enter the story world" and ultimately find pleasure and meaning in reading literature.

A Good Girl (From the Bronx)
by Amberdawn Collier

❖ **About the Story**

Sharing a home and attending the same school as her cousin Sasha has never been easy for Jenelle. But when Sasha gets in trouble with the law, Jenelle is torn between her allegiance to family and her dream of attending college.

I know it's going to be a bad day when my cousin Sasha takes off her earrings at the bus stop and hands them to me. They are 18-carat gold hoops, huge and heavy, with "Sasha" written in script across the diameter. I just learned about diameter in Math A. It means the distance across a circle. Not that words matter now. Sasha has already whipped her jar of Vaseline out of her bag and she's rubbing it thick on her face and bare arms.

"I'm gonna mess that bitch up," Sasha hisses.

"Who?" I really have a hard time updating the list of people Sasha is mad at. She has a new boyfriend every week, so there's tons of ex-girlfriends, new girlfriends, wifeys and baby-mamas that want to fight her.

"Keianna." Sasha squints as a group of girls move our way. "She thinks she can mess with my man and not get beat down."

WORDS TO CONSIDER
posturing: (1) posing for effect; (2) striking a body posture or facial expression in order to express an artificial or pretend attitude. Example: Edwin put his hands up like he wanted to fight, but I knew that he was just posturing.
endearment: a word or an act intended to express affection. Example: Don't be surprised if a store clerk or taxi driver calls you "mami." It's just a term of endearment here in Washington Heights.
unnerving: (1) depriving someone of courage, strength, or steadiness; (2) causing someone to become nervous or upset. Example: It was unnerving to hear wolves howling before we entered the woods. Example: I find it unnerving when a teacher tells the class that there are only 10 minutes left to complete a test.

Sasha claps her hands together. They make a strange squelching sound. She looks at her jeans—brand new, tight as skin Rocawear with raised lettering across the butt. She looks at me.

I'm wearing the school uniform—white button-down shirt and navy blue pants, but they ain't from no dime store. They're Dickies and I have to take a stand. "Un uh. Not on me."

The girls are almost on us and Sasha balls her hand into a fist. She gives me her nasty look—the one that scares just about everybody.

"Fine," I mutter and put out my hands. Sasha rubs the cold, gloppy crap onto my palms.

"OK," she breathes. "I'm ready." Her nearly flat chest stuck out, she marches up to the group of girls. They're only about 15 feet away and if they don't fight fair, I can always jump in—but that's a joke. I can't fight for nothing, Sasha says. Still, she knows her cousin's got her back.

Keianna steps away from her cluster, and she and Sasha begin throwing insults. They're doing what my mom calls posturing. I'm trying to keep an eye on Sasha and rub the sticky Vaseline into my skin. I pull up my pant legs carefully and put some on my ankles and knees. Most of it goes away, but my hands are so oily, I can barely keep a grip on my plastic Metrocard.

I see the bus coming down the road just as Sasha throws her first punch. I want to look away, but I can't. My job is to be Sasha's witness and I have to live up to it. Even though Sasha is the size of a 12-year-old fed only on government cheese, and Keianna is a tall, thick girl, Sasha has her on the ground in a matter of seconds. Keianna's associates are screaming all kinds of things and looking like they want to jump in. Sasha screams at them to stay back.

"The bus is coming!" I yell, and my voice sounds empty because it doesn't have the anger or panic of the other screams.

Sasha lifts Keianna's head and brings it down on the pavement. The girl twitches strangely. Sasha is astride her. "Keep your skanky hands off my man!"

Keianna doesn't answer, but her friends look ready to break the rules of fighting and kill Sasha.

"The bus!" I shout again as it pulls up to the stop. The two older women who were waiting with me shake their heads as Sasha runs up to join me.

One of them looks hard at me. "What's a good girl like you doing with trash like that?"

Making my face as mean as possible, I say, "She's not trash; she's my cousin." I want to add "Mind your own business, you old biddy," but I just can't be that rude.

We get on the bus and Sasha glares at a middle school boy until he moves. She sits, I stand beside her. Under her shiny coat of Vaseline, Sasha is glowing. You'd think she just won the lottery. She puts out her hand and I silently give her the gold hoops.

I would've been on time to first period if Sasha had been wearing her uniform. She never does. When we enter the school, we get sent to the office—or in reality, Sasha gets sent to the office and I go with her because I'm her cousin.

It's always been like that. We are each other's built-in chaperones. Our moms are sisters and they raised us like sisters.

It takes the office lady 10 minutes to tell Sasha that she's a bad, ungrateful girl and if she doesn't start wearing her uniform, she'll be kicked out of the school next year.

"Good," Sasha mutters, her arms crossed in front of her chest.

The office lady frowns, trying to decide whether it's worth her time to lecture Sasha more. After a minute, she sighs. Pulling out a pad of paper, she writes Sasha a pass. "Get to class."

Sasha waits for me to get mine. The office lady frowns again, deeper this time, so deep that the lines around her mouth seem to cut into her skin like scars from a knife fight. "What are you? Her shadow?"

Why is everyone giving me grief this morning? Before I can answer, Sasha growls, "She's my cousin."

"Sasha, go to class. Jenelle, stay right there. I want you to talk to Miss Caridad."

I was brought up to listen to adults, and Sasha was too. She might mutter back talk, but direct orders are a different story. Shrugging her shoulders at me, she says, "I'll see you third period in Math," and disappears around the corner.

My mom says that I have a bad habit of sulking. So, I guess I am sulking for the next 20 minutes until I get called into the school social worker's office. Like I need to talk to a social worker. My mom's got a job—a good job. She's a bus driver for the MTA. My dad doesn't live with us, but he pays child support every month and I see him every other weekend. He lives in Manhattan with his new girlfriend.

Miss Caridad Benitez is a scary woman. She's taller than most Hispanic women and she doesn't play. It's like she can read minds. When something's going on at home, she just knows. Plus, she's got lots of friends at children's services and she can cause serious trouble in a hurry if she wants to.

"Jenelle, Jenelle." She is distracted. As she repeats my name, she shuffles through files on her desk, her long, perfectly manicured nails spray-painted with pink and blue lines, clicking against each other. Finally, she stops and opens one file. After reading for a good five minutes, she looks up at me. Her eyes are brown, but she has blue-colored contacts in. The effect of the brown showing through the blue is unnerving.

"Sasha Delgado is your cousin." This isn't a question, but I nod anyhow.

"You are a straight-A student. One of only 15 kids in tenth grade on the honor roll." I nod again.

"Sasha is failing every class except Math A. Ms. Henry tells me Sasha sits beside you in that class."

Before I can nod, Miss Benitez says, "Can I have a verbal response, please?"

"Yes, Sasha sits beside me in Ms. Henry's class." I get a little defensive. "But Sasha's good at math—she doesn't copy off me."

Miss Benitez smiles. "I didn't accuse you of anything." She folds her hands together, a flash of pink and blue against her brown skin. "Actually, Jenelle, I've been meaning to talk to you for a while."

"I didn't do anything!" Now I'm getting upset. My skin feels hot and tight. I wonder if that's the way Sasha feels before a fight.

"No, you haven't. You are a good girl. A great student. Your teachers love you. They think you have great potential—to get scholarships and have a wonderful future. However, we're all a bit concerned about your relationship with Sasha."

"Sasha's my cousin."

"We've already established that." She points to several framed pictures on her desk of large, smiling women and happy-looking kids. "Family, Jenelle, is a blessing."

"Yes."

"But family can cause us difficulties, too. Sasha is a wild girl. She gets into a lot of fights; she cuts her classes; she spends too much time with older guys." Miss Benitez pauses. "You and Sasha are on two different paths. It may seem like you have a lot of time before college, but right now you are making the records that will determine your educational future. You spend too much time looking after Sasha, and if you don't put a little distance between the two of you, you're going to end up getting into serious trouble because of her."

I'm silent. It's not like I haven't heard this speech before. In nearly every grade, some teacher or counselor or someone has pulled me aside and told me that Sasha is bad news or a rotten apple or a lost cause or whatever. But Sasha's my cousin. I'm older by two months. It's always been my job to look out for her. It always will be my job. I can't just cut her out of my life.

"I can't stay away from Sasha—we live together."

"You do?" Miss Benitez looks down at her file. "Since when?"

Squirming in my chair, I know I've said too much. My aunt won't like that. Or my mom. "My aunt's boyfriend wasn't treating her right. So, about six months ago, Sasha and Aunt Francesca came to live with us."

"Sasha's been living with you since the beginning of the school year?"

"Yes." My lips are so tightly pressed the word almost doesn't come out.

"Do you share a bedroom?"

"Yes." I want to tell her that it doesn't matter, that Sasha's bony elbows in the small of my back can somehow be comforting.

I'm ready for the interrogation to continue, expecting that she'll get really personal, but Miss Benitez just stops right there. She looks at the clock. "You've missed enough class today. " As she writes out my pass and stamps her special "Caridad Cares" logo with a rose on it, I breathe a sigh of puzzled relief.

"Think about what I said. You might have to live with Sasha, but you don't have to live her life." She hands me the square of paper.

The bell for second period rings as I'm walking to class. I have to switch directions and head to Spanish, which is a waste of time since I already speak Spanish, though usually just to my grandparents. I mostly do Math homework in that class. Ms. Pagan doesn't seem to care. She spends the period yelling at the boys in the front for throwing their books. If you stay quiet in the back, she doesn't notice you.

I finish a few geometry problems with circles. I draw random shapes on the front of my Spanish notebook and think about what Miss Benitez said. No one gets it. My mom takes care of her little sister and I take care of my little cousin. Sasha would laugh if I said that out loud. She thinks she takes care of herself. But I braid her hair and pierce her ears and rub lotion on her elbows when they get ashy. She'd have trouble keeping the little things together if I wasn't there.

In Math, Sasha walks in 10 minutes late, her low-cut red shirt almost falling off her shoulder and her face mad red. Ms. Henry gives her a disgusted look.

"Sign the late sheet, Ms. Delgado."

"Whatever," Sasha mutters as she picks up the pen to sign the log. She winks at Eric Lopez and slides into the seat beside me.

"I met a real hot one nigga from Hunts Point last period." She whispers from the side of her mouth.

I tap my math textbook to remind her to get hers out. She pulls her tiny drawstring book bag from her shoulders and searches. "Oh, snap! I musta left it on the table this mornin'." She unwraps a piece of gum and sticks it in her mouth. Her jaw muscles throb as she chews.

Moving my book to the center of the table, I tear out a sheet of notebook paper for her to use. "You can share with me." I say softly. She forgets her math book at least twice a week.

"Anyway, like I was sayin', I met this guy, he's mad cool." Pausing, she looks at me from the side. "He's black."

I don't respond. There's nothing I want to say. Our grandparents were really mad at my mom when she married a black man and had me. Grandpa still refers to me as "la negra" when he thinks I can't hear him. Aunt Francesca stayed in their good graces by only dating white or Hispanic men, and she told Sasha to stay away from the "blacks."

No one thinks I'm black. My dad's pretty light-skinned. Everyone figures I'm Dominican, even though Mom's family is Puerto Rican all the way. Sasha's so pale she looks like a white girl—or at least she would if she put on preppy clothes from a white store like Abercrombie and Fitch or someplace like that. Grandpa's nickname for her is "la rubia" because her hair is almost blonde.

I draw the angles in dark, angry lines. It has always bugged me that I work hard at school and don't cause trouble and Sasha is still "la rubia" or "la princesa" or some other endearment from my grandparents. My grandparents live just five blocks away and we're over there for dinner three or four times a week. Mom has told me since I was little that mis abuelos do love me, they just have a hard time admitting it. Her favorite comforting statement is "They'd really miss you if you died." We laugh together every time she says that one.

"Did ya hear me?" Sasha is poking me with the pencil she borrowed from me. It's green with gold stars, a quarter from the pencil vending machine in the school library. "He's *black*," she hisses.

"So?" I'm feeling defiant. "I'm half-black."

"And you know I ain't got no problem with that. You my *blood*. Mi *prima*." Sasha's voice is fierce and I feel bad. One thing I've got to hand to Sasha is that she isn't prejudiced and she never ever let anyone tease me about being half and half.

"His name's Anthony. He wants me to meet him at Skate Key on Friday night."

"What about Jorge? You just fought Keianna over him this morning!" I try to keep my voice down because Ms. Henry shoots me a look from the board covered in pi and circumference equations.

"I'm done with him. Jorge is a dick. He was cheatin' on me with Keianna." Sasha inspects her nails, which I can tell I'll be painting tonight. "It's time for a new man—maybe a husband."

"You're too young for a serious man" I suddenly realize what Sasha means. "You thinking about doing it with a guy you just met for 10 minutes?" It's all I can do not to shout this across the room.

"Maybe." Sasha grins like it's no big deal, like our moms haven't told us the troubles of being young and pregnant—my mother had me when she was 19 and Aunt Francesca was 16 when she had Sasha.

I swore in blood to my mother that I wouldn't have sex until I got married and I've kept that promise. I just turned 16 and I've only kissed two boys. One on a dare in sixth grade and the other a year ago at a party when we were playing spin-the-bottle. It was OK, but I'm not going to throw away my future over some five-second burst of good feeling.

My mom hasn't had a boyfriend for three years, and she says she likes it that way. "Baby, you don't need a man, trust me. They only make things complicated."

Aunt Francesca, on the other hand, is like Sasha, and has a different guy for every day of the week. They try to keep it a secret, but me and Sasha know that Aunt Francesca's had at least two abortions since Sasha was born.

"You're being stupid." I breathe, knowing that I'm going to make her angry, but not caring.

Sasha hisses several bad words at me and grabs my book.

I don't bother trying to wrestle it away from her. Instead, I get up and go to Julissa's desk and share with her.

She and I work in silence for a while. "Your cousin's *pissed* at you." Julissa shakes her head. "Lucky you're her cousin; anybody else say that to her and she'd beat the crap outta them."

"Yeah, well, she is being stupid." I steal the calculator out of Julissa's hand and punch in a few numbers. "I don't care if she's mad. She'll get over it."

Julissa looks down at my paper. "How'd you get number 12? That don't make no sense."

I start to show her the steps when the door opens. Principal Morris walks in, followed by two NYPD officers. They are not the school safety NYPD, who wear specially marked badges and don't carry guns. These guys are the real thing.

"Sasha Delgado and Jenelle Stewart, please come with us." Principal Morris's voice is loud in the suddenly quiet classroom.

Sasha and I have both lived in the Bronx long enough to know not to talk to cops. We didn't do nuthin'; we didn't see nuthin'—that's the code. I wouldn't snitch on anyone, let alone my own cousin, so the whole questioning me in the guidance office while Sasha's in the principal's office doesn't change my answers.

I can tell that the cop, a black woman with really wide eyes and a slight gap between her front teeth, is annoyed with me.

"You walk with your cousin to the bus every morning?"

"Yes, ma'am." I'm not stupid enough to be rude with a cop.

"You walked with her this morning."

"Yes, ma'am."

"You saw her fighting with a girl named Keianna Hughes?"

This is tricky, but I think I know what to say. "You know, I was busy watching for the bus. There were other people around, but I wasn't paying much attention to Sasha."

That isn't exactly a lie, but I can see that the cop is wise to me.

"Mm-hm." She mumbles and writes something on her note pad. "Your name's Jenelle?"

"Yes, ma'am."

"You've got pretty manners, Jenelle." She leans a little closer to me, trying to intimidate me. It works. "Your principal, Mr. Morris, he vouched for you. Said you're a great student, never any trouble. I can tell, just by the way you speak, the way you carry yourself, that you are not planning on spending your life in this neighborhood." She pauses and points at me. "Am I right?"

"I'm not ashamed of my neighborhood." My skin feels so tight it itches.

"But you aren't proud of it, either, are you?"

"It's good enough for my family; it's good enough for me."

"Okay, don't get defensive." She offers me a small smile. I can see the gap in her teeth. It isn't an ugly gap. "My point is, you have a future, girl. Now, lying to the police isn't going to help that future."

I feel trapped. My head is pounding. It isn't even fourth period yet. I need some water. All these people telling me what to do, talking to me about my future. Everything is confused except for the fact that Sasha is my cousin and I need to protect her.

"I wasn't paying attention to Sasha. I was watching for the bus." My tone is stubborn, I can hear it myself. Sasha would be proud. I wonder if that's a good thing.

If I had known how all this would have ended up, I would have stopped Sasha—really, I would have. Sasha's beat lots of people up, why should this girl have been different? I'm sitting in la sala de mis abuelos and they are not pleased. Mom and Aunt Francesca are at the juvenile detention center, visiting Sasha, who is going to be spending the night there.

Somehow, Grandpa is convinced that it's la negra's fault that la rubia is in trouble. Yeah, like I forced Sasha to beat Keianna's head against the pavement and put her in a coma.

"Ju," my Grandpa waves a finger at me, "Ju are supposed to look after tu prima!"

"I did, papi. She was fighting, not me." Staring at the crucifix above his chair, I feel empathy with Jesus's pained expression.

"Caesar, leave Yeni alone." My grandma enters with a little tray. Neither of my grandparents can ever seem to put the "j" sound in the right places. "Sasha is a bad girl." She shakes her head as she pours the strong coffee my grandpa loves, coffee that makes me gag.

"Mi rubia is not a bad girl!" Indignant, he snatches the cup from her.

"She spends too much time on the street, not in the house studying, like Yeni does." Grandma smiles at me. I've always suspected that if I wasn't half black, I'd be her favorite hands-down.

Grandpa starts to rant in rapid Spanish. Even though I can't understand every word, I know he's talking about me and what a mistake my mother made marrying my father. Whenever anything bad happens to the family, he finds a way to connect it with what my mom did 16 years ago.

Listening to him, trying not to inhale the thick smell of coffee, his aftershave mixed with sweat and the scented candles Grandma has lit underneath the picture of La Virgen, I want to cry. I can feel the pressure of the tears, welling up underneath my eyeballs.

"Excusa me," I mumble, and head to the bathroom. Like the rest of the apartment, it is incredibly clean, but the air is hot and close. I shut the door and lie down on the linoleum floor, the surface smooth and cold against my face. Tears run across my face, sideways past my nose, and pool on the floor.

One of the reasons I love school so much is because no one there compares me to Sasha, at least not in a bad way. To the teachers, I'm the good one, the one they want. I love Sasha, but sometimes I hate her so much. I hate her when my Grandpa smiles at her and pats her hair and says, "Ah, mi rubia preciosa."

Maybe it's a good thing that Sasha has to spend the night in teen jail. Maybe she'll think twice before she bashes someone's head in again.

I get to the bus stop early the next morning. It's strange to be there alone, to be anywhere alone. The office lady was right. I was Sasha's shadow. It's hard for shadows to walk by themselves.

Keianna's friends are over on the other side of the street, staring at me. I don't think they'll bother me, since I didn't do anything, but who knows? Focusing on the ground, I'm careful not to look their way.

Aunt Francesca was hysterical last night, crying how her baby was going to be locked up. Mom was pretty quiet. She stroked my aunt's hair and gave her two Tylenol P.M. s to get her to sleep.

I made her tea while she put her sister to bed. When she came out, I noticed she looked a lot older than usual. The circles around her eyes were so dark, almost purple.

"Mom? You want honey in your tea?" I got the squeezie bear out of the cupboard.

"Yeah. Honey sounds nice. That's not caffeinated tea, is it?"

"Nah," I stirred in the honey. "Sleepytime." My smile felt lopsided.

"Good girl." She sipped and her eyes were vacant for a while. "What are we going to do, Jenelle?"

"What do you mean?"

"Sasha's facing some serious charges, especially if that girl doesn't come out of her coma soon." My mom put her cup down and drummed her fingers on the table. "Lawyers are expensive. Francesca's got no money. She can't keep a job more than a month at a time."

"Don't you have some money saved up?" I had seen the statements from the bank before.

Mom's brows knitted together in a frown. "That money's for you. For college. No one is touching that." She reached across the table and grabbed my hand. Her grip was tight, but I liked the pressure.

It has always been my mom's dream to send me to college—a nice college, not some two-year community thing. She talks big about Columbia or NYU, but I know it'll probably be more like a CUNY school. If I go, I'll be the first person in my family to make it further than high school. Since she started working for the MTA, we could have moved to Queens or someplace a little nicer in the Bronx, but Mom stayed here to save money. All the little corners, all the Tasty O's and off-brand chips are to put a little extra into that savings account.

I knew, deep down, that my mom wanted me to say, "It's okay. Use the money for Sasha—she really needs it. We'll save more; I'll get a scholarship."

She was watching me with those tired eyes, waiting for me to do what the two of us do best, sacrifice our dreams for la familia. I wet my lips with a sip of tea. The liquid was hot and thick with the taste of honey. It was like the heaviness of the honey tied my tongue, wouldn't let it move.

"I can get a job after school," I said finally. It was a compromise. I did want to help Sasha, but I couldn't give her that money.

My mom seemed shocked, but she smiled. "Yeah, okay." She squeezed my hand again. "And I'll work some extra shifts, try to get some overtime."

Taking her empty cup, I walked over to the sink and rinsed it out. I could feel her standing behind me. I knew she was still confused about what I hadn't said.

"I'm tired. See you in the morning," I kissed her cheek.

"I'm working second shift this week, so I'll make you breakfast. You want pancakes?" Her smile was genuine that time.

"Yeah, that sounds good." Morning would be a strange time without Sasha's hair dryer and frequent cursing at the mirror. I didn't want to think about it. "Goodnight."

Mom kissed my forehead. "Hasta mañana," she whispered.

I have to talk to Miss Benitez about getting work papers. It's pretty easy to find a job on the down low, since I look a bit older than 16. Still, I don't need any more trouble with the cops.

"You want to get a job?" Miss Benitez looks at me like I asked for permission to get AIDS.

"Yes."

"Your mother isn't in financial trouble, is she?" Those blue contacts are very distracting.

"I can get a job. I'm 16. You don't need to know all that. Please just give me the papers. I've got to get to gym."

Her silver and burgundy nails tap on the desk. They must have cost her 50 dollars, easy. My mom only gets her nails done in a salon on special occasions. We do each other's nails at home with a kit from the drugstore.

"Jenelle, I know from experience that when students get their work papers, their attendance drops and their grades drop. For some students, it's the difference between a 70 and a 65. With you, a drop could mean the difference between college paid for and college you have to pay for." She pushes back a piece of highlighted curl, tucking it behind her ear, which has three piercings.

"Unless there is a desperate financial need, I would advise you not to get a job now. Concentrate on keeping straight A's. You know, a minority girl from the Bronx with above a 90 average can do a lot of things."

If I hear someone else tell me that, I might just join a gang and live the rest of my life on the streets. Where do these people get off telling me how great my future's going to be when I've got to worry about my cousin going to prison right now?

My face must have shouted out my thoughts because Miss Benitez digs through her files and pulls out two forms. "Bien. I'm just telling you that you need to be careful. Work for a big company that will follow the hour restrictions for minors." Silver flashes as she wags her finger at me. "No bodegas. They'll want you to stay till one or two on school nights."

So if I eat one more doughnut, I'll puke. Three weeks ago, getting a job at Dunkin' Donuts sounded like a great plan. I thought I could be sipping on one of those frozen coffee drinks and munching on those little munchkins all night long.

Not really. We've got a greasy-ass manager who pinches the butts of all the girls and counts the munchkins so we can't eat any unless he gives them to us. He goes around tasting them and when he says, "Oh, you can have some," you know they're stale and nasty.

I'm always working the shift after school, so we get a lot of stupid guys coming in and trying to flirt with us or trying to get us to give them free doughnuts. Sergimar, the girl who works with me, gives in some times if the guy is really cute.

I just stand by the Dunkaccino machine and do my homework if no one's around. Since Sasha got arrested, people give me a weird distance, like I'll go crazy and slam their heads into the ground. It's annoying that everyone assumes I'm like my cousin, but it's also nice to be left alone.

The third scene of *Julius Caesar* is giving me trouble when the bell over the door rings and two cops walk in. One of them is the lady cop who tried to get me to talk about Sasha. Sergimar is messing with her hair in the corner by the sink, so I go over to the counter.

"Welcome to Dunkin' Donuts. How may I help you?" It took me a week to train myself to say 'may' instead of 'can'. I think it sounds classy.

"Hello. Jenelle, isn't it?" The cop smiles at me, that gap showing. I wonder if it bothers her at all when she looks in the mirror. I kind of like it.

"Yes, ma'am. What can I get you?" I try to steer the conversation away from questions about my cousin.

"I'll have an iced coffee and a wheat bagel, toasted with cream cheese." She turns to her partner. "Parker, what you want?"

The other police officer, a white man with a crew cut, is staring out the window, keeping his eye on the corner. "Hot coffee with cream."

He continues to scan the block. "And a donut with jelly filling."

Finally looking at her, he hands her a five-dollar bill and says, "I'm gonna wait in the car, Kinesy."

"Fine, I'll be out in a minute." She turns back to me and smiles again. "Getting a job to save up for college?"

"Yeah, something like that," I mutter, heading over to the toaster with her wheat bagel. I suppose I don't have to worry about her since they talked to all Keianna's friends and they know what happened without me saying a word. Having a cop smile at me, though, is still a new thing and I'm nervous as she watches me fill her cup with ice.

"So did your cousin get a public defender yet?" She asks this like we're friends, chatting away.

"We're payin' for a lawyer, that guy Thomas with the ads on the buses." Her bagel slides out of the toaster and I grab the cream cheese. "Heavy or light?"

"Light, please." Officer Kinesy is frowning now. "You aren't working here to pay for her lawyer, are you?"

This woman, like the guidance counselor, creeps me out with how she just seems to know what's going on. She'll probably give me the same lecture as Miss Benitez. "She's my cousin; I have to help her out. Everyone in the family is pitching in."

"You do a lot for your cousin. That's real nice of you."

I look down at the bagel I'm wrapping up. I don't want to see if her face has a sarcastic look or not. "Sasha's like my sister. We're only two months apart."

"I think you're more like worlds apart, Jenelle." She hands me the money and doesn't say anything about how I shouldn't work or how bad it is for my grades.

Instead, as I hand her the change, she smiles thinly, and says, "Take good care of *yourself*, Jenelle. In order to help other people, sometimes you have to be selfish first."

She walks out and ducks into the squad car. Her partner laughs at something as she passes him his coffee. I watch the car turn away and think.

"Is it bad to be selfish, Sergimar?"

She turns around from the mirror, where she's been this whole time, playing with the fraying ends of her braids, trying to get the tiny rubber bands around them so they don't come undone.

"I don't know," she mumbles. I come up behind her and take the rubber bands from her. Her hair is fine, like Sasha's, and it slips out of the braids faster than thick hair like mine. Not that I ever get braids. Mom's always too busy, Sasha can't do it right and it's too expensive to have them done in the salon. Twisting and pulling, I manage to get Sergimar's hair all into place.

She turns around and puts the rest of the rubber bands in her pocket. "I guess it depends," she says, checking herself out in the mirror.

"Sometimes, you gotta do for yourself, ya know? Like get your nails done to look fine or get some braids or a new pair of jeans." Sergimar's smile is very wide and her teeth are mad white, like a movie star's. Boys love her and she knows it, but she isn't crazy over them like Sasha. She just flirts and sends them all away empty-handed.

"But what about helping out family? Should family always come first?"

"What're you?" She laughs, "A Hallmark card?"

She laughs some more at her own joke. "Nah, I guess family's important, like you kids or you mom, but not just anyone who says he's family. I mean, I got tons of cousins and half and step—relatives. I wouldn't be goin' crazy, bendin' over backwards to help 'em all, ya know?"

I nod, even though her answer doesn't help. Sasha is close family.

"You thinkin' 'bout you cousin?" Sergimar tilts her head so she can see my downturned face. "Girl, you doin' the right thing. You workin' so she can get a good lawyer. That's pretty nice, like that cop said."

"What if I said that my mom's got money saved, enough to pay for an even better lawyer, but she won't use it 'cause it's for my college and I told her not to?" This spills out of me before I can think about it. Sergimar goes to school with me, but I don't really know her that well.

Sergimar goes over to the frozen drink machine. "I say it's time for a Coolatta, girl." She gets down a cup. "Hand me the whip cream out the fridge."

I open the little mini fridge and get out the canned whip cream. She sprays it all over the top of our drinks and passes one to me.

"Now, let me get this." Sergmiar pauses to put a straw in her drink. She sips deeply. "Okay. You got some money for college and you feelin' guilty that you not using it for Sasha?"

"Well, basically, yeah." I hadn't really boiled it down to such a simple thought.

"You was with Sasha when she beat that girl, Kia, Kaya, whatever her name is?"

"Keianna. Yeah, I was at the bus stop, but I didn't see anything." I feel obliged to continue the lie.

"Mmm-hmm." Sergimar sucks on the straw. "Anyway, how I see it—she did it, right? I mean, Sasha did beat that girl so bad she in a coma, right?"

There was no way around that. "Yeah, she did."

"So, unless the cops be beatin' confessions outta her with a rubber hose, she goin' do some kinda time or somethin', right?"

"Probably, I guess."

Sergimar puts down her cup and waves her hands in the air in a "duh" kind of way. "So then why you feelin' guilty? Spendin' money on her would be like wastin' it. It don't matter how fancy a lawyer she got 'cause there be witnesses and everyone know Sasha's crazy."

"Girl," she continues, "bein' selfish is different from just bein' dumb."

"Speaking of dumb, I know I ain't seeing two dumb girls not doin' their work." Ranaldo, the manager has finally come out of the office. I throw what's left of my drink in the trash and Sergimar slides hers behind the microwave.

"Don't call us names, or I'll call the corporate office." I stick my chin out.

"That won't matter if you've already been fired," Ranaldo threatens. "Now, do something. Sergimar, make some new coffee and scrub out the pots. Jenelle, put out some more muffins and bagels." He leans over and pops a munchkin into his mouth. He makes a slight face. "You girls can have the rest of those. I'll get some fresh ones."

We're both giggling when he leaves.

Sunday is a big family dinner at mis abuelos, with Uncle Carlos, his wife and kids, Aunt Tina and her boys, Aunt Francesca, her latest boyfriend, me and Mom and like 50 thousand other people related to us in some way. All the guys are in the front room, the older ones playing dominoes and smoking cigars and the younger ones watching a basketball game.

The women are either in the kitchen or the dining room and the little kids are running around the apartment, chasing each other. Grandma has turned on salsa music on her radio in the kitchen and my aunts and cousins dance around each other with bowls and plates, getting dinner ready.

My mom is in charge of the tamales and she's in the corner, pretty quiet. I'm at the table, cutting up vegetables for the salad. Aunt Francesca is beside me, chain-smoking and flicking her ashes into her empty coffee cup.

"So, you heard from Sasha's lawyer?" Aunt Tina asks as she does the merengue and sets the tables (two long wooden ones and three fold-out card tables—the kids have to eat at those).

"Nah, he's busy a lot." Taking a long drag, Aunt Francesca gives me a sideways look. "But he's all we can afford."

I stare at the cutting board, wishing to vanish. My mom's voice comes from the corner. "Mr. Thomas is a good lawyer. He has a great record. I looked him up online at the library. No complaints about him."

"Yeah, but I woulda liked to get Joe Schuster." I feel Aunt Francesca shift towards me again.

"No way, mami," Aunt Tina laughs, "That guy's mad expensive. He represents druggies, anyhow. You don't want it lookin' like Sasha needs some drug lawyer."

"We coulda afforded it," Aunt Francesca hisses softly. The cigarette smoke blowing up my nose and mouth makes me want to choke, plus the onions I'm chopping are already making me cry. "If someone wasn't so *selfish*, thinkin' she's a big star, goin' go to Harvard—like she needs that much money to go to Bronx Community College."

Aunt Tina looks a little lost. I don't think she knew about the savings account, but it's clear that Grandma does because her face is turning red. This is bad, I know, 'cause Grandma never gets mad and even though I know she doesn't love me as much as Sasha, I still don't want to hear her scold me. I start to rise, thinking I'll run and hide in a closet or something, anything to get away.

"Yeni, sientate!" Grandma's voice snaps, and I immediately follow her order, sitting back in my seat.

"I'm only going to say this once," she continues in her thickly accented English. I know she wants everyone in the kitchen to hear her or she'd have switched to Spanish.

"I love all my children and all my grandchildren, but some mothers," she looks pointedly at Aunt Francesca, "have not done as good a job raising their kids as others."

"Mama!" Finally putting down her cigarette, Aunt Francesca is clearly angry.

"Quiet, Francesca!" Grandma continues. "Nothing," she slams her fist down on the counter, "Nothing—is more important than an education. When I came to this country, I couldn't speak any English or read in any language. Mi padre said that education was a waste on niñas, that we should just be pretty and find a husband. I had three children before I learned to read. You can't live that way anymore." Grandma pauses to wipe her eyes. "You have to have an education. It is free for 12 years in this country! Twelve years! Yeni is a good girl and she deserves to go to a good college. She will!"

She stops and points her finger at Aunt Francesca. "And she is such a good girl that she's giving her paycheck to you for Sasha! What has Sasha ever done for Yeni? Digame! Nada, but Yeni is like her mother. Eva always takes care of you, Francesca, and Yeni takes care of Sasha. God blessed you, Francesca, but you are abusing your blessings."

Aunt Tina has her head down in the doorway, but I can tell by her shaking shoulders that she's trying not to laugh. She's always complaining about how my mom babies Aunt Francesca. She raises her head and adds, "Yeah, Frannie, why don't *you* get a job? Sasha is *your* daughter, not Jenelle's."

"Shut the—" Aunt Francesca stops when Grandma makes a warning sound. "I did have a job at Key Foods, but they was workin' me like a dog." Her face crumples like she's been punched.

"If you care about Sasha, you won't mind working hard. Eva works hard. Tina works hard, even Yeni works hard. It's your turn, Francesca." Grandma looks around the room, making eye contact with all of us.

"Basta. I've said what I need to say." She turns the music back up and continues breading the pork chops.

Aunt Francesca mutters something about the bathroom and leaves. Aunt Tina sits in the empty spot and helps me finish cutting the vegetables. She smells sweet, like cocoa butter and vanilla. I don't see her as much 'cause she lives in Brooklyn, but I've always liked her best of my aunts and uncles. She's the manager of a clothing store in Greenwich Village and she wears the best clothes. She's also the only girl who will stand up to Grandpa.

"So, that was a surprise, huh?" Aunt Tina whispers. No one can hear us over the salsa, which is blaring now.

I smile at her. "Yeah, I didn't think Grandma liked me that much."

"All this family loves you, Jenelle. Papi is just a prejudiced fool who is too old to change the way he thinks. Mama doesn't like to disagree with him out loud 'cause she was raised that you follow your husband's beliefs. But, she's still got some cojones of her own, on the really important things—like just now." She pops a raw green pepper slice into her mouth and stands up, carrying the bowl of veggies with her.

I watch Aunt Tina dance over to my mom and kiss her on the cheek. When my mom's face turns, I see that she's been crying. I get up and join the hug Aunt Tina started. Before I know it, my face is buried in Mom's chest, and I'm crying too.

"No crying on my tamales!" Grandma chides. I think she's a little embarrassed by her speech. She never talks that much at once.

"I'm proud of you, Jenelle," My mom says into my ear. "You're better at takin' care of yourself than me. I know you're gonna do something great with your life, baby."

"Mmm-hmm," nods Aunt Tina. She's stealing a piece of the tamale off the sheet. "Jenelle'll be the rich one, the famous one."

It's a little strange to hear my family talking about my great future instead of my teachers or Miss Benitez, but it's nice, too. Coming from them, it seems easier to believe.

"Well, if I am rich, I'm gonna buy all of you big mansions and nice cars." I move in to steal a piece of tamale as well, but mom slaps my hand.

"I want a BMW convertible," she says. "Red, with black leather interior."

"A Hummer for me," Aunt Tina puts her hand on an imaginary steering wheel, looking content.

"What about you, Grandma? What kinda car do you want?"

Grandma looks at me and I feel like she's really seeing me for the first time ever. She smiles. "I want a station wagon, to fit all my grandkids."

"To fit all your grandkids, Mami, it's gonna have to be a limo," Aunt Tina teases.

They're all laughing and joking, but I think they really believe in me. This is the good part, the blessing that Miss Caridad talked about, and I know it's where I'll find my strength.

✄ Teacher Focus Group Discussion: Girlz in the Hood: Gender Representation in Urban Literature

> Bakhtin (1981) suggests, as have others, that we experience ourselves within a liminal space between what is and what could be . . . Developmentally, there is an emergent ability to imagine ourselves as different from how we have been imagined and how we have been named.
>
> "Fantastic Self: A Study of Adolescents' Fictional Narratives, and Aesthetic Activity as Identity Work," Cynthia Lightfoot (2004)

Ratner: "A Good Girl (From the Bronx)" depicts a young girl growing up in the Bronx and the competing demands made upon her by her family, school, and neighborhood. I just thought we would start with some basic comments about the impact this story may have on girls in the schools where you teach, or might be teaching in the future. Specifically, compared with other young adult and classic fiction used in schools, to what degree would a story like

Discussion Questions

In the Lines

1. How are Jenelle and Sasha related?

2. Describe the appearance of the two girls.

3. How does Jenelle respond when the older woman waiting at the bus asks, "What's a good girl like you doing with trash like that?"

4. What information does Janelle reveal during her meeting with Miss Benitez?

Between the Lines

5. Describe Jenelle's behavior and thoughts during the fight. What do they suggest about her relationship with Sasha?

6. How do Jenelle and Sasha's grandparents feel about their granddaughters?

7. Janelle's mother explains that Jenelle's grandparents do love her but that "they just have a hard time admitting it." What does Jenelle's mother mean by this? Discuss whether or not you think Jenelle should accept her mother's explanation.

Beyond the Text

8. At various points in the story, Jenelle is advised or questioned by an older woman, the school principal, the policewoman, and her mother. Compare what the various women had to say to Jenelle and her responses. Whose advice and/or questioning do you think was most helpful to Jenelle? If you were a friend, a relative, or concerned community member, what advice would you give to Jenelle?

9. Cultures share certain beliefs and values concerning what it means to be a "girl." They may also carry expectations for how a girl should conduct herself within various settings. Compare how Jenelle and Sasha behave and present themselves in the family, school, and neighborhood. To what degree do their words and actions reflect expectations for how a girl should conduct herself in these various settings?

10. What elements of Jenelle and Sasha do you see in yourself? What elements of their characters do you appreciate or seek to emulate?

"A Good Girl (From the Bronx)" foster your students' "emergent ability" to imagine themselves as different from how they have been imagined and how they have been named? What impact might the story have on a student's concept of what it means to be female?

Colleen: I think it depicts the lives of these two polar opposite girls, one the punk-ass girl who is just always getting into fights all the time and the other who is just trying to do her work and still stay involved with her family. I think it would be—assuming that a girl this age is able to get into the story and be invested in it and believe that it was authentic—I think that it would be easy for them to identify with one or the other and just decide whether or not they fit into that role. And then, from there determine whether or not they could imagine themselves breaking out of that role.

Holly: Perhaps it's even more the case for students in urban communities, but I was thinking that certain kids everywhere—adolescents in general—feel that they are too cool for school. But I don't think that girls will necessarily relate to one versus the other. In fact, they might relate to both these girls because a lot of students experience that inner struggle between, "Well, do I want to be accepted by my peers and fit in, or do I want to focus on my studies?" Does caring about school, or being perceived as one who cares about school, get in the way of my ability to do other things that are very important for my coexistence with peers in my school and in my community? Can I be both? Can I be cool and care about my education or do I have to be one way or the other?

Christina: I definitely think that the majority of the female students in a classroom see themselves as Sasha, though of course there are maybe one or two students who see themselves as more like Jenelle. That would be the case in my current classroom—most of the girls would like to look in the mirror and have Sasha reflected back at them, while perhaps two of the girls are actually like Jenelle and would be proud to see such a depiction in writing. I would also say that when the reality of what Sasha has done lands her in jail, some of the same kids who would say, "Hell yeah, I'm Sasha, that chick was written after me," would then say, "Nah, I wouldn't be stupid enough to get caught."

Laila: I just want to make a distinction between what someone is, what someone sees themselves as, and what a person wants to be. When I think of the girls in my class, I suspect that they would have a range of responses to Sasha. Some of them are very much like her but don't recognize it, some see themselves as like her but are actually quite different. Then there are some who want to be like her but are well aware that they just can't be. It's very complicated. We can't assume that just because a student seems drawn to a character like Sasha or purports to be like her, that she really is that way. Maybe it's just a pretext. Maybe deep down inside she wants to be more like Jenelle but just can't pull it off for some reason. Look, I recently saw *Lara Croft, Tomb Raider* (2001), and I have to admit that I was really into her character, but that doesn't mean that I'm about to get into gunfights and jump off buildings.

Debbie: But isn't that just the point of the quote that we read at the beginning of the discussion? It says, "Developmentally, there is an emergent ability to imagine ourselves as different from how we have been imagined and how we have been named" (Lightfoot 2004, p. 37). What it means is that a story like this lets students imagine themselves in a variety of ways, even ways that are different from their true character.

Laila: No, I understand that. I agree. My point is that as teachers and adults we can't just conclude that a student who gravitates towards a Sasha is like Sasha, or really wants to be like her. Sometimes you have to dig a little deeper and think about what a student's expressed desires tell you about the student's true character.

Colleen: To me, the driving element in terms of a reader relating to a character is the writing itself. I think that it might be easier for people to relate more with Sasha because she doesn't have much depth. Everything is on the surface and so they can fill in their own gaps. Jenelle is so developed, or at least more developed than Sasha, so there's not a lot of room for them to step into her shoes. Or, at least I felt as I was reading it that I couldn't maneuver within her. I find it easier—and I think it will be easier for students—to relate to a character that is more stereotypical because they would be able to sort of fill in the gaps for themselves.

Debbie: That may be true, but I think it's a problem if our students connect too easily and quickly with Sasha. The quote says that fiction helps us "imagine ourselves as different from how we have been imagined and how we have been named," but I would argue that Sasha is very much how city kids, particularly students of color, are imagined and named all the time. As the kids say, she's "gangsta." She fights, she's promiscuous, she's got the big hoop earrings and the big attitude.

Ratner: But she's also light-skinned, whereas Jenelle has a dark complexion, right? Where does that fit into the stereotypes you're describing?

Debbie: That's true—and that's one of the elements of the story that I find most interesting—but other than skin color, Sasha is pretty much textbook "ghetto"; she's what TV, the music videos, and all the other types of so-called "mirrors" present to city kids all the time. That's why I would hope that more students, particularly girls, would find something appealing about Jenelle. It's not just because she's "good"; in fact, she's not stereotypically good. She has more than one dimension to her. She's prideful at times. She talks back and she's envious. She doesn't give Sasha away to the police or the principal. For better or worse, I know that a lot of my students would respect that and then they might be more willing to play with the idea of assuming the less "cool" elements of her character. You see, that's what I think the quote is about. Good fiction lets a reader "try on" or, as the quote says, "imagine," other ways of being, not just the clichéd and narrow ways presented in popular media. There are kids like Jenelle in our classes—good kids who aren't perfect. They just never get the airtime and press that the Sashas get.

Holly: But I would argue that even the stereotypical elements of the characters have a purpose in this story and offer good reasons for teaching it. The fact is that appearance and other superficial aspects of life have a huge impact on our students. There were a couple of situations where Jenelle was confronted by adults telling her that she should separate herself from her cousin basically because of the way she would be viewed by society and what would happen to her as a result. They were painting a very negative picture of Sasha and, at least in part, their opinion of her is based on her "look." But what if Jenelle was the one dressed in tight jeans and hoop earrings, and Sasha had the school uniform on? Would the adults still treat Jenelle like the straight-A student, the one who is going to succeed and be the first person in her family to go to college? I think the story allows a teacher to get into these kinds of issues.

Ratner: Just one comment: Jenelle says that her schoolgirl looks don't help her too much especially when it comes to her family, especially with her darker skin, right? So it is a little complicated. She moves in different worlds and her appearance has different consequences in those worlds.

Ed: I think it's helpful for our students to discuss our chameleonlike natures where in one world you are wearing uniforms in school while on the street, you might be wearing earrings or a doo-rag, or whatever. In a sense, we're all wearing uniforms wherever we go. They're just different kinds of uniforms for different situations. And I think our kids need to know that this is OK. That's life. I get more worried when a kid thinks that dressing conservatively in a situation that calls for it is a kind of selling out while when someone dresses in an inappropriately casual way, they'll say he or she is "keeping it real" or "ghetto," which is code for "authentic." And then, by the way, there are some students who think, "Well, if I wear the uniform, that's all I need and therefore I am that straight-A student." There are some teachers who also think this way. What I like about Jenelle is that she "gets it"; she understands that appearances do matter—both in school and in the street—but she also knows that there's more to it than just appearances; there has to be some substance, too.

Christina: I agree. I think that Jenelle isn't above the pack but she doesn't follow it either. She might help girls her age to better navigate between the two worlds and get their priorities straight. She has Apple Bottoms jeans[1] but doesn't wear them to school because it doesn't fit with the purpose of going to school, which is to get an education and have an opportunity to do better. She realizes that and isn't about to jeopardize it, which is why she doesn't let her aunt use her college money to get Sasha a better lawyer. And I think that is being smart, not selfish.

Ratner: OK, let's return to the topic of female identity in the story. Can someone just read the first page out loud? [Debbie reads the first page.]

[1] A fashion line launched in 2003 by hip-hop artist Nelly.

So, here is a depiction of two girls, blood relations, but obviously very different in terms of personality, interests, etc. You have your students sitting in a classroom and doing some "imagining" in the sense that Lightfoot uses it in the quotes above—the sense of filling a space between what is and what could be. What is a female? What could it be? What is a teenage girl? What could a teenage girl be? Literature offers us the opportunity to explore this "liminal space," as Bakhtin puts it. What do these two representations of the girls have to offer our students, if anything at all, in terms of "imagining" the "female"?

Holly: I have to be honest, at the beginning part of the story I thought that the speaker was a girl, but then when she describes the school uniform as having pants and not a skirt, I was little confused. And then there's this fight and I'm thinking that these must be guys mixing it up. It took me until the end of the page to establish that the narrator was not the one fighting and that there were only girls involved in the fracas.

Ratner: Well, that's interesting in its own regard. I imagine that for some of us, our schema for the afterschool fight invokes boys, not girls, which may in part explain Holly's confusion. I wonder how confusing this opening scene would be for your students.

Ed: From my own experience in schools, I don't think students would have any trouble recognizing this as a "girl" fight. It's definitely in their schema. There might even be more girl fights than boy fights in my school.

Helena: Yeah, I think the notion of a physically aggressive girl is much less foreign to our students than to many of us.

Ratner: OK, so back to the original question. What do you think would be going through the minds of the girls in your classroom as they read through this scene?

Kevin: I think that the majority of them are preoccupied by Sasha because she's the cool chick and because I think for this generation, in and out of the city, the idea of "ladylike" is gone. I'm from the South originally and people think that Southerners still have this genteel notion of womanhood, but that's not true. It's like if you mention "ladylike" now, teenagers have no referent for it. It's gone. That being true, I think Jenelle would not even enter their minds at the beginning of the story. But I think later they might become drawn to Jenelle, later when she's more feisty and defiant of the various authorities in the story.

Ginette: I don't think that the desire to be ladylike is gone. I just think that more girls nowadays are afraid to own up to that desire—they don't want to be that "good girl" because nobody wants them to be that good girl.

Ratner: Who is "nobody"?

Ginette: I just mean that times have changed. There was the feminist movement, women in the workforce, women in positions of power in government, etc. Women playing sports and boxing, etc. So, I think in society in general there is a lot of pressure for girls not to "act like a girl" in the traditional sense. But that doesn't mean that the desire is gone. And then when you're speaking of urban culture, there are other pressures as well. A lot of the female rappers present themselves as "roughnecks" who don't take shit from anyone. They're verbally aggressive, sexually aggressive, physically aggressive. The same reason that girls latch on to a rapper like Foxy Brown and Remy Ma is why they would gravitate to Sasha.

Angela: Yeah, but they also love Beyoncé and Mariah Carey. They're hardly roughnecks.

Ginette: But then you're talking about the other end of the spectrum—the sex object. Everything they see is extreme. The women and girls who make it on TV and the radio, the ones that high school girls obsess over, are either sex objects sitting on the hoods of men's sports cars or they're wannabe gangsters. That's why we need to expose girls to as many alternative gender models as possible. This story is good because Jenelle represents a female "type" that is familiar to them in some ways but different from the typical fare they're fed in the media and lowbrow literature. I also think, though, that they need to read classics like *Pride and Prejudice* (Austen 1813) alongside a story like "A Good Girl (From the Bronx)." Then they can see that females have always faced struggles, and they can compare what it means to be a woman in various places and times.

Ratner: OK, right now I'm going to put myself in the seat of a girl that has been in classrooms where I have taught and that I imagine you have encountered as well. I'm basically a good kid, not that different from Jenelle. I get decent grades, dress and act in ways deemed appropriate by authority figures, don't get into fights, stay out of trouble if I can help it. And as I'm reading this story, I'm thinking, I love Jenelle. I love the fact that she's totally uncomfortable with the predicament Sasha has put her in, but is somehow figuring out a way to negotiate her way through the situation; I love the fact that she is aware of how out of control her cousin is but not willing to write her off. I love the fact that she has some sense of humor about this stuff, as crazy as it is. I love the fact that she shares the same dilemmas and insecurities that I do, which, as with most adolescents, usually centers around social status and how to present oneself in front of peers. I'm feeling this kid, Jenelle, because there is a lot of her in me, and, frankly, I haven't read many books in or out of school with a character that reminds me of me.

Debbie: I basically was that girl in high school, and honestly, I do appreciate a character like Jenelle. She's kind of stuck in the shadows, and a story like this could help girls like her step out a bit.

Ratner:	I heard a couple of you say that Sasha is the cool one and Jenelle is uncool. Does everyone see it that way? More importantly, how would your students view Jenelle? Do you think they would see her as uncool?
Holly:	I don't think it's an issue of cool. Jenelle is just one of those students who when they are sitting in a classroom, they are just sort of there; the office lady described her as Sasha's shadow. And then on the day that Sasha wasn't in school, Jenelle herself says that she feels strange without her cousin there and that it's hard to be alone when you're someone's shadow. And I kinda get the feeling that when she wasn't with Sasha she was just one of those kids who blended in. She didn't really seem all that outgoing, she doesn't really mention other friends or anything. I don't really think that makes her anything other than one of the faces in the crowd. She didn't seem unhappy with that role.
Debbie:	There are definitely some students who would admire Jenelle; I would have been one of them. I'm just not sure that they would admit it in a class discussion. Another thing that certain girls, and boys for that matter, would appreciate about Jenelle is that she shows how even the "good" kids have serious problems to deal with, like the whole racial thing going on in Jenelle's family.
Ginette:	I see Sasha as the kind of person who acts from the heart, someone who I guess you could say has more spunk to her. Whereas Jenelle, I feel, would be the one who would get away with murder one day, like, she's that type of a person.
Ratner:	Jenelle would get away with murder?
Ginette:	Yeah, because Jenelle finds ways to manipulate around situations. Whereas Sasha would just go headfirst into a situation, Jenelle would work around the situation. So as a teenage girl growing up in this world, which one do you admire: the one who can get away with things and get around things or the one that goes headfirst into things?
Ed:	Woman who do that kind of thing are considered cunning and deceitful; if a man does it he's just being practical or clever.
Debbie:	I don't know. I don't think Jenelle is manipulative or getting away with anything. She didn't do anything wrong. She's just trying to protect her cousin, which is admirable in a way.
Ed:	No, I agree with you. I'm just saying that I can see how certain readers would interpret Jenelle's behavior as manipulative or cunning because we've been conditioned to see it that way.
Holly:	Yeah, but you can also argue that readers will see Sasha's directness as "boyish." Girls aren't supposed to plow headfirst into situations.
Ratner:	Speaking of Sasha, let's focus on her now. Personally, I'm also feeling Sasha and if I was that high school girl sitting in the back of a classroom, I might also find Sasha alluring.
Ed:	She's more passionate.

Ratner: She's an asskicker, what can I say? I don't like what she is doing or approve of it by any means, but there is something free
about her—I don't know what it is—but I'm feeling her, too. And
I'm fairly certain that many students I've taught—both boys
and girls—would find her aggression thrilling. So, if that's the
primary kind of imagining that the story activates in a young
reader—if that's how the story engages students and allows
them to "enter the story world"—does that justify teaching it? Is
that enough?

I don't think so. And I don't think that's what Lightfoot
intended by "imagining" in the sense of readers entertaining new
ways of being and "trying on" new identities, ones that do not
necessarily conform to "how we have been imagined and how we
have been named." But of course there is much more to this story
than the opening fight scene.

Ginette: When you said that you are feeling Sasha, I think that's what the
kids get out of it. You might not agree with what she does and
how she goes about doing things, but while you are reading that
story it's kinda like they say—you give her her "props" for the
way she goes about things. You would! But again, that's because
when you enter the story world you are no longer part of your
reality, you become a part of that reality. So it's OK to appreciate
a character like that. In the real world or even in your classroom
as a student, you might not appreciate the person who kicks the
other kids' asses every day. But, you know, in the story world you
would be able to appreciate them as a character.

Colleen: Well, this also raises the issue of female aggression and where
such behavior fits into the space carved out by society in terms of
acceptable behavior. If you bring gender into it, I would consider
Sasha to be a much more masculine person. She is just so aggressive, and so if you are defining gender in terms of being passive
or aggressive, she is just so utterly self-centered and in her own
space. She's going to do what she wants and she doesn't care.
In all these ways, she comes off as more boyish.

That said, I think there is a general pressure within adolescent groups to portray oneself as aggressive. I don't see it so much
as a gender thing or a city versus suburban thing, but just a part of
growing up. Teenagers imagine themselves as more independent
than they actually are, and they see aggression and rebelliousness
as forms of independence.

Ed: But you yourself said that you see Sasha as masculine.

Colleen: True. So I guess it's just a matter of degree. I'm actually very curi-
ous how students would react to Sasha and Jenelle. I really can't
say for sure.

Ratner: Let's stay with Sasha for another moment. I'm sure that there are
parents out there, probably some kids as well, and many teachers

who would just be horrified by Sasha. This wasn't some little slap fight; she really hurts this girl and leaves her twitching on the sidewalk. Pretty rough stuff. Given this, how do you feel about bringing this story into a high school classroom, and how would you justify teaching it?

Ginette: How many times do we read about situations where you have two men fight to the death over a woman? I mean, you read about that and parents have no issue with it. I think we have to reanalyze the society in which we live today, where on the one hand females are pushed to be more aggressive because they are taught that that is the way to succeed in a male-dominated world, supposedly. And on the other hand they are pushed in subtle and direct ways by families and media to be "feminine" in the sense of sexually and socially submissive. How do you go about doing both? It must be pretty confusing for girls these days.

Ratner: For me that's what justifies teaching the story, and particularly the opening scene. I mean, you are right—this isn't two guys getting into a fight, in which case you wouldn't have batted an eye.

Olympia: We wouldn't have even discussed it.

Ratner: Right. But now here you've got something very, very different going on and we could at least consider the value of that in itself. In my view, this isn't some gratuitous fight scene; there's a young girl who has done something terribly, terribly violent and as I read the scene, I find myself stopping and thinking, "What is going on here?" Now, will the kids say, "Well, what is going on here?" or will they just be like, "Yeah, that sounds about right." For me, starting with that opening scene, the story puts you in a questioning stance. It carves out space for analyzing questions of gender identity, responsibility to family versus personal interest, racial issues. Any last thoughts?

Holly: I see another value to the story, a fairly straightforward one. Kids fight. I don't know if it happens more or less in city schools, I just know that kids fight a lot. And they, just by nature, don't often think things through because there is so much emotion behind it. Hormones, rage, whatever it is, they are ready to go at it. But how often does someone wind up in a coma from fighting? Probably not that often. But could a kid wind up in a coma? Yes, and sometimes they do. So it's not so far-fetched to imagine two girls fighting for a guy and how the consequences of this can be very serious. The details in the writing make the scene convincing, and I could see teenagers buying into it. If they buy into the fight, maybe they'll also buy into the outcome and think, "This is the kind of thing that could happen to me." I suppose some will turn around and say, "Nah, that couldn't happen to me," but even if it plants that little seed of doubt, I think that is probably a good thing.

✻ Classroom Activities: A Good Girl (From the Bronx)

Introductory Activity: Anticipation Guide

When readers pick up a new novel or story, their reading of the text is mediated through knowledge and experiences they have collected through a lifetime of prior encounters with people, places, and other texts. In the sense that readers—including adolescent readers—are not blank slates, it is helpful to think of the act of reading as an interchange of two texts: the actual story and the mental text, or perhaps more accurately, the multimedia library of texts, images, ideas, beliefs, and values stacked in our minds. The technical term for the mental map upon which we transpose new information and ideas is "schema." Schema theory—the concept that all human beings possess categorical rules or scripts that they use to interpret the world—can explain, for instance, how our students' and our own prior notions of what it means to "be" or "act" like a girl will have a great impact on our "reading" of characters like Sasha and Jenelle in "A Good Girl (From the Bronx)." Anticipation Guides (Herber 1978) are useful instructional tools for cultivating in students three learning strategies that schema theorists identify as essential to the reading process: activating schema, building schema, and adjusting schema.

The Literature Anticipation Guide prepares students for the concepts and content that they will read about in class. I have found Anticipation Guides to be particularly effective when used in conjunction with literature that presents issues or events about which students have preconceived notions and strongly held beliefs. Anyone who spends time with teens knows how quickly and emphatically they are willing to express their opinions on a range of topics, even ones they have spent little time examining. Literature Anticipation Guides invite students to voice their beliefs on important matters and then to reflect upon and reexamine these beliefs after encountering perspectives on these matters in the context of a poem, novel, story, or play.

Figure 5.1 provides directions for creating a Literature Anticipation Guide and using it during the prereading stage of a literature lesson or unit. Figures 5.2 and 5.3 present Parts 1 and 2 of a Literature Anticipation Guide that can be used in conjunction with "A Good Girl (From the Bronx)."

According to Widmayer (2004), learners respond to new information in three different ways: In *accretation,* learners take the new input and assimilate it into their existing schema without making any changes to the overall schema. Learners are *tuning* when they realize that their existing schema is inadequate for the new knowledge and modify their existing schema accordingly. *Restructuring* is the process of creating a new schema addressing the inconsistencies between the old schema and the newly acquired information.

Used routinely, Literature Anticipation Guides enable young readers to utilize, and observe others utilizing, literature as a vehicle for assimilating, tuning, and restructuring new concepts into previously held notions about the world and human experience. There is a side benefit for teachers: It affords us the opportunity to tune and restructure our own previously held notions about what students know and believe in regard to issues, events, and cultural domains showcased in literature.

FIGURE 5.1

Directions for Preparing and Facilitating Literature Anticipation Guides

1. Identify major concepts or issues that students will encounter in target literature.

2. Create a short list of statements reflecting beliefs concerning the identified concepts or issues. It is helpful to include statements that you anticipate are consistent with students' beliefs or experiences and others you anticipate will contradict their beliefs or experiences.

3. List the statements on a handout or chart and provide space for students to indicate whether they agree or disagree with each statement (see Figure 5.2).

4. Facilitate whole- or small-group discussions in which students share their responses and their justifications for them.

5. After students have read portions of the target literature, or after they have finished reading the entire selection, ask them to reassert or change their original responses to the statements and locate specific evidence in the text to support their current perspectives (see Figure 5.3).

6. Facilitate a second session of whole- or small-group discussions in which students share their responses and their justifications for them.

Writing Project: Narrative Detours

As students move into upper-grade English classrooms, a gradual shift in instructional focus occurs as analytic responses to literature begin to take precedence over creative responses. Elementary school teachers readily have students draw, dramatize, or compose their own poems, stories, and plays in conjunction with the reading of literature. Secondary English teachers, out of convention or in response to what they view as "real world" concerns (i.e., standardized tests, preparation for college), tend to regard the secondary years as time to get "serious," which in the English classroom means instruction and assignments focused on analytic writing, most notably the "literary essay." This, I believe, is a mistake.

First, the distinction between analytic and creative responses to literature is a flimsy one. A major contribution of scholars associated with the reader-response school of English studies was to demonstrate that reading literature *and* writing literature both entail, at least in part, acts of invention (Iser 1978; Fish 1980). Meaning is not encased in the printed text waiting for the reader to simply unpack it. A reader must transpose his or her own meaning upon the author's text. In her seminal *The Reader, the Text, the Poem*, Louise Rosenblatt (1938, 1978) described this process as a "transaction" which results in an autonomous third text "co-created" by author and reader.

When facilitated with purpose and forethought, classroom assignments and activities involving creative response to literature can also demand that students employ reason, logic, goal-setting, metacognition, and other habits of mind

FIGURE 5.2

Literature Anticipation Guide for "A Good Girl (From the Bronx)" (Part 1)

What do you think?

<u>Directions:</u> Before you read your class assignment, read each statement in Part 1.
  If you believe that a statement is true, place a check mark in the *Agree* column.
  If you believe that a statement is false, place a check mark in the *Disagree* column.
  Be ready to explain your responses.

Statement	Agree	Disagree	Why?
1. Girls who fight are not "ladylike."			
2. Parents and grandparents always love children equally.			
3. Adults outside of the family are more suited to advise children than family members because family members cannot see their own children objectively.			
4. You should never report a crime that you have witnessed if doing so will put yourself or loved ones in danger.			
5. People of different races, religions, and cultures should not have children together as it often leads to problems for these children.			
6. Family always comes first.			

more closely associated with analytic or critical thinking. I qualify this statement because creative responses to literature such as dramatizing scenes from stories or novels ("story theater") and writing alternative endings to literature (also known as "ghost chapters") are often treated frivolously by students, especially when a teacher assigns such activities as "supplementary" work or just to give students a break before getting back to the serious stuff. When creative activities are given such low priority by the teacher, it is not surprising that students will thoughtlessly scribble a drawing in response to *Heart of Darkness* (Conrad 1902), or write an absurdly improbable alternative ending to *Of Mice and Men* (Steinbeck 1937), one having little connection with the chapters that preceded it. When teachers expect little more from their charges than staying "on task" during these activities, they sacrifice opportunities to develop in students a range of generative and analytic thinking skills. Again, there is nothing innately fluffy about creative responses to literature; students are just as likely to write thoughtless literary essays when teachers assign them as busy work. When teachers

F I G U R E   5 . 3

Literature Anticipation Guide for "A Good Girl (From the Bronx)" (Part 2)

What do you think now?

<u>Directions:</u> You have just read a story related to each of the statements in Part 2. If you believe that a statement is true after reading the story, place a check mark in the *Agree* column. If you believe that a statement is false, place a check mark in the *Disagree* column. In the "Textual Support" column, note lines or passages from the story that you believe support your opinion.

Statement	Agree	Disagree	Textual Support
1. Girls who fight are not "ladylike."			
2. Parents and grandparents always love children equally.			
3. Adults outside of the family are more suited to advise children than family members because family members cannot see their own children objectively.			
4. You should never report a crime that you have witnessed if doing so will put yourself or loved ones in danger.			
5. People of different races, religions, and cultures should not have children together as it often leads to problems for these children.			
6. Family always comes first.			

approach creative work in the English classroom rigorously and thoughtfully, however, students will respond in kind. In a moment, I will describe "Narrative Detours," an activity that requires students to respond creatively *and* analytically to classroom literature. Before I do so, here are some general guidelines for ensuring that when students are invited to produce any type of imaginative work in the English classroom, they approach such work seriously and thoughtfully:

1. When introducing tasks that involve creative responses to literature, make sure to emphasize the "why" behind the activity. What is the rationale for the project or task? How does it fit with other activities that the class has conducted around literature? How will it facilitate students' understanding of literature or their growth as readers and writers?
2. Develop and discuss with students a rubric that helps them define what counts as quality in terms of both the process of completing a creative

task and the product. Your students need to know that approaching tasks creatively means taking risks and thinking generatively; this does not mean, however, that anything goes. Students also need to see (literally, *see*) what "good" looks like. You should, if possible, share previously completed student work ranging from poor to outstanding, as well as exemplary work from outside your classroom in the target genre.

3. Approach creative tasks as a process and allow sufficient time to treat them as such. Process writing is widely encouraged and practiced in English classrooms for nonfiction writing projects. Yet, when secondary English teachers facilitate poetry, fiction, and dramatic writing (if they do so at all), students are often given as little as a class period or less to complete their work. This sends the wrong message; if the production of outstanding literary essays or personal narratives requires brainstorming, drafting, revising, editing, and conferring, why wouldn't a student writing a ghost chapter or a group of students preparing a dramatic interpretation of a short story undergo a similar process of refinement?

Narrative Detours

I tell my students that I met my wife at a party on Ludlow Street on Manhattan's Lower East Side. Before the party, I had a previous engagement uptown that exhausted me. I could have just as easily headed back to my apartment in Brooklyn and called it a night. How different would my life have been had I not forced myself to go to the party on Ludlow, or had I not stood in that line for the bathroom behind my future wife? Fictional stories, like our lives, present decisive moments that leave us to wonder, in retrospect, what if? What if?

What if Jenelle had stopped Sasha from going after the girl at the bus stop? What if the girl that Sasha fought at the bus stop had come out with just a few bruises rather than falling into a coma? What if Jenelle had admitted to the policewoman that she witnessed her cousin's fight? What if Jenelle's mother had used the money for an expensive lawyer to represent Sasha instead of saving it for Jenelle's college tuition? What if Jenelle had been born with a light complexion and Sasha a darker one? How would this have changed their interaction with the grandparents? What if the social worker or the policewoman had given different advice to Jenelle or had given the same advice but in a different manner? What might they have said and what might have been the result of these conversations?

The Narrative Detour assignment described in Figure 5.4 asks students to write fiction in response to fiction by pursuing the types of hypothetical questions that naturally emerge from a story like "A Good Girl (From the Bronx)." I have found a few advantages to facilitating the Narrative Detour creative response to literature as opposed to the more common Alternate Endings and Ghost Chapters. More so than these related activities, the Narrative Detour reinforces the idea that characters, and the writers who animate them, make choices as they travel along the path of a story. Choosing a specific decisive moment, tinkering with that moment, and then considering the implications of the chosen "detour" helps students recognize the interconnectedness of narrative events as well as that of the characters inhabiting the story world.

FIGURE 5.4

Sample Narrative Detour Assignment for "A Good Girl (From the Bronx)"

Writing Assignment—Narrative Detour

<u>Directions:</u> Choose an episode from "A Good Girl (From the Bronx)" that contains one of the many "decisive moments" in the story. It can be a scene that we discussed or one that we did not explore in class

<u>Part 1: Narrative Detour.</u> Identify the decisive moment in the episode—for example, the moment that Sasha tells Jenelle to back her in the fight or the moment when the policewoman asks Jenelle if she witnessed the fight. Next, take a narrative detour from the original text by changing the direction chosen by the author. This could mean altering a character's words, thoughts, or behavior. If you like, you may choose to change an event in the episode or include a completely new one. Once you have taken the Narrative Detour, rewrite the rest of the episode as you envision the detour would take it. **Note:** You do not need to rewrite the entire story, just the decisive moment and the episode that contains it!

<u>Part 2: Reflection.</u> Attach a two- to three-page reflection on your Narrative Detour. The reflection should address the following points:

- Describe why you chose this particular decisive moment for your Narrative Detour.
- Considering what we know about the characters and events from reading the original story, how plausible (likely, believable) is your detour? What other events or episodes in the story suggest that your change is plausible?
- Discuss how the detour you made would affect different characters in the story, including ones that were not involved in the episode. How does your Narrative Detour change the overall story in terms of its themes, meanings, and/or overall impact on readers?

I have found that when students attempt to author large expanses of fiction, they become overwhelmed by the task. The writing they produce often amounts to a listing of events with little attention to crafting compelling images or developing characters. By focusing students' creative efforts on a smaller expanse of text, the Narrative Detour affords students the opportunity to "paint a picture with words" rather than piece together the bare bones of a story. The result is usually more gratifying for both writer and reader. Writing a more manageable expanse of fiction also allows more time for the type of reflective writing described in Part 2 of the Narrative Detour assignment.

Community of Readers Extension Activities: Reader Reinvention (a.k.a. "Madonna" or "Diddy")

Chapter 4 introduced activities that encourage students to walk around in the skin of fictional characters (Heart-to-Hearts and Chance Meetings) and writers of fiction (Copy/Change). Reader Reinvention, by contrast, asks students to assume the roles of other *readers* of literature.

For years I have called this activity "Madonna," in honor of the Material Girl's well-publicized makeovers every few years. Currently, I refer to it as "Diddy," the most recent moniker of hip-hop mogul Sean Combs, because it seems to get the point across to this generation of teens.

Kindergarten through eighth grade teachers customarily assign students cooperative learning roles that are primarily designed for discussion management (Leader, Collector, Recorder, and Reporter) or that correspond with specific reading strategies (Summarizer, Questioner, Predictor, and Clarifier). Particularly at the high school level, I avoid these types of role assignments because my goal is for students to conduct "teacherless" literature discussions in which participants independently, spontaneously, and organically choose from an array of response styles individuals might adopt when reading and discussing literature. Assigning students to restrict themselves to one particular discussion management function or to a single reader response works against this goal. Therefore, if I assign roles at all, which I do only occasionally, they are the types of roles that participants naturally assume during group discussions. The goal of Reader Reinvention is not behavior management or topic control, but rather to provide students with an opportunity to "try on" a new social identity in a group discussion context. In light of the unique pressure to fit in during the high school years, Reader Reinvention provides students with a risk-reducing "cover" to experiment with new ways of interacting and communicating with peers.

To begin the activity, ask the class to discuss the various "roles" that they have noticed individuals typically perform during group or whole-class literature discussions. Figure 5.5 includes some of the roles that my students have identified over the years in which I have facilitated this activity.

Directions for Reader Reinvention

1. As a class, identify and create a list of class literature discussion roles.
2. Ask students to reflect in their reading journals on which types of literature circle roles they tend to assume and why this is so.
3. Pass out strips of paper, each with the name of one of the discussion "roles" written on it.
4. Direct the students to "reinvent" themselves during the literature circle and assume their assigned role during the discussion.
5. In the middle of a literature circle or at the beginning of the next one, assign students new discussion roles.

❧ Language In Context Study: Code Switching

Jenelle, Miss Caridad Benitez (the social worker) and Jenelle's grandparents are all English speakers, but when we study their respective lines of dialogue in "A Good Girl (From the Bronx)," it is clear that they do not speak English in the same manner. A language, like a fruit or vegetable, can come in many varieties. Like taking a few bites of a Macintosh apple before casually putting it aside

FIGURE 5.5

Sample Roles for Reader Reinvention

The Initiator—Tends to speak first and introduce new topics of discussion during the literature circle.

The Clarifier—Rephrases or seeks clarification on other participants' comments and questions so that she and/or the group as a whole can follow the discussion.

The Devil's Advocate—Tends to take an opposing point of view on perspectives voiced by other participants, sometimes voicing sincere differences and other times playing the provocateur.

The Mother Hen—Tends to affirm the perspective of other participants by providing interpersonal or text-based support. He/she is also sensitive to the literature circle experience of all participants and strives to ensure that all members of the group participate and feel included in the discussion.

The Still-Waters-Run-Deep Girl/Guy—Doesn't say much but listens carefully. When he/she does speak, it is usually to contribute an unusual or overlooked perspective on the literature or literature discussion itself.

The Pull-It-All-Together Guy/Girl—Has a knack for following the flow of the conversation and at essential moments refocusing the group on themes, essential questions, or conclusions that have emerged over the course of the book group. He/she also likes to relate the current discussion to central themes, questions, and concerns from previous literature circle sessions.

---

and switching over to a Golden Delicious, a speaker can communicate in one variety of a language and switch, even mid-sentence, to another variety. The linguistic term for using more than one language or language variety within conversation is code switching.

When Jenelle's grandparents speak, they use English and Spanish interchangeably:

> Grandfather: "Mi rubia is not a bad girl!"
> Grandmother: "What has Sasha ever done for Yeni? Digame! Nada, but Yeni is like her mother."

Any student who has spent time on the streets and public transportation systems can attest to the wealth of English language variations spoken in major American cities. It is important, however, for students to understand why speakers alternate between language variations, when they do so, and how multiple language varieties affect individuals and cultural groups who use them.

If Jenelle's grandparents are the first generation of the family to move from Puerto Rico to the United States, for example, they may switch from English to Spanish whenever they cannot think of an equivalent English word or phrase. They may also, however, use Spanish interchangeably with English as a means of (a) retaining their Puerto Rican heritage, (b) signaling their identity as bilingual-bicultural individuals, or (c) conveying specific meanings, because words and phrases have different connotations in the two languages or when encountered in different settings.

Not all code switching involves alternating between two distinct languages such as Spanish and English. Consider, for example, the following exchange between Jenelle and Sergimar as they work in Dunkin' Donuts:

> Jenelle: "But what about helping our family? Should family always come first?"
>
> Sergimar: "What're you, bitch?" she laughs, "a Hallmark card?"

During their conversation, Sergimar speaks to Jenelle in English but it is phonologically, grammatically, and syntactically different from the English spoken between Jenelle and Miss Caridad Benitez in the school office. While some would argue that the word "bitch" is a demeaning vulgarity that should never be used in conversation, the word is often used and understood by contemporary urban teenagers in a far different manner from the way it has been used in other times and contexts; Sergimar clearly does not intend it as a slur against her co-worker and peer. Gumperz's (1982) model of code switching suggests that speakers use language variations to establish "in-group" identity and create solidarity between members of language minority communities. By using the word "bitch" in this instance, Sergimar may be signaling to Jenelle that they can engage each other on a personal, more intimate level. By contrast, when Miss Benitez and Jenelle speak to each other in language closer to the standard English of society at large, they are signaling that they will engage each other on a more impersonal, detached level.

To help your students explore the nature, function, and impact of code switching, ask them to choose a dialogue in "A Good Girl (From the Bronx)" and study the language patterns of the characters in terms of word choice, grammar, syntax, and phonology. Then, direct students to rewrite the dialogue using different combinations of language variations during the conversation. What happens, for example, if Sasha speaks to Jenelle in English words and phrases that approximate Miss Caridad Benitez? What happens if Jenelle responds in the voice of Sasha? How does it change the tone of the conversation, or the reader's perceptions of either character?

⚔ Text Connections

For Students

Ferrell, Carolyn. "Proper Library." In *Don't Erase Me*. New York: Houghton Mifflin, 1997.

Told in the voice of Lorrie, a gay, black teenager from the Bronx, "Proper Library" is a moving account of one youth's struggle to give and receive love, and to find a language for making sense of his life as an outsider in the schools and on the streets of inner-city New York. Both "Proper Library" and *The Basketball Diaries* (see p. 26) contain strong language and sexual content. For this reason, teachers may choose to share selected excerpts of the stories rather than the entire text.

Gautier, A. L. "Palabras." *Crab Orchard Review*, 2001.

Gautier has created a tapestry of immigrant themes. Written in English with phrases of Spanish, this story begins with a heartfelt and mushy letter from the narrator's grandfather (Papi) to his son in Puerto Rico. Then Papi receives a postcard that simply states, "Papi, No comprendo ingles. Signed, tu hijo." The narrator, Esteban, reveals that his grandfather moved to Brooklyn, abandoning the life he'd led as a young man, selling "mango, coconut, pineapple, and cherry ices from a handcart" and opening a bodega for the sake of his son. Dichotomies abound in the story: between the grandparents and their children, speakers of Spanish and speakers of English, and the quarrels between lovers and husbands. Esteban's sensitive nature and bilingual orientation leads him to discover there is a word for everything, and in the case of his father there is a Spanish word that "translates pretty tamely into English." Throughout the story, Gautier introduces the reader to a bilingual way of thinking of the culture of America in Brooklyn and the second-generation father who "wants all of the things [his parents] left behind."

Ortiz, Judith. "American History." In *Big City Cool: Short Stories About Urban Youth.* Edited by M. Jerry Weiss and Helen S. Weiss. New York: Persea Books Inc., 2002, pp. 64–73.

"American History" describes the day John F. Kennedy was shot, from the perspective of Elena, a Puerto Rican teenager who lives in a massive Puerto Rican housing project in Paterson, New Jersey. Elena is studious and thoughtful, gangly and awkward. On the day Kennedy is shot she was supposed to go to Eugene's house to study. Eugene is new in Paterson and white. Elena is infatuated with him. When she arrives at Eugene's house, his mother says that she may not come inside. Though she doesn't say it, it's clear that this is because Elena is Puerto Rican. This is her lesson in American History.

Geha, Joseph. "All Alone and Together." In *Big City Cool: Short Stories About Urban Youth.* Edited by M. Jerry Weiss and Helen S. Weiss. Persea Books Inc, 2002, pp. 51–64.

Labibeh, a third-generation Christian Arab, lives with her depressed mother in Chicago. Her sister is in Brooklyn with their father on September 11, 2001. Both girls experience sadness, fear, prejudice, and solidarity after the attacks. The story is also a good jumping-off point for conversations about assimilation and cultural identity. The girls' father has Americanized his name, and both girls have English and Arab names. Labibeh is taking Arab lessons, enjoys cooking Libyan food, but still has many of the same family and social struggles as any teenage girl. She is figuring out how to be an Arab American in a loaded cultural moment.

For Teachers

Blau, Sheridan. *The Literature Workshop: Teaching Texts and Their Readers.* Portsmouth, NH: Heinemann, 2003, 242 pp.

Through re-creations of actual workshops that he holds for teachers, former NCTE president Sheridan Blau introduces readers to the rationale, theoretical framework, and instructional implications of the literature workshop. Blau is adept at explaining the complex relationship between reader, text, and teacher; he provides great insights into why students often see themselves as incapable of penetrating sophisticated texts, and he explores how literature teachers unknowingly promote this view. Using engaging anecdotes and literature "experiments," Blau presents helpful guidance on how English teachers can address the problem of background knowledge in teaching literature that students often see as inaccessible, and how to allow for a diversity of responses to texts while establishing standards for the intellectual merit of student interpretations.

Lopez, Nancy. *Hopeful Girls, Troubled Boys: Race and Gender Disparity in Urban Education.* New York: Routledge, 2002, 223 pp.

Lopez's ethnographic study of Dominican, Haitian, and West Indian youth in New York City seeks to understand "the dynamics that contribute to race and gender disparities in urban education" amongst these immigrant populations. Her rich descriptions of life in the homes, leisure spaces, schools, and workplaces of Caribbean youth reveal how gender-specific systemic and institutionalized forces of oppression rather than "natural" differences between men and women in these communities have resulted in such marked differences in educational attainment. Lopez's perspective as a sociologist sheds new light on an issue of great concern to urban educators.

Snitch

by Grace Park

There was a groove in the table where someone had scratched out "FAT A--."
Mo rubbed the well-worn cuts and wondered what they must've been looking at when they carved out this little piece of boredom. His eyes settled on
DeLayla's shirt in front of him and the pants that didn't cover her butt. He
traced the letters F, A, T, in mindless loops. After a while he sat up straight,
breathed out slowly and slumped back down on his desk. It was 5 minutes in.

Ms. Bancroft stood at the front of the classroom next to their teacher,
Ms. Wong, arms crossed in front of her sizeable frame, brows crossed on her
face. Ms. Wong stood mimicking the assistant principal, arms crossed in front
of her, but much less convincingly. Her face was too full of concern, too earnest.
Silence hung heavy in the room, like the inside of a casket.

Ten minutes past the hour and the air was thick. A warm breeze floated
in, bringing with it the scent of summer and dirt and freedom.

"You have a choice," Ms. Wong said to the room.

"We know there were witnesses to the incident; we know that some of
those people are in this classroom."

Why did he have to go through this? It wasn't like he'd done anything. He
never did anything. And yet, here he was, sitting in an overheated classroom—
in the middle of June, why, God, was the heater still on!?—listening to the
sounds of the seventh graders playing outside on the tarmac. They screamed
and yelled and laughed while Mo sat in silence waiting for someone to give
Ms. Wong an answer. Or rather, for her to fold and the lesson on possessives
to continue.

Mo cleared his throat, scratchy and dry, thought about asking for some
water, and then thought better of it. He looked up to find Janelle giving him a
look from the corner of her eye—she sat in the row next to his. She didn't say a
word but there was no mistaking her message:
"Don't snitch."

Not that she had to worry, he rolled his eyes. No idiot was going to
squeal—everyone knew what would happen if they did.

When he saw four boys jump Jerell O'Neal outside the schoolyard on the
way home yesterday, the first thing Mo did was dart into Ramon's Deli. If no
one saw him, no one could say he'd snitch. And so he sat with his mouth shut,
fingers absentmindedly tracing the letters again.

His mom always said to tell the truth. But even she would understand
this situation—you don't betray friends. One of the boys in the group, though

he wasn't doing the punching, was his friend Justin. Or Justin who used to be his friend. After this past summer, Justin stopped hanging out with him. At first Mo was confused and hurt, but then he realized that Justin was just hanging out with the cooler kids and he couldn't blame him. He told himself, "I'd ditch me, too, if I could."

He remembered the last time he'd made the effort.

Crossing the lunchroom, soggy tater tots on a Styrofoam tray, Mo motioned for Justin to join him. Without even acknowledging Mo, Justin abruptly broke into a jog in the direction of Alberto, whom he slapped on the back and passed a handful of sunflower seeds. For a brief moment, Mo could see Justin looking back at him, but he didn't come over.

That would be the last time he'd try that.

Mo thought some more about his mom and what she would say.

"Mohammed, it's not like we're going to be here forever," she'd say, puttering around the house fixing up the ragged furniture she had received from the Morales' next door when they moved out. "If your father were here he'd put things straight. But you have to be the man of the house now and stay out of trouble."

Another wipe-down of the frames they had on the bookshelf.

"You know your father was a brave man, and he always did what was right. Even though he's not with us anymore, you can still learn from him. Think about what your father would have done."

But at the moment he was thinking about Jerell and the 15 stitches he needed on his head. He was thinking about Justin and the stupid jokes they used to make up and laugh about; the way they used to watch out for each other.

He thought some more before lifting his head from folded arms and sitting up straight. He looked up at Ms. Wong and their eyes met.

✎ Teacher Focus Group Discussion: Now You Try It

An overworked and overwhelmed first-year teacher recently asked me if other professions demand that one make so many on-the-job decisions. "Sometimes," he confessed, "I think about how nice it would be to just take orders at a coffee shop."

Considering my limited experience in professions outside of teaching, I did not have a wide enough perspective to answer his question. Still, I knew exactly what he meant: Should I seat my students in rows or tables? Should I cover more material or less material in greater depth? Should I slow down for the students who need more time? But what about the kids who know their stuff already? How should I start tomorrow's lesson? How should I end it? Now that my students look bored and confused, should I wrap the lesson up and come back to the topic tomorrow? Am I being structured enough, or do I need to give my students a little more freedom? Should I send Marta to the principal or give her one more chance? Should I take a sick day tomorrow or save it for when I get the inevitable flu?

Should I work in a Starbucks next year?

Teaching *is* a profession of decisions, and the list seems even longer and more complicated for English teachers. Should I teach the classics or alternative literature? Do I have enough time for both? Will my students find anything to relate to in *Ethan Frome* (Wharton 1911)? Can I really afford to teach *A Clockwork Orange* (Burgess 1962) instead of Shakespeare's *A Midsummer Night's Dream?* I love Carolyn Ferrell's "Proper Library" (Ferrell 1997) but should I teach it in a high school class? What about my principal? What about parents? Should I remove some of the vulgarities and some of the sexual content? But then what's the point? And if I do teach it, how will I handle my rampantly homophobic boys when they figure out that the main character is a gay teen?

So how did I answer the student contemplating a career change from schoolteacher to coffee server? I told him that the time to think about getting out of teaching was when he no longer found himself struggling with these decisions that were plaguing him. "When your most pressing concern of the week is changing the border on your bulletin board," I explained, "then you might as well work at Starbucks."

I was able to tell him without exaggeration that I have *never* been bored in all my years of teaching—routinely frustrated, discouraged, and exhausted in mind and body, but never bored. The teachers I know have more than their share of complaints about the profession, but boredom is not one of them. This is precisely because teaching consistently presents them with intellectually and emotionally challenging decisions, the kind where you lose track of how long you've been in the shower or space out on your wife mid-sentence during dinner conversation.

Beyond sheer volume, it is the weightiness of our decisions that makes the profession both draining and resistant to boredom. I have never appreciated the educational cliché (often spoken by those who have not done much teaching), "If you reach even one child, it makes it all worth it." What about the other 25 kids? What if your own child was in the unreachable group? The expression also presupposes what Mayher (1989) describes as "one of the controlling myths of schooling: That which is learned has been taught; (and its corollary) that which has been taught has been learned" (p. 274). A former student once phoned me 15 years after he attended my tenth-grade English class to inquire why I had invoked Jesus' Sermon on the Mount while teaching *The Merchant of Venice.* During college he had become an observant Christian and suspected that I had taught the lesson back then to plant the seeds for his religious awakening. The point of my story (see Ratner 2008 for a detailed account) is that the choices we make as teachers *matter;* they matter even if we don't always know to whom they matter, to how many, or in what capacity; this is what makes teaching both a daunting and consistently engaging way to spend your working hours.

Because every educational context and educator is unique, the types of choices and questions that teachers wrestle with from moment to moment defy uniform, easy answers. Earlier chapters presented focus groups of English teachers discussing *Street Lit* stories and the issues they raised for the teaching and reading of literature in urban schools. Having read these discussions,

I hope that you have gained some insight into how teachers think through the instructional, moral, and ethical considerations surrounding the teaching of *one* particular piece of literature, for *one* particular population of students attending a specific type of educational institution.

Now I invite you and your classmates to engage in your own focus group discussion in response to your reading of "Snitch" by Grace Park. Appendix A contains a second version of the story that I wrote with input from students in my graduate English and English Education courses. Appendix B contains an alternative ending to the second version of "Snitch" suggested by a former student and soon-to-be New York City public school teacher, Ferva Syad. Before participating in the focus group, you should read both the second version of "Snitch" and the alternate ending and prepare to discuss the following question:

Which version of the story (*Snitch 1*, *Snitch 2*, or *Snitch 2* with alternate ending), if any, would you teach to your current or future students?

To complete this pre-focus group assignment, you will need to synthesize your understanding and current thinking on the major topics addressed in the previous focus groups. The topics—along with guiding questions to help you explore them—are grouped under the following categories: Appropriateness; Authenticity and Responsible Representation; Writing Quality and Literary Merit; and Instructional Value.

Appropriateness

1. Which of the three versions of "Snitch" is most appropriate for teenage readers?
2. To use Feingold's expression (see Focus Group Discussion, Ch. 2), are any of the versions "too much, too often, too early" for teenage readers? If so, which particular version and elements of the story do you find inappropriate?
3. Are any of the versions of "Snitch" (or elements of the three versions) inappropriate for a particular age level or demographic of students?
4. What are the criteria by which you decide on the appropriateness of stories targeting teenage students?

Authenticity and Responsible Representation

Raymond Carver, a master of the short story genre, professes to have taped an index card on the wall by his desk with the following quote attributed to Ezra Pound: "Fundamental accuracy of statement is the ONE sole morality of writing" (1991b, p. 88). Carver himself put it this way:

> That's all we have, finally, the words, and they had better be the right ones, with the punctuation in the right places so that they can best say what they are meant to say. If the words are heavy with the writer's own unbridled emotions, or if they are imprecise and inaccurate for some other reason—if the words are in any way blurred—the reader's eyes will slide right over them and nothing will be achieved. (p. 90)

While most writers and readers would agree that precision in language and observation are crucial elements of great literature, accuracy in representing individuals and cultures is a more complicated process—morally, ethically, politically—than simply "getting the words right." While there have been many other acclaimed writers—Henry James and Gustave Flaubert, to name two—who have championed precision of expression, it is worth noting that Ezra Pound, a major twentieth-century poet and intellectual figure, was also an avowed fascist and propagandist for the Axis governments during the World War II era; apparently, he meant it literally when he declared accuracy of statement to be the sole moral consideration for writers.

Perhaps as a result of the unprecedented slaughter of millions over two world wars, in recent decades writers and thinkers have taken a more equivocal approach to the issue of representation in art. What does it mean for a painter, filmmaker, or novelist to "get it right"? Does a fiction writer have any moral and ethical responsibilities to readers or the world at large beyond "accurately" observing and recording his observations of this world and its inhabitants? If there are no universal truths but only perspectives, what are the historical and culturally bound narratives through which the artist arrives at a perspective? When fiction or nonfiction writers depict the experiences of a black family from the South Bronx or a Mexican family from a Los Angeles barrio, what preexisting stories, concepts, and beliefs do they carry with them through which they filter their observations of these subjects? To what degree does a writer's rendering of these families knowingly or unknowingly buy into, or even advance, historical constructs that maintain cultural disparities and further alienate marginalized groups?

Even if we ignore issues of morality and ethics for a moment, and focus on accuracy as a function of craft, representation in fiction remains a complicated matter. If we consider, for example, writers known for having a great "ear" for dialogue (Carver, for one), there is a significant difference between how their characters speak and how their speaking would appear in transcriptions of actual dialogue. Realistic is not the same as "real." The achievement of writers like Carver is "verisimilitude" (see Figure 6.1) or creating an impression of reality rather than accurately recording human speech. Whether the intent is a lifelike portrayal of human interaction, a vivid description of a place, or a moving evocation of an emotion, writing that aims for realism rests on the writer's ability to convince the reader that there is something *true*—in the sense of authentic, rather than factually verifiable—about their observations of the world. And because readers, like writers, exist in time and place, we also need to consider how historically and culturally transmitted constructs shape their perspectives on fictional subjects, and how in turn fiction shapes their perspectives on history and culture.

In the context of the *Street Lit* stories, these questions regarding authenticity and responsible representation are not academic ones. Although they contain universal themes and topics of interest to all students, they were written for and about students in urban classrooms, particularly those populated with the black and brown faces of working-class and low-income communities, including English language learners and newly arrived immigrants from nations relegated to "third world" status. What are their notions of "reality" and authenticity, and how did they arrive at these notions? What does it mean for them to act, speak, and think "American," "black," "Dominican," "urban," "poor," like a boy, girl, and student? How do their own concepts of race, ethnicity, gender, and class mesh with the depictions of people and places in the *Street Lit* stories, some written by authors who share the cultural characteristics and experiences of these students, others who come from very different experiences and heritages?

In addition to the questions above, here are three more questions to discuss in your focus group related to authenticity and representation:

1. Which version of "Snitch" comes closest to matching Yokota's (1993) criteria for culturally authentic multicultural literature (i.e., richness of cultural details; authentic dialogue and relationships; in-depth treatment of cultural issues; inclusion of members of minority groups for a purpose)?
2. In reflecting on the stories in this book and other literature you have read targeting teens and young adults, what other criteria would you use to assess authenticity of multicultural literature?
3. "Snitch" depicts an episode in the lives of students attending school in a poor and working-class inner-city neighborhood. To what degree have the authors of the three versions of "Snitch" created responsible representations of their subjects? What, in general, are the responsibilities of fiction writers to their subjects and readers?
4. Were there elements in the versions of "Snitch" that you viewed as authentic in terms of the author's treatment of characters and/or events but potentially harmful to students? Were there any elements in the stories that you viewed as inauthentic but potentially beneficial for your students? (In a more general sense, are there occasions in youth fiction when authenticity not a virtue, and conversely, when contrivance *is* a virtue?)
5. Specifically, which of the three versions of "Snitch," or elements within the versions, do you think your students would regard as authentic? How do your students' notions of authenticity in regard to these stories, and fiction in general, compare with your own?

Writing Quality and Literary Merit

In addition to assessing the appropriateness of a literature selection for a particular group of students and determining its usefulness for instructional purposes, teachers also consider the artistic merits and writing quality of a story, play, or poem when choosing literature for instruction.

There are nearly as many perspectives on what makes a story good as there are stories, but as Sondra Perl and Mimi Schwartz (2006) remind us, "deeper discussions" about writing quality and the success of a story are only possible when readers have a shared and critical language at their disposal beyond "'It flows!' or 'It needs more!'" (p. 80). Perl and Schwartz's "Twenty Ways to Talk About Creative Nonfiction" is a glossary of terms that seasoned writers use to talk effectively about their craft. "Talking Points for Analysis and Discussion of Narrative Writing" (see Figure 6.1) condenses their glossary and adapts it for analysis and discussion of fictional narratives. You may consult the "Talking Points" as you prepare to discuss the following questions with your focus group:

1. Based solely on the quality of the writing, which version of "Snitch" would you select for use in an English classroom?
2. What specific recommendations would you make for improving the respective versions of "Snitch"?

Overall Impact

Stories are more than the sum of their parts, so as you compare the three versions of "Snitch," you should also consider the overall impact each version had on you as a reader. Describing his selection process for a short story anthology he edited, Carver (1991a) wrote: "the best fiction ought to have, for want of a better word, *heft* to it. (The Romans used the word *gravitas* when talking about a work of substance.) . . . When a reader finishes a wonderful story and lays it aside, he should have to pause for a minute and collect himself." (p. 223)

Another measure of the overall impact of a fictional work is the degree to which a reader "cares" for the characters that inhabit it. Caring, in this sense, does not necessarily mean liking a character but rather the level of investment a reader has made in exploring the inner-life of the character and turning the pages to discover what will become of him or her. Regardless of whether or not we like an Iago or Shylock, for example, Shakespeare has compelled legions of readers and theatergoers to tune into the same emotional bandwidth as these characters.

Here are three more questions to consider as you prepare to discuss the literary merits of "Snitch":

1. Which version, if any, would you describe as having *heft,* or having compelled you to pause at the end and collect yourself?
2. To what degree did you care about the characters, particularly the protagonist, Mo?
3. Which version of "Snitch," if any, took you on a journey that left you in a different place—emotionally, intellectually—from where you were before you read it?

Instructional Value

Teachers usually choose literature for use in the classroom with some kind of instructional agenda in mind. The agenda might include highlighting a literary device such as irony or modeling an element of writing such as how to craft an effective lead or conclusion. A play or poem might be selected to promote discussion of an essential philosophical question or promote an ethical stance or ideology to which the teacher subscribes. Sometimes English teachers work within an interdisciplinary model of instruction and choose

FIGURE 6.1

Narrative Writing "Talking Points"

1. **Back-Story:** A story never occurs only in the moment; it has a context. The characters had lives before the readers met them; the events discussed had forces that shaped them. The back-story provides this context. If you hear, "But what's the back-story?" the reader desires more history about the characters (who they were) and the events (what happened) before the story begins.

2. **Cliché:** Writers should avoid the obvious in their observations and their use of language. Readers want to be surprised, and obvious sentiments like, "Falling in love was the best part of growing up" and stock phrases like "sparkling blue water" offer readers no surprises.

3. **Delivering on a Promise:** Every piece of writing sets up a promise in the first paragraph that it must fulfill by the last paragraph so that readers feel satisfied.

4. **Flatness of Dialogue:** This phrase is used when the language doesn't sound as if real people are talking. The usual problem: either every voice sounds the same or the dialogue is being used as exposition (to provide information) rather than to re-create a scene.

5. **Foreshadowing:** Even with surprise endings, readers like to feel as if they could have guessed what was coming. If there are no clues, there is no foreshadowing—that is, the hints that make what happens next seem inevitable, at least in retrospect.

6. **Narrative Arc:** Where did the writing end up vis-à-vis its beginning? How have characters changed? What's been learned by writer and reader?

7. **Narrative Tension:** Every piece of writing has tension points that draw the writer toward the subject and, if well developed, keep the reader engaged. Too often the tensions are avoided, leaving readers asking, "What's at stake here?"

8. **Pacing:** How quickly or slowly does the writing move along? If someone says, "It takes too long to get there!" the pacing is too slow. If someone says, "It goes by too quickly!" the pacing is too fast. Tip: The latter often happens at key moments, full of tension that needs exploring.

9. **Riffs:** Borrowed from jazz, the word in writing refers to digressions that give back-story about characters and events—and/or offer scenes and reflections by the writer. A riff can move away from the main story for a paragraph or several pages before returning to it.

10. **Serving the Story:** Every part of the writing, be it a short essay or a full-length book, should add something to the whole. Someone who says, "This doesn't serve the story" is suggesting that the story could use some cutting or the author needs to consider how each episode in the narrative serves the whole.

11. **Showing and Telling:** This pair refers to the need to re-create scenes (showing) and to reflect on them (telling). They must be in balance for the writing to work. If someone says, "Show more, tell less!" that means you are summarizing events without letting readers experience them. If someone says, "But what do you think? Where do you stand?" he or she is asking for reflection that reveals your point of view.

12. **The Story:** What's the story here? That is a central question for writer and reader alike. "Story," in this context, does not refer to the plot, but to the meaning of the piece: why the writer wrote it, why the reader should care.
13. **Trusting Your Readers:** Writers need to have faith in their readers' ability to "get it." If you hear, "No need to beat me over the head!" the writer may need to be subtler in word choice and refrain from repeating the same thing over and over again.
14. **Verisimilitude:** Verisimilitude means "the appearance of being true." An event may have happened as described on paper, but that is not good enough. In narrative writing, what is true must also *seem* true so that readers feel that the story is credible.
15. **Voice:** If a piece of writing does not have a strong authorial presence, a sense that an individual has written the words, it lacks "voice." If voice is "off," the writer must adjust it. If the prose sounds anonymous, like an automaton, the writer had best start again.

(Adapted from "Twenty Ways to Talk About Creative Nonfiction," in Perl and Schwartz's *Writing True: The Art and Craft of Creative Nonfiction,* 2006)

literature that furthers students' understanding of a topic covered in social studies or science class. The following questions will help you to critically examine the potential instructional value and uses of the respective versions of "Snitch."

1. Which version of "Snitch," if any, holds the most instructional value? As you read them, which version presented "teachable moments" or opportunities for addressing your instructional objectives as a current or future English teacher?
2. What specific academic knowledge or skills can you envision developing in students through the use of "Snitch" in a middle school or high school classroom?
3. Which version of "Snitch" furthers beliefs, values, or attitudes that you would like to develop in students? Conversely, which version furthers beliefs, values, or attitudes that you would not want to develop in students?

Classroom Activities: Now You Try It

After reading and discussing *Snitch, Snitch 2* and the alternate ending to *Snitch 2,* design a series of instructional activities around one version of the story. Your lessons may follow a format similar to that used for the preceding *Street Lit* stories (discussion questions, introductory activity, writing project, community of readers extension activity, language in context study) or some other model for lesson planning. Whichever format you choose to employ, I encourage you to create lessons that aim to develop in students the two dispositions that have been highlighted in earlier chapters: empathy and independence.

Empathy

Speaking at a town hall meeting in the swing state of Pennsylvania during the 2008 presidential campaign, Democratic candidate Barack Obama called for increased support for arts in education. "Part of what arts education does," he explained, "is that it teaches people to see each other through each other's eyes; it teaches us to respect and understand people who are not like us, and that makes us better citizens and it makes our democracy work better" (Obama 2008). With news headlines and campaigns dominated by the collapse of the financial markets and the wars in Iraq and Afghanistan, it is heartening that a candidate found cause to highlight an issue that has been outside the public consciousness yet fundamentally connected to matters that Americans identify as most concerning in 2008. Both the foreign policy miscalculations of the Bush regime and the market miscalculations of financial corporations can be viewed at least in part as failures to "see each other through each other's eyes." Would the first decade of the millennium have turned out differently had Americans on both "Wall Street" and "Main Street" been reading and discussing important works of art as eagerly as stock listings? Surely there are many who would view this question as naïve, even silly. But it is hard to argue with the premise that goodwill and empathy for those "who are not like us" have been in short supply in recent years, and that the arts, as Obama suggested, are uniquely positioned to develop these dispositions.

With its reliance on standardized test scores in math, science, and reading, the Bush administration's No Child Left Behind legislation has led to widespread elimination of nontested school curriculum such as art, music, and physical education (Meier & Wood, 2004). Despite the increased attention in schools to reading and literacy instruction, we should not assume that the subject of English has escaped NCLB unscathed. Wood writes, "School people are no fools. Tell them what they will be measured on and they will try to measure up" (p. 42). This holds true for English teachers, who are devoting disproportionate amounts of instructional time to preparing students for the discrete subskills that appear on standardized reading tests such as inferencing, sequencing, and identifying theme or literary elements. Tests like the Stanford 9 do not assess a "soft" skill like reading literature empathetically, so English teachers may reasonably conclude that focusing on it would be a waste of valuable instructional time. Woods, however, reports the skills and aptitudes that are assessed on these tests do not "predict anything about a child's success in life after school" (p. xii). Rather than disregarding the merits of teaching students to "see each other through each other's eyes," perhaps English teachers need to be asking why we are wasting valuable instructional time on preparing students for tests like the Stanford 9. When reading a Robert Frost poem becomes an occasion for eighth graders to mechanically "identify the main idea" rather than develop a depth of feeling for nature or humanity, it is time that English teachers take issue with the dominant pedagogy.

Obama's sentiments demonstrate an understanding that developing empathy in students *will* affect their lives outside of school, whether in the home, workplace, or civic arena. Empathy, however, is not synonymous with altruistic acts, and we cannot assume that helping students respond to fictional characters at a visceral level will prepare them for a life of good deeds. In *Empathy and the Novel* (2007), Suzanne Keen writes that "fictional worlds provide safe zones for readers' feeling empathy without experiencing a resultant demand on real-world action" (p. 4). While Keen makes a strong case for not overstating the impact of novels on a reader's capacity for good acts, she needs to consider that reading literature is not solely an autonomous pursuit; it also occurs in social arenas where it functions as a conduit for consequential human exchanges. As I write this, readers are discussing literature with other readers in book groups, across dinner tables, via blogs and chat rooms, and in classrooms. When students voice an opinion on a character like "Mo" in "Snitch," they will routinely do so in the presence of their peers. When they write about a character, they will often share their writing with their teacher and classmates. Classrooms are not the fictional "safe zones" that Keen describes as insulating readers from the "suspicion and wariness" invoked by real-world appeals for "assistance (p. 4)." Depending on the text and classroom context, a student's public stance on a fictional character or event may in fact require considerable courage and demonstrate genuine personal growth. Considering the potentially vulnerable position in which we place students when we encourage them in classroom settings to connect deeply with characters, I advise teachers to plan and facilitate this type of literature instruction deliberately and sensitively. I also impress upon them, however, not to avoid it altogether in order to spare students (and themselves) from the potential discomforts of responding deeply and personally to fiction in a public arena like the classroom. I have found that the lessons of literature are most powerfully delivered when woven through the very fabric of a classroom community.

Independence

Referring to her first years as a classroom teacher, Glenda Bissex (1996) writes, "If only I could have envisioned myself as a model learner rather than a model knower" (p. 12). The shift in professional identity noted by Bissex describes precisely what I have come to regard as a key marker of progress in the development of pre-service and novice teachers. When I start working with an English teacher or teacher candidate, they often present themselves as "model knowers"—ones who see their job as revealing to students the subtleties in stories, plays, and poems that they would never discover without a teacher present. Others will initially gravitate to a version of "Socratic" questioning described by Blau (2003) wherein they lead students to say "the very things that [the teacher] would otherwise have said in a single uninterrupted turn, if he had been inclined to lecture" (p. 25). While pontificating on the finer points of literature and leading pseudo-Socratic discussions may have certain instructional benefits, teachers who routinely position themselves as model knowers may be teaching their students an unintended and undesirable lesson: Don't work hard at understanding a play or poem because the teacher will explain it to you anyway.

I consider it positive growth when I observe those same teachers or teacher candidates positioning themselves as a "model learners"—ones who view their jobs as that of modeling and guiding students in practicing the skills, habits, and dispositions that will enable them to become independent, self-sufficient readers, writers, and problem solvers. Effective readers of literature, including teachers of English, monitor their own thought processes to assess the quality and purposefulness of their ideas and interpretations. They regard uncertainty and confusion as a normal part of the reading process, and they work off of tentative interpretations to form more complete understandings through rereadings of text. They also take part in everyday conversations around literature and seek outside sources such as literary scholarship and cultural media to enrich their reading lives. Effective readers of literature do these things independently and not simply when they are directed to do so by a teacher or other authority. As long as they are willing to present themselves as model learners, English teachers are in an optimal position to model the strategies, attitudes, and effort that facilitate what many students assume come naturally and effortlessly to the "experts" who teach them: understanding and enjoyment of challenging literature.

It is far easier to tell students what they need to know about a particular play or poem than to cultivate in them the skills and habits of mind that will enable them to independently make convincing and meaningful interpretations of challenging literature. It is also far easier to prescribe for students how they should feel about a particular character in a story or novel than it is to develop in them the capacity to connect strongly and viscerally with a range of fictional personas, including ones with whom they do not readily identify. As you plan lessons for your chosen version of "Snitch," I hope that you will take up the challenge of employing literature as an instructional tool for cultivating empathy and intellectual independence. Here are guiding questions to assist you in designing your lessons:

- Empathy is defined as identification with, understanding of, and vicarious experience of another person's situation, feelings, and motives.[1] To what degree do the instructional activities you have designed around "Snitch" enable students to not only understand characters from the story, but also *experience* their situations, thoughts, and emotions?
- Walking in the shoes of fictional characters while in the presence of other students can be a risky prospect for teenage readers of literature. To what degree will your "Snitch" lessons invite or discourage such risk taking? Why?
- Wilhelm (1996) writes that most high school literature instruction involves "seatwork and recitation that focus on cracking codes instead

---

[1] empathy. Dictionary.com. The American Heritage® Stedman's Medical Dictionary. Houghton Mifflin Company. http://dictionary.reference.com/browse/empathy (accessed: October 28, 2008).

of creating meanings" (p. 14). To what degree do the lessons you are designing position you as the source of "correct" readings of "Snitch" rather than providing students with the freedom to arrive at their own perspectives on a story, as well as the responsibility and intellectual tools to independently account for their perspectives through sound reasoning and reflection?

- Thinking about one's thinking (metacognition) is a central factor in determining a student's capacity to independently manage challenging intellectual tasks, including the reading and interpretation of complex texts (Paul & Elder 1999; Livingston 1997). What opportunities do your lessons give students to self-reflect on the accuracy, fairness, relevance, and consequences of their positions on "Snitch"? What opportunities are they given to revise and rearticulate, in written or spoken forms, their views on the story?

Appendix A
Snitch (Version 2)

There was a groove in the table where someone had scratched out "FAT A- -." Mo rubbed the well-worn cuts and wondered what they must've been looking at when they carved out this little piece of boredom. It couldn't have been Angelique. She was just right as far as Mo was concerned . . . and nice too, which wasn't always the case with girls who were that good-looking.

His eyes settled on DeLayla's shirt in front of him and the pants that didn't cover her butt. He traced the letters F, A, T, in mindless loops. After a while he sat up straight, breathed out slowly and slumped back down on his desk. It was five minutes after the final bell.

Ms. Bancroft stood at the front of the classroom next to their teacher, Ms. Wong, arms crossed in front of her sizeable frame, brows crossed on her face. Ms. Wong stood mimicking the assistant principal, arms crossed in front of her, but much less convincingly. Her face was too full of concern; too earnest. Silence hung heavy in the room, like the inside of a casket.

Ten minutes past the hour and the air was thick. A warm breeze floated in, bringing with it the scent of summer and dirt and freedom.

"You have a choice," Ms. Wong said to the room.

"We know there were witnesses to the incident; we know that some of those people are in this classroom."

Why did he have to go through this? It wasn't like he'd done anything. He never did anything. And yet, here he was, sitting in an overheated classroom on a Friday in the middle of June—why God, was the heater still on!?—listening to the sounds of the seventh graders playing outside on the tarmac. They screamed and yelled and laughed while Mo sat in silence waiting for someone to give Ms. Wong an answer.

Mo cleared his throat, scratchy and dry, thought about asking for some water, and then thought better of it. He looked up to find Janelle giving him a look from the corner of her eye—she sat in the row next to his. She didn't say a word, but there was no mistaking her message: "Don't snitch."

Not that she had to worry. He rolled his eyes. No idiot was going to squeal—everyone knew what would happen if they did.

One of the boys in the group that Mo saw messing around with Oswaldo's iPod was his friend Justin. Mo's mom always said to tell the truth. But even she would understand this situation—you don't betray friends.

But was Justin really still his friend? After this past summer, Justin stopped hanging out with him. At first Mo was confused and hurt, but then he realized that Justin was just hanging out with the cooler kids and he couldn't blame him. He told himself, "I'd ditch me, too, if I could."

He remembered the last time he'd made the effort.

Crossing the lunchroom, soggy tater tots on a Styrofoam tray, Mo motioned for Justin to join him. Without even acknowledging Mo, Justin broke into a jog in the direction of Alberto, slapped him on the back and passed him a handful of sunflower seeds. For a brief moment, Mo could see Justin looking back at him, but he didn't come over.

That would be the last time he'd try that.

In the silence of the room, Mo could hear the ticking of the second hand on the classroom clock posted above the blackboard. "Damn," he kept saying under his breath, "Why today?" It was already 3:20, which meant that even if Ms. Wong let them out now, he still wouldn't get home until close to four o'clock.

Any later and there was a good chance that he would miss Angelique.

She said she would look for him on the playground after school. But how long would she wait? Mo tried to find a clue in the words he couldn't get out of his head since Wednesday when he caught up to her with the Metrocard she had left behind in fifth period science.

"You live in the Grant Houses, right?" Angelique had asked him as he handed her the Metrocard. "I think I seen you there on Friday when I was watching my cousin, Ashley."

"Who me?" Mo responded, scratching his jaw. "You saw me?"

"Yeah, I know it was you. I was pushing my baby cousin on the swings when I seen you walking into the building."

It wasn't every day that Mo had a conversation with a girl, and almost never with a girl like Angelique Curry. He searched for words, but before he could find them Angelique started off down the hallway. After a few steps, she turned back in Mo's direction: "I'll be there this Friday. You should come by and meet us at the swings."

"Look. We'll stay here for as long as we have to," Ms. Bancroft announced. Her booming voice brought Mo back to the moment. Arms still folded across her chest, she had resumed her threats. "I'll just call homes and let everyone know you'll be coming home late today. And you—" Ms. Bancroft was speaking in the direction of Latrell Fields, seated directly to the right of Mo. "Mr. Fields! Sit up straight and look forward." Latrell did as he was asked but not before turning his head accusingly at Mo. It was true. Mo also had his head down, but Ms. Bancroft either didn't notice or care to call him on it. Mo almost wished that Ms. Bancroft would scold him, even kick him out of the room where maybe he could sneak out of the school and keep his date with Angelique. But Mo was invisible. He couldn't get in trouble even if he tried.

As soon as Ms. Bancroft drifted to another area of the room, Latrell put a finger up his nose and flicked a booger at Mo. It fell short, landing on the floor between their two desks. Mo could care less anyhow. He was thinking about how good Angelique looked in gym shorts earlier in the week.

Now the clock read 3:26. Mo reached in his pocket and ran his fingers over the glassy surface of his own iPod. Unlike Oswaldo, he knew better than to take it out during school. Only two things could happen if you didn't have the sense to keep it in your pocket: a teacher would confiscate it, or if they saw it first, kids like Ray Shaun and Alberto would jump you and take it for themselves. Part of Mo thought that Oswaldo got what he deserved—flashing around that iPod in the hallways, singing and dancing like a fool. But Oswaldo wasn't a bad kid, just a little slow in the head and annoying.

Mo thought more about what his mom would say.

"Mohammed, it's not like we're going to be here forever," she'd tell him, puttering around the house fixing up the ragged furniture that she had received from the Morales' next door when they moved out. "If your father was still around he'd put things straight. But you have to be the man of the house now and stay out of trouble."

Another dusting of the frames they had on the bookshelf.

"You know your father was a brave man, and he always did what was right. Even though he's not with us anymore, you can still learn from him. Think about what your father would have done."

But at the moment he was thinking about Oswaldo and the 200 bucks that he must have spent on that iPod. He was thinking about Justin and the stupid jokes they used to make up and laugh about; the way they used to watch out for each other. Mostly, though, he was thinking about Angelique. He was thinking about what it would be like to kiss her.

He thought some more and then lifted his head off his arms and sat up straight. He looked up at Ms. Wong and their eyes met for a split second before Mo buried his face back in his arms. Not even Angelique was worth the beating he would take for squealing. Just a few weeks ago he saw Ray Shaun, Alberto, and a ninth grader jump Jerell O'Neal outside the schoolyard on the way home. The first thing Mo did was dart into Ramon's Deli. If no one saw him, no one could say he'd snitch. Later he found out that Jerell needed over 30 stitches to close up the cut on his head. And so this time he again kept his mouth shut, fingers absentmindedly tracing the letters as Ms. Wong and Ms. Bancroft waited in vain for a witness to come forward. Mo looked over at the clock and hid his face again in disgust. It was 3:34.

He stayed that way until he felt something tickle his ear. A Latrell booger had found its target and now rested on Mo's desktop. Having nothing with which to knock it to the floor, Mo left the snot in place; there it stood like a crusty green monument to Mo's helplessness. Latrell the artist grinned with satisfaction at his handiwork. Mo glared at Latrell but they both knew it was the kind of glare weak kids give stronger kids when there is little else they can do.

It was killing Mo to watch the minutes go by on the clock so he distracted himself by imagining he was The Thing from the *Fantastic Four* comics. "It's clobberin' time!" he would announce and pulverize Latrell with his massive stone hands. Or if he was Reed Richards, Mr. Fantastic, he could stretch and contort his body into any shape he wanted; he could extend his arms until his hands were clasped around Latrell's head and then rub the bigger boy's face in the booger still sitting on his desk.

But if Mo was being honest with himself, the closest thing he had to a superpower was invisibility, the same as Sue Richards, the one female member of the Fantastic Four. He could slip in and out of situations with nobody paying much attention. It had its advantages, Mo thought, but why couldn't he be The Thing at these times, or Johnny Storm, the Human Torch, who just by saying "Flame on!" could transform himself into a flying inferno of molten heat.

Ms. Bancroft began pacing slowly between the aisles of desks looking over students' shoulders. "Okay, since not a single student here feels the need to cooperate, this is the way we are going to handle this unfortunate situation: In a moment, Ms. Wong and I will walk out of the room. We will wait exactly five minutes. At the end of those five minutes, if nobody returns the iPod, or lets us know who has it, I will contact the police and let them handle it. To make things even easier, you do not even need to speak to us directly. Just leave the iPod on Ms. Wong's desk, or write a note and let us know who has it."

Ms. Bancroft headed for the door with Ms. Wong a few steps behind her. When the two were out of sight, Donnie James, a friend of Ray Shaun and Alberto, left his seat and peeked through the small window into the hallway before turning toward the class. "Nobody snitches. Nobody!" he announced, scanning the room. Eliza stood up from her chair and leaned in Donnie's direction. "Shut up, Donnie! I ain't staying here all day. Don't you think I got things to do?"

"You shut up, bitch!"

"You're the bitch, bitch."

Seeing that Donnie and Eliza might come to blows, Tre Portis planted a foot on Mo's lap to catapult himself closer to the combatants. Mo, who had been keeping to himself as he always did in these moments, instinctively reached into his pocket to check for damage to his iPod—a black Shuffle, the same color and model as Oswaldo's. Satisfied that it was still in one piece, he slapped at his thighs to remove Tre's sneaker print off his lap. Mo then rose like a sleepwalker from his chair and maneuvered through a maze of desks, chairs, and students to the side of the classroom. When he reached the windows, he looked down Union Street and could see the bus stop where a small group of students and adults had gathered waiting for the M11. It had not arrived yet, but surely it would any minute. *And then it will be too late,* Mo thought. *There's nothing I can do about it.*

But then Mo remembered his superpower.

Stopping only to grab his book bag and jacket, he walked in slow, determined strides down the aisle towards Ms. Wong's desk. Behind him curses and accusations ricocheted off the classroom walls; students got in each other's faces or watched others get in each other's faces. Nobody noticed Mo as he arrived at the desk and stood before it with the iPod in his palm. Mo stared for a moment into the black glass on the face of the device; he could see his reflection in it. He grinned and the reflection grinned back at him. Mo then placed the iPod flatly and delicately on the desktop; he was taken aback by how sharply the sound of metal on wood cut through the classroom noise. But still nobody heard it or noticed Mo at the head of the class. When Mo walked over to the classroom door, opened it and let it close behind him, nobody saw or heard that either, not even Ms. Bancroft and Ms. Wong who stood in the hallway just steps from the door huddled in conversation. As he walked by the pair taking care not to let his sneakers squeak on the polished surface, Mo wondered whether he had taken full advantage of his invisibility. Perhaps it hadn't even been necessary to give up his iPod. This entire time could he have walked right of the classroom without raising an eyebrow? Could he have been with Angelique an hour ago instead of holed up in detention for a something he had nothing to do with?

But then Ms. Bancroft noticed. "Where are *you* going, Mr. Agee?" she asked.

"Someone did what you said, Ms. Bancroft."

"Did what, Mr. Agee?"

"Someone left Oswaldo's iPod on Ms. Wong's desk."

A smiling Ms. Bancroft turned to Ms. Wong. Pleased by her own handling of the situation, she invited Ms. Wong to lead the pair back into the classroom. As the door shut behind them, Mo walked to the end of the hallway looking only once over his shoulder. Then he jogged. When he reached the stairwell leading to the exit, he came to an abrupt stop and turned back in the direction of Ms. Wong's classroom. Laughter echoed down the hallway—the sound of students reenergized by the mysterious turn of events. Then he could hear Ms. Bancroft's baritone voice rising above those of his classmates. Although he could not make out her words, he knew that she would be commending them at this point for "doing the right thing" and "working together as a community to solve the problem." For a moment, Mo felt an urge to head back to the classroom and set the record straight. The whole thing wasn't sitting right in his stomach. Had anyone gotten what they deserved? Slow as he was, Oswaldo would sooner or later figure out that the iPod wasn't actually his, not the same music, probably less gigabytes. And the boys who took it . . . what would stop them from doing that kind of thing again, maybe something worse? Wasn't it time someone stood up to Alberto and the rest? It even bothered Mo that Ms. Bancroft would feel more right than ever for keeping the whole class hostage and threatening to call the police.

And what about his mom who always taught him to do the right thing even when it was the hard thing to do? And what about his dad, who Mom always reminded Mo was brave and righteous before he took off on them? Both of his parents had forbidden Mo to use curse words, and to this day he felt uneasy swearing even when not in their presence. To his surprise, then, the words "screw them" rolled easily off his tongue, as easily as saying "two slices and a Coke" at the pizza place; then, as he bounded down the stairwell three, four steps at a time, he said with even greater ease, "Fuck 'em all." As Mo sprinted down Union Street to the awaiting M11, repeating "fuck them, fuck them" between drawn breaths, he had the sensation that the legs which carried him—stronger and sturdier than he could remember—were not in fact his own.

Appendix B
Snitch (Version 2, Alternate Ending)

Mo climbed the steps to the M11, chest heaving, shirt clinging to his back. He spotted an empty seat near the front of the bus, but chose not to take it. In his mind, sitting down would only delay his arrival at the Grant Houses.

Through the passenger windows, Mo could see the Union Street sidewalks bustling with their usual late afternoon activity. African men in brightly colored garments sold carved animals and incense lined neatly on bamboo mats. Neighborhood women inspected mangos and tomatoes from the outdoor bins in front of supermarkets and Korean groceries. As the bus left the curb, Mo fixed his gaze through the front windowpane on the two lanes of Union Street heading eastbound. Never before had he so hated the Dollar van pulling over to pick up passengers taking up an entire lane on the already congested street. Just as the bus cleared the van and began to pick up speed, it was thwarted by an SUV double parked in front of the Golden Crust Bakery. By the time the M11 ambled past the SUV, the green light had turned yellow.

A rage bubbled up in Mo towards every vehicle, every man, woman, or child that stood between him and Angelique. But soon the rage turned to defiance. Enough was enough, Mo thought, and he transformed himself into The Thing picking up delivery trucks like they were toys and heaving them to the sidewalk. At cross walks, he became Mr. Fantastic, kneading his torso through a half open window and arching it to form a pedestrian bridge over Union Street. Shirtless teenage boys on tricked out bicycles, do rags flapping in the wind, girls in short shorts and T-shirts tied in knots above the navels, mommies with babies and toddlers in strollers streamed across the human bridge allowing traffic to pass freely. Soon the M11 had reached Comely Station and begun the final leg, skip stop, all the way to Forest Avenue. Approaching the station, Mo made his way to the back exit and pushed against the double doors until they gave way; he jumped to the pavement and without breaking stride began running to the projects. It was three short blocks to the Grant Houses, but Mo wasn't taking any chances. "Flame on!" he said to himself and he was Johnny Storm, the Human Torch, rocketing into the sky; a white hot projectile trailed by a streak of yellow and orange. In seconds he was approaching Building 6 on the eastern perimeter of the Grant Houses. "Flame off!" Mo said, and returned to earth in his school clothes just steps from the walkway leading into the projects.

Before Mo could see the playground situated just on the other side of building 6, he could hear it. Flip flops and bare feet slapped through puddles left by the water fountain that had been dormant since September. Over the screams and laughs of children, he recognized the voice of Ms. Price. "Devon!" she shouted, "Didn't I tell you to stay away from that sandbox?" As Mo turned the first corner, he could hear the rhythmic cranking of metal chains pulling on the frame of a swing set, making that heeee-haaaaw sound that always reminded Mo of donkeys. Then he heard a voice above all the other play-ground noises: "Not—so—HIGH!" said the voice struggling to get the words out between spasms of laughter.

It was Angelique.

Mo gathered himself before turning the back corner. He didn't want to appear too excited, but he was—not only about Angelique, but about the whole day: his daring escape from the classroom, the fact that it was only the beginning of June and already felt like mid-summer with sprinklers on and fire hydrants cracked. He wondered if Angelique liked roller coasters. Maybe in a few weeks they could take the bus to Six Flags and ride The Scorpion together.

Mo started to turn the corner and stopped again. Angelique was not only one of the prettiest girls in school, she was also known for her style. Mo thought about running up to his apartment and changing out of his school clothes, but he decided it was too late to risk it. What was the use of throwing on his Coogi shirt if Angelique was gone before she could even see it? He loosened his belt two notches, let his polo shirt hang free, dropped his pants a few inches lower on the hips, and turned the corner.

Now he was standing directly in front of the swings. The voice he had heard *was* Angelique's, but she wasn't alone on the swing. Even with Angelique on his lap, her curls concealing half his face, Mo could recognize Jimmy Perez, a tenth grader from Building 7.

"Hey, Mo!" waved Angelique. "Say hi to Mo, Ashley," Angelique called over to her cousin who was circling the swing set on her tricycle.

Jimmy also acknowledged Mo with a nod. Mo nodded back but said nothing. He stood in place, only his head rising and falling with the pair as they cut the blue sky in slow looping arcs. Each time he followed the swing to its apex, the sun, still bright in the late afternoon, blinded him. As Mo turned to walk away, his eyes shut and still stinging, he was certain that he could hear the hiss and crackle of its scorched surface.

Works Cited

Atwell, Nancie. 1998. *In the Middle: Writing, Reading and Learning with Adolescents.* 2nd ed. Portsmouth, NH: Boynton/Cook Publishers-Heinemann.

Austen, Jane. 1813. *Pride and Prejudice.* New York: Penguin, 2005.

Bailin, Sharon, Roland Case, Jerrold R. Coombs, & Leroi B. Daniels. 1999. "Conceptualizing Critical Thinking." *Journal of Curriculum Studies* 31(3): 285–302.

Bakhtin, Mikhail M. 1981. *The Dialogic Imagination.* Ed. Michael Holquist. Trans. Caryl Emerson and Michael Holquist. Austin, Texas: University of Texas Press.

Bissex, Glenda. 1996. *Partial Truths: A Memoir and Essays on Reading, Writing and Researching.* Portsmouth, NH: Heinemann.

Blau, Sheridan. 2003. *The Literature Workshop: Teaching Texts and Their Readers.* Portsmouth, NH: Heinemann.

Brown, Dan. 2003. *The Da Vinci Code.* New York: Doubleday.

Burch, Jennings Michael. 1985. *They Cage Animals at Night.* New York: Signet–New American Library.

Burgess, Anthony. 1962. *A Clockwork Orange.* London: William Heinemann–Pearson.

Burgin, Richard. 1978. "Isaac Bashevis Singer's Universe." *New York Times Magazine* (Dec. 3), pp. 39–47.

Calkins, Lucy, with Shelley Harwayne. 1991. *Living Between the Lines.* Portsmouth, NH: Heinemann.

Carroll, Jim. 1987. *The Basketball Diaries.* New York: Penguin.

Carver, Raymond. 1991a. "Fiction of Occurrence and Consequence" (with Tom Jenks). *Call If You Need Me: The Uncollected Fiction and Other Works.* New York: Vintage.

———. 1991b. "On Writing." *Call If You Need Me: The Uncollected Fiction and Other Works.* New York: Vintage

Chiles, Nick. 2006. "Their Eyes Were Reading Smut." *The New York Times.* Retrieved September 17, 2008 from <http://www.nytimes.com/2006/01/04/opinion/04chiles.html>

Cisneros, Sandra. 1991. *The House on Mango Street.* New York: Vintage.

Clark, Wahida. 2003. *Every Thug Needs a Lady.* New York: Black Print Publishing.

———. 2006. *Payback Is a Mutha.* New York: Dafina Books.

———. 2007. *Thug Matrimony.* New York: Dafina Books.

Conrad, Joseph. 1902. "Heart of Darkness." In *Youth: A Narrative, and Two Other Stories.* London: Blackwood; New York: Penguin, 2005.

Curtis, Christopher Paul. 1995. *The Watsons Go to Birmingham—1963.* New York: Delacorte Press.

Daniels, Harvey. 2002. *Literature Circles: Voice and Choice in the Student-Centered Classroom.* Portland, ME: Stenhouse Publishers.

De Trevino, Elizabeth Borton. 1965. *I, Juan de Pareja.* New York: Farrar, Straus and Giroux.

Diaz, Junot. 2007. *The Brief Wondrous Life of Oscar Wao.* New York: Riverhead Books.

Dickens, Charles. 1861. *Great Expectations.* London: Penguin Classics, 1996.

Elbow, Peter. 1998. *Writing Without Teachers.* 2nd ed. New York: Oxford University Press.

Ellison, Ralph. 1953. *Invisible Man.* New York: Random House.

Ervin, Keisha. 2006. *Hold U Down.* Columbus, OH: Triple Crown Publications.

Esquivel, Laura. 1992. *Like Water for Chocolate: A Novel in Monthly Installments with Recipes, Romances, and Home Remedies.* Trans. Carol and Thomas Christensen. New York: Doubleday.

Feinberg, Barbara. "Reflections on the 'Problem Novel': Do These Calamity-Filled Books Serve Up Too Much, Too Often, Too Early?" *American Educator* 28 (Winter 2004– 2005): 8–19.

Ferrell, Carolyn. 1997. "Proper Library." In *Don't Erase Me* (pp 1–20). New York: Houghton Mifflin.

Fish, Stanley. 1980. *Is There a Text in this Class? The Authority of Interpretive Communities.* Cambridge, MA: Harvard University Press.

Fishkin, Shelley. 1995. "Teaching Mark Twain's Adventures of Huckleberry Finn." *Public Broadcasting System Huck Finn Teacher's Guide.* Retrieved September 15, 2008 from <http:// www.pbs.org/wgbh/cultureshock/ teachers/huck/essay.html>

Frey, James. 2003. *A Million Little Pieces.* New York: Doubleday.

Friedman, Thomas L. 2006. "As Energy Prices Rise, It's All Downhill for Democracy." *The New York Times* (May 5). Retrieved October 13, 2008 from http://select.nytimes .com/2006/05/05/opinion/ 05friedman.html

Gaines, Ernest. 1993. *A Lesson Before Dying.* New York: Vintage.

Gautier, A.L. 2001. "Palabras." In *Crab Orchard Review* (pp. 67–73). Carbondale, IL: Southern Illinois University Press.

Geha, Joseph. 2002. "All Alone and Together." In *Big City Cool: Short Stories About Urban Youth.* Ed. M. Jerry Weiss and Helen S. Weiss. New York: Persea Books.

Gilmore, Dewitt, a.k.a. Relentless Aaron. 2004. *Platinum Dolls.* Mount Vernon, NY: Relentless Content.

———. 2006. *Extra Marital Affairs.* New York: St. Martin's Press.

Golden, Arthur. 1997. *Memoirs of a Geisha.* New York: Knopf.

Golding, William. 1954. *Lord of the Flies.* New York: Perigree Books–Penguin.

Gumperz, John (Ed.). 1982. *Language and Social Identity.* Cambridge, U.K: Cambridge University Press.

Hansberry, Lorraine. 1959. *A Raisin in the Sun.* New York: Random House.

Herber, Harold. 1978. *Teaching Reading in Content Areas.* 2nd ed. Englewood Cliffs, NJ: Prentice Hall.

Herbert, Bob. 2005. "Blowing the Whistle on Gangsta Culture." *The New York Times* (December 12). Retrieved October 13, 2008 from http://select.nytimes .com/2005/12/22/opinion/22herbert .html?scp=1&sq=Blowing+the+Whistle +on+Gangsta+Culture&st=nyt

Hill, Marc Lamont, Biany Perez, & Decoteau J. Irby. 2008. "Street Fiction: What Is It and What Does It Mean for English Teachers?" *English Journal* 97(3): 76–81.

Hirsch, Jr., E.D. 2003. "Reading Comprehension Requires Knowledge—of Words and the World." *American Educator* 27(1): 10–31.

Holman, Felice. 1974. *Slakes Limbo.* New York: Atheneum-Simon and Schuster.

Hugo, Victor. 1862. *Les Misérables.* New York: Signet–New American Library.

Ice-T. 1991. *O.G.: Original Gangster.* Sire/ Warner Bros. Records.

Iser, Wolfgang. 1978. *The Act of Reading: A Theory of Aesthetic Response.* Baltimore, MD: Johns Hopkins University Press.

Johnson, Angela. 2003. *The First Part Last.* New York: Simon Pulse–Simon and Schuster.

Kahari, Asante. 2004. *Homo Thug.* New York: Black Print Publishing.

Keen, Suzanne. 2007. *Empathy and the Novel.* New York: Oxford University Press.

Kennedy, Randall. 2002. *Nigger: The Strange Career of a Troublesome Word.* New York: Pantheon Books.

King, Deja. 2007. *Bitch Reloaded.* Columbus, OH: Triple Crown Publications.

King, Martin Luther, Jr. 1964. "Letter from Birmingham Jail." *Why We Can't Wait.* New York: Signet–New American Library, 2000.

King, Stephen. 1982. "Rita Hayworth and Shawshank Redemption." In *Different Seasons* (pp. 1–102). New York: Viking Press.

Kristof, Nicholas D. 2006. "Disposable Cameras for Disposable People." *The New York Times* (February 12), p. D14 .

Labov, William P. 1973 *Language* in *the Inner City: Studies in the Black English Vernacular.* Philadelphia: University of Pennsylvania Press.

Lara Croft, Tomb Raider. 2001. Dir. Simon West. Perf. Angelina Jolie, Jon Voight, Iain Glen, Noah Taylor and Daniel Craig.

Lee, Harper. 1960. *To Kill a Mockingbird.* Boston: Grand Central Publishing–Hachette Book Group, 1988.

Lightfoot, C. 2004. "Fantastic Self: A Study of Adolescents' Fictional Narratives, and Aesthetic Activity as Identity Work." In C. Daiute and C. Lightfoot (Eds.), *Narrative Analysis: Studying the Development of Individuals in Society.* Thousand Oaks, CA: Sage Publications.

Livingston, J.A. 1997. *Metacognition: An Overview.* Retrieved September 15, 2008, from <http://www.gse.buffalo .edu/fas/shuell/cep564/Metacog .htm#Top>

Lopez, Nancy. 2003. *Hopeful Girls, Troubled Boys: Race and Gender Disparity in Urban Education.* New York: Routledge-Taylor and Francis Group.

Lynch, Tanika. 2006. *Whore.* Columbus, OH: Triple Crown Publications.

Mackler, Carolyn. 2003. *The Earth, My Butt, and Other Big Round Things.* Cambridge, MA: Candlewick Press.

Macrorie, Ken. 1988. *The I-Search Paper: Revised Edition of Searching Writing.* Portsmouth, NH: Boynton/Cook Publishers–Heinemann.

Markandaya, Kamala. 2002. *Nectar in a Sieve.* New York: Signet–New American Library.

Mayher, John. 1989. *Uncommon Sense: Theoretical Practice in Language Education.* Portsmouth, NH: Boynton/ Cook Publishers–Heinemann.

Meier, Deborah, & George Wood (Eds.). 2004. *Many Children Left Behind: How the No Child Left Behind Act Is Damaging Our Children and Our Schools.* Boston: Beacon Press.

Morrison, Toni. 1987. *Beloved.* New York: Penguin Books.

Myers, Walter Dean. 1999. *Monster.* New York: Harper Tempest/Amistad–HarperCollins.

The National Council of Teachers of English and the International Reading Association. 2006. *Standards for the English Language Arts.* Urbana, IL: The National Council of Teachers of English.

Oates, Joyce Carol. 1994. *"Where Are You Going, Where Have You Been?"* Ed. Elaine Showalter. New Brunswick, NJ: Rutgers University Press.

Obama, Barack. 2008. "Barack Obama in Wallingford, PA." Retrieved September 17, 2008 from http://www.youtube .com/watch?v=yN2Zy_68RcY

O'Brien, Tim. 1990. *The Things They Carried.* Boston: Houghton Mifflin.

Ortiz, Judith. 2002. "American History." In M. Jerry Weiss and Helen S. Weiss (Eds.), *Big City Cool: Short Stories About Urban Youth.* New York: Persea Books.

Orwell, George. 1946. *Animal Farm.* Orlando, FL: Harcourt Brace & Company.

Paul, Richard W., & Linda Elder. 1999. *Critical Thinking Handbook: Basic*

Theory and Instructional Structures. Dillon Beach, CA: Foundation for Critical Thinking.

Paul, Richard, & Linda Elder. 2001. *The Miniature Guide to Critical Thinking Concepts and Tools.* Dillon Beach, CA: Foundations for Critical Thinking.

Perl, Sondra, & Mimi Schwartz. 2006. *Writing True: The Art and Craft of Creative Nonfiction.* New York: Houghton Mifflin.

Plath, Sylvia (writing as Victoria Lucas). 1963. *The Bell Jar.* New York: Bantam, 1971.

Pradl, Gordon. 1996. *Literature for Democracy: Reading as a Social Act.* Portsmouth, NH: Boyton/Cook Publishers.

Ratner, Andrew. 2008. "That Which Is Taught, That Which Is Learned." *Journal of Adolescent and Adult Literacy* 51(7): 533–537.

Rickford, John R. 1999. *African American Vernacular English: Features, Evolution, Educational Implications.* Malden, MA: Blackwell Publishers.

Rose, Mike. 1990. *Lives on the Boundary: A Moving Account of the Struggles and Achievements of America's Educationally Underprepared.* New York: Penguin.

Rosenblatt, Louise M. 1938. *Literature as Exploration.* 5th ed. New York: Modern Language Association, 1996.

———. 1978. *The Reader, the Text, the Poem: The Transactional Theory of the Literary Work.* Carbondale, IL: Southern Illinois Press, 1994.

Salinger, J.D. 1951. *Catcher in the Rye.* New York: Little, Brown and Company.

Sapphire. 1996. *Push.* New York: Knopf.

Schoenbach, Ruth, Cynthia Greenleaf, Christine Cziko, & Lori Hurwitz. 1999. *Reading for Understanding: A Guide to Improving Reading in Middle and High School Classrooms.* San Francisco: Jossey-Bass.

Sendak, Maurice. 1963. *Where the Wild Things Are.* New York: Harper & Row.

The Shawshank Redemption. 1994. Dir. Frank Darabont. Perf. Tim Robbins, Morgan Freeman, Bob Gunton, William Sadler, Clancy Brown, and Gil Bellows. Columbia Pictures.

Shteyngart, Gary. 2006. *Absurdistan.* New York: Random House.

Smith, Betty. 1943. *A Tree Grows in Brooklyn.* New York: Harper & Bros.

Smith, Frank. 1997. *Reading Without Nonsense.* New York: Teachers College Press

Soto, Gary. 1991. *Taking Sides.* San Diego: Harcourt Children's Books.

Sparks, Beatrice, ed. 1971. *Go Ask Alice.* New York: Simon and Schuster.

———. 1994. *It Happened to Nancy: By an Anonymous Teenager.* New York: Avon Books.

Steinbeck, John. 1937. *Of Mice and Men.* New York: Covici, Friede, Inc.

Stowe, Harriet Beecher. 1851. *Uncle Tom's Cabin.* Ware, England: Wordsworth Editions, Ltd.

Suskind, Ron. 1998. *A Hope in the Unseen: An American Odyssey from the Inner City to the Ivy League.* New York: Broadway Books.

Thomas, Lewis. 1979. *The Medusa and the Snail: More Notes of a Biology Watcher.* New York: Penguin.

Turner, Nikki. 2007. *Forever a Hustler's Wife.* New York: One World–Ballantine.

Twain, Mark. 1885. *Adventures of Huckleberry Finn.* New York: Harper & Bros.

U.S. National Endowment for the Arts. 2007. *To Read or Not to Read: A Question of National Consequence.* Research Report #47. Washington: NEA.

Walker, Alice. 1982. *The Color Purple.* San Diego, CA: Harcourt Trade.

Waxler, Robert, Jean Trounstine, & Meghan McLaughlin. 1997. *Success Stories: Life Skills Through Literature.* Washington, D.C.: U.S. Department of Education.

Wharton, Edith. 1911. *Ethan Frome.* New York: Signet–New American Library, 2000.

Widmayer, Sharon. 2004. *Schema Theory: An Introduction.* Retrieved October 16,

2008, from <http://www2.yk.psu.edu/~jlg18/506/SchemaTheory.pdf>.

Wilhelm, Jeffrey. 1996. *"You Gotta Be the Book": Teaching Engaged and Reflective Reading with Adolescents.* New York: Teachers College Press.

Williams, Lori Aurelia. 2005. *Broken China.* New York: Simon and Schuster.

Williams-Garcia, Rita. 1997. "Wishing It Away." In *No Easy Answers: Short Stories About Teenagers Making Tough Choices* (pp. 261–268). New York: Random House.

Wilson, Harriet. 1859. *Our Nig; or, Sketches from the Life of a Free Black.* New York: Penguin, 2004.

Wells, Gordon. 1997. "Learning to Be Literate: Reconciling Convention and Invention." In S. I. MacMahon and T. E. Raphael (Eds.), *The Book Club Connection: Literacy Learning and Classroom Talk.* New York: Teachers College Press.

Yokota, Junko. 1993. "Issues in Selecting Multicultural Children's Literature." *Language Arts* 70: 156–167.

Index